Praise for *My River Chronicles*

"Jessica DuLong has captured the essential energy, grace, and beauty of the Hudson. Through her travels she discovers the place of the river and valley in America's past and present, as well as the essence of her own life. DuLong's is a personal journey that resonates with all of us."

—Tom Lewis, author of *The Hudson: A History*

"Whether you know the Hudson intimately or have yet to make her fine acquaintance, Jessica DuLong's soulful narrative will make you crave a journey on the river. The author's vivid portrayals of her fireboat's inner workings are rendered with such precise tenderness that as a reader I sat mesmerized by descriptions of motors and magnetism. *My River Chronicles* is a heartfelt ode to the increasingly lost art of expert craftsmanship and understanding the beauty of the mechanical world arond us."

—Gwendolyn Bounds, author of *Little Chapel on the River: A Pub, a Town and the Search for What Matters Most*

MY RIVER CHRONICLES

REDISCOVERING AMERICA ON THE HUDSON

⤳

JESSICA DuLONG

FREE PRESS
New York London Toronto Sydney

*f*P

FREE PRESS
A Division of Simon & Schuster, Inc.
1230 Avenue of the Americas
New York, NY 10020

First Free Press hardcover edition September 2009

FREE PRESS and colophon are
trademarks of Simon & Schuster, Inc.

For information about special discounts for bulk purchases,
please contact Simon & Schuster Special Sales at
1-866-506-1949 or business@simonandschuster.com.

The Simon & Schuster Speakers Bureau can bring authors to your live event. For
more information or to book an event contact the Simon & Schuster Speakers Bureau
at 1-866-248-3049 or visit our website at www.simonspeakers.com.

Book design by Kelvin P. Oden / Oh Snap! Design

Manufactured in the United States of America

1   3   5   7   9   10   8   6   4   2

Library of Congress Cataloging-in-Publication Data
DuLong, Jessica.
My river chronicles: rediscovering America on the Hudson / Jessica DuLong.
p. cm.
1. Hudson River (N.Y. and N.J.)—Description and travel. 2. Hudson River
Valley (N.Y. and N.J.)—Description and travel. 3. DuLong, Jessica—Travel—Hudson
River (N.Y. and N.J.). 4. John J. Harvey (Fireboat). 5. Hudson River Valley (N.Y. and
N.J.)—History. 6. Hudson River Valley (N.Y. and N.J.)—Social life and customs. 7.
Community life—Hudson River Valley (N.Y. and N.J.)—History. 8. Work—Social
aspects—Hudson River Valley (N.Y. and N.J.)—History. 9. Social change—Hudson
River Valley (N.Y. and N.J.)—History. I. Title.
F127.H8D85 2009
917.47'30444—dc22   2009011610

ISBN 978-1-4165-8698-2
ISBN 978-1-4165-8717-0 (ebook)

To Bob, for showing me the meaning of
in for a penny, in for a pound

For Ben, with boundless gratitude

CONTENTS

My River Chronicles

PROLOGUE

IF THE CANARIES found it in their hearts to sing, no one could hear them. One minute they were flitting about the treetops in Germany's Harz Mountains. The next they had been netted and stowed in the belly of the steamship *Muenchen*. Each bird perched in its own tiny wooden cage that hung side by side with six other birds in six other cages, all swinging from a single wooden rod. Then another rod with seven cages, and another, and another. Seven thousand caged birds swayed in the cargo hold as the ship's bow cut through the squally sea.

Twelve storm-tossed nights after the birds—involuntary immigrants—had departed Bremen, Germany, they arrived in New York harbor, two days behind schedule. On Tuesday, February 11, 1930, as the ship approached Manhattan's Pier 42, no one knew that the cargo in nearby Hold Six had already begun to smolder. The 499 sacks of potash, forty drums of shellac, 386 rolls of newsprint, 234 bales of peat moss, along with steel and aluminum, all stored side by side, were a recipe for a mighty conflagration.

✦ ✦ ✦

Two hours after the steamship's arrival on Manhattan's West Side, four longshoremen stood in Hold Six, unloading bags of potash—fertilizer bound for New England farms. They heard a crackling noise, and a streak of blue flame shot up from the sacks at their feet. They stamped on the smoldering bags trying to smother the flames, but soon thick black smoke filled the hold. The men, coughing and choking, scrambled for safety as huge tongues of flame began to lick out above the deck. The blaze spread quickly to other cargo holds, and within minutes fire consumed the whole rear of the ship.

An electric pulse from the New York City Fire Department's dispatch office snapped through telegraph wires to ring a bell in the station house at Pier 53, fourteen city blocks away. A specific sequence of clangs summoned Engine Company 86 to the scene. Firefighters readied hoses and engineers stoked the boilers of fireboat *Thomas Willett*, and pilot John Harvey hurried to the helm. Surely he could already smell the burning. With more than two decades' experience on the job, Harvey took the wheel, signaled the engine room, and the *Willett* steamed south at full throttle.

Meanwhile, the *Muenchen*'s crew, with the aid of longshoremen, hooked up a hose from the pier and raised it on a boom to reach the upper deck. But the hose line was frozen. Soon the billowing smoke was so dense that the men standing near the hatch were scarcely visible to spectators gathering on the pier, a crowd that by day's end would number ten thousand. None of the firefighters rushing to the scene, by land or by river, knew then what Hold Six contained.

At 11:30 a.m., fireboat *Willett* rounded up on the south side of the pier. The whole stern of the *Muenchen* was aflame. Directed by the battalion chief, Harvey brought the boat as close to the fire as he could. He had no idea he was sidling up to a bomb.

Part I

~

FOUR CENTURIES,
ONE RIVER

Mark Peckham

Chapter One

NAMESAKE

SEVENTY-TWO YEARS later, nothing more than a pegboard forest of disintegrated pilings remains of Pier 42, where pilot John Harvey met his fate. Today is Memorial Day 2002, and we, the crew of retired New York City fireboat *John J. Harvey*, are preparing to pay homage to our boat's namesake.

Pilot Bob Lenney, who steered this vessel for more than twenty years while the boat still served the FDNY Marine Division, noses her slender bow toward the stubby remnants of the covered pier—a grid of timbers, their rotting tips sticking out just a foot or so above the water's surface. Chief engineer Tim Ivory swings a leg over the side, clutching a small bouquet of all-white flowers that he has duct-taped to the end of a broken broom handle. A crowd gathers on the bow as he leans out over the water, holding on with just one leg, to stab the jagged handle-end into the top of one of the crumbling piles.

I know all this only by way of hearsay and pictures. From where I stand belowdecks, my fingers curled around the smooth brass levers that power the propellers in response to Bob's commands, I can't watch it unfold. Because I, fireboat *Harvey*'s engineer, stand in the engine room the whole time we're under way, this ceremony, like all the rest, is to me just another series of telegraph orders: Slow Ahead on the starboard side; Slow Astern on the port.

Between shifts of the levers, I steal glimpses of the harbor through the portholes—round windows just above the river's rippled surface. Above decks, pilots use the Manhattan skyline for their points of reference, to know where they are or where they're headed. Here, belowdecks, I use low-lying landmarks: the white tents where fast ferries load, the numinous blue lights in South Cove, the new concrete poured to straighten Pier 53 (which firefighters call the Tiltin' Hilton) where, on February 11, 1930, FDNY Marine Division pilot John Harvey signaled his deck crew to drop lines and shot south at the helm of fireboat *Thomas Willett* on his final run.

Nearly three-quarters of a century after his death, as the fireboat named in his honor leaves the pegboard forest, I hold my own private memorial service, issuing a silent prayer. It's something of a thank-you and something of a nod of acknowledgment: We remember. I whisper about the work we've put into preserving the boat over the past year. I tell him about rewiring shorted-out circuits. About our efforts to dis- and reassemble failing, rusty pump parts. About coating her steel surfaces with protective epoxy paints. All this, I explain, is done, in part, to pay homage to him—the man who lives on through this fireboat.

As the boat pushes through the water, I stand at my post, sweating. Though I can't hear the slosh of bilgewater over the growl of the engines, I can watch it through gaps in the diamond-plate floor. Like every steel vessel, this boat fights a constant, silent battle with the salt water that buoys her. The river seeps through little openings in her seventy-one-year-old skin. It trickles, etching burnt orange stains into the thick white paint that coats the riveted hull. Sometimes the boat rolls and sways and a splash of green overwhelms my porthole view. That's when I remember that I'm underwater. Less than a half-inch of steel plate separates me from the river.

Only after we've pulled away can I make out, through a porthole, a small speck of white where the flowers stand tall in the May sunshine. As the speck disappears against the muted gray of the concrete bulkhead at the water's edge, the significance of the ceremony fades into the everyday rhythms of the machinery.

✦ ✦ ✦

When I moved to New York City from San Francisco in 2000, I had never heard of a fireboat. Now I have found a home in the engine room of a boat born four decades before I was. During long stretches at the controls, when the drone of engines drowns out the mental clutter of my landside life, I wonder about the men stationed here before me. Did they feel left out of the action down here in the cellar? Did they chain-smoke, read, play cards to pass the time while they waited for the pilot's next command? Career guys, most of them. Firefighters, with an engineering bent. Irish and Italian. Their uncles, fathers, and brothers—firefighters before them—had laid down the paving stones that marked their nepotistic path.

There were no paving stones for me. My father is a car mechanic in Massachusetts. I'm here only by blissful accident, having stumbled aboard in February 2001—a naive young upstart with a university degree. A bubble-salaried dot-commer. A striving, big-city editor. A woman.

When I look at the black-and-white photographs of old-time crews—ranks of short-haired men, some young, shirtless, and grinning; others defiant; a few older ones, impassive, their stern expressions suggesting what a handful the younger ones can be—I want to know them. But I'm not sure the feeling would be mutual. These men probably never imagined that someone like me would be running their boat, their engines. All my compulsive investigations began as an attempt to bridge that gap. The distance between us is what first fueled my fascination with the fireboat's history—a fascination that escalated to obsession, then swelled to encompass the history of the Hudson River, whose industries helped forge the nation. I've since fallen in love with workboats, with engineering, with the Hudson.

As American society continues to become more virtual, less hands-on, I'm a salmon swimming upstream. I have come to view the transformation of our country through a Hudson River lens. More and more, my days are defined by physical work—shifting levers, turning wrenches, welding steel. As I work and research, a picture begins to form of the history of American industry mapped through personal landmarks. As the United States faces economic upheaval that challenges us to rethink who we want to be as a nation, I have discovered that it pays to take stock of who we have been: a country of innovators and doers, of people who make things, of workers who toil, sweat, and labor with their hands.

My own, personal compulsion to understand the country's progression was born out of the ashes of the steamship *Muenchen*. Maybe not being able to witness, firsthand, the leaving of the flowers is what drives me to dig up the details.

✦ ✦ ✦

Classic Fireboats in Action 1900–1950 isn't available on DVD, so when it arrives in a brown padded envelope, I have to pull the TV down from a shelf in the closet instead of just sliding a disc into my laptop. Perched in front of the twelve-by-eight-inch screen that I've wired to an old VCR, I rewind the tape over and over again, playing back the same scenes, dredging for details. I slow it down, letting the video advance frame by frame, watching the billowing smoke head toward heaven in a sequence of awkward jumps. The boat I'm straining to find is fireboat *Thomas Willett*.

The raw footage is grainy. Long scratches gouged into the original film squiggle across the television screen. Abrupt lighting shifts flash every few seconds, casting the images in new shades of black, white, and gray. At the center of the frame, the SS *Muenchen* lists precariously to port. The North German Lloyd passenger and cargo ocean liner is not only afire, it's sinking under the weight of all the water the firefighters are using to try to save her. I scoot my chair in closer and squint, my face inches from the screen. Even though I know how this story ends, it doesn't diminish the knot in my gut as I prepare to watch it unfold.

According to newspaper reports, the *Willett* (named after New York's first mayor, who served in the 1660s) was the first of New York City's fireboat fleet to respond to that morning's alarm call from her station, fewer than ten piers away. The court records I dug up at the National Archives revealed that the *Willett*'s pilot, John Harvey, a forty-eight-year-old career firefighter with nearly twenty-four years on the job, was unmarried and lived at 82 Jane Street with his "permanently crippled" brother William F. and his unwed sister Sadie V.; John J.'s salary, it seems, supported them all. But it's the *Classic Fire-*

boats narrator who reveals that February 11, 1930, happened to be Harvey's last day before retirement.

Alongside Pier 42, at the foot of Leroy Street in Manhattan's West Village, the *Muenchen* sits tipped disconcertingly close to the building on the pier. Her masts, taller than the two-story pier shed beside her, disappear in cumulus clouds of smoke. Firefighters pummel her with water from all sides. Multiple streams—at least five, maybe more—surge through pier-shed windows. Where the water makes contact with the fire's heat, bursts of smoke leap out, then head for the sky. Less than a hundred feet off the ocean liner's starboard side, a fireboat delivers still more water, sending ferocious jets of spray onto the ship's superstructure. But through the haze of the smoke, I can't tell which boat it is, and the narration—generalities with no play-by-play—offers little assistance.

In the next shot, I watch a few nameless, faceless, helmeted firefighters shifting equipment on the aft deck of a fireboat positioned off the *Muenchen*'s stern. This low-quality footage has the film-speed hiccups characteristic of early motion-picture photography, which makes it hard not to assume that people actually moved all Chaplinesque and chicken-like back then, in an age before color existed. The entire shaky video has a security-camera quality to it. Even my frame-by-frame viewing isn't enough to bear witness. But at least I can make out the nameboard on this boat that's just moving into view: the *James Duane*, sister ship to the *Willett*. I'm getting closer.

But then, as quickly as it begins, the two minutes of tape just ends, midblaze. The video skips ahead to 1932, to the next big fire—a five-alarmer at the Cunard Line's Pier 54, at the corner of Eleventh Avenue and Fourteenth Street, that was one of the worst pier fires in New York City history. This was the first chance the rookie fireboat, the new flagship of the fleet, had to demonstrate that the $582,500 invested in building the largest, most powerful fireboat in the world was worth every city penny. Making her on-screen debut is the FDNY Marine Division's first internal combustion–powered vessel, "my" boat: fireboat *John J. Harvey*. My chest fills up at the sight of her. But with her arrival, I realize that the story I'm so hungry to see has happened off-camera.

Instead, I will hunt down the details of that day in the electronic databases, on microfilm viewer screens, and in archives, with their dusty docket books of tissue-thin pages filled with elegant, slanted script.

Before the *Muenchen* departed Bremen, I learn, dockworkers had loaded the ship's cargo spaces with thousands of different items: thirty-five cases of hosiery, five cases of artificial flowers, thirteen cases of hollow glassware (pharmacy vials for Eli Lilly), an entire household's worth of goods—from linens to bric-a-brac, belonging to a Mrs. Hilda Schaper—and seven thousand canaries.

Back then this assemblage of mismatched break-bulk cargo was the norm. Uniform products like coal or grain that could be sent tumbling loosely down into ships' holds constituted bulk cargoes. But break-bulk comprised diverse items of all shapes, weights, and sizes packed side by side, one on top of the other, in the gaping maw of a ship's hold—everything from easels to kid gloves to crockery.

Newspaper articles offer some clues about the fire. Short "reaction" snippets tell about the thousands in New Jersey who "gathered at scores of vantage points along the Palisades [to watch] huge billows of smoke rising from the liner." Feature stories reconstruct events in full, lurid detail. It is in one of these longer pieces, tucked into a little sentence at the end, that I first read about the canaries. Along with Harvey's fate, the birds' story has me transfixed. I can picture the birds in the dark hold, lonely for their lost mountain home.

More details surface at the National Archives, where my big break comes, by chance, in one of the docket books on the rolling cart that the researchers drag out to a special pencils-only (to protect the documents from ink) room. The docket book leads to an extensive paper trail: files full of court claims for lost-property damages or, in Harvey's case, a loss of life. Sadie Harvey filed a claim for her brother, and stacks of other documents reveal innumerable quotidian details about the lives of *Muenchen* passengers: masons, housewives, barbers, carpenters, and tailors with names like Otto, Heinrich, Kasper, Barbara, August, and Paul. Along with foreign tourists and returning American vacationers, the steamship carried scores of immigrants planning new lives in the United States. These pages catalog the lives and property that pilot John Harvey had been called upon to save.

✦ ✦ ✦

Reported by wireless:

February 10. S.S. Muenchen, Bremen to New York (North German Lloyd Line), was 500 miles east of Sandy Hook, due 11th, 9 a.m.

Landfall was still a night away when the *Muenchen* steamed past New Jersey's Sandy Hook, through the Narrows, and into the open mouth of New York's Upper Bay at nine thirty p.m. on Monday, February 10. According to law and tradition, Captain Feodor Bruenings dropped anchor at New York's Quarantine, the public health station where, for decades, inbound steamers had been stopping for inspection by immigration and public health officials. In the predawn darkness, a mail tender tied up alongside, and 1,757 mail sacks shot down canvas chutes onto the tender's deck for delivery to the General Post Office the following morning. In their cabins, vacationers savored their last night aboard, enjoying the calm seas inside the protected harbor, while immigrants tossed and turned with anticipation, knowing that no familiar bed awaited them ashore. All the while, Gotham's lights twinkled in the distance.

When dawn broke on Tuesday morning, the weak winter sunlight did little to warm the frozen air. As engineers down below fired up the ship's two triple-expansion steam engines, a rhythmic throb and hiss vibrated up through the decks, telling passengers their wait was over. A pack of assist tugs, with their snub-nosed bows and tall, cylindrical stacks puffing white steam and black coal smoke, shepherded the *Muenchen* into New York harbor. Upon entering the mouth of the Hudson, passengers could see the moss-green Statue of Liberty standing guard on the left as they passed Governors Island on the right. Straight ahead, at the very tip of Manhattan Island, a squat, round fort at the water's edge, Castle Clinton, came into view. Built for the War of 1812, Castle Clinton served as America's first official immigration center from 1855 to 1890, before passing that torch to Ellis Island. Here, at the tip of Manhattan Island, the feet of ten million immigrants first touched American soil.

✦ ✦ ✦

Sitting in the glow of a microfilm reader, I scan the ship's manifest, silently pronouncing passengers' names, wondering which of them braved the wind on the deck to watch the seemingly endless expanse of ocean give way to the bustle of New York harbor as they followed a path taken by millions before them. How long did they plan to stay in the United States? inquired immigration officials. "Always," came the reply.

A few months earlier, on October 29, 1929—Black Tuesday— the stock-market plunge had rattled the city and the nation. Then, as now, the U.S. economy was in a state of flux. But New York City still buzzed with activity. Each morning, men in hats and ties filled the avenues on their way to work. In the Wall Street district alone, half a million commuters continued to staff banks; railroad corporations; insurance and telegraph companies; steamship builders; and coal, iron, steel, and copper dealers. Ticker tape machines rattled off trades, and meanwhile, all along the waterfront, and up and down the Hudson River, the world's cargo changed hands.

1904 view of West Street and the Hudson River looking north. *(Collection of The New-York Historical Society, neg. 56570)*

Shipping had fueled the city's economy, making Manhattan the dominant American seaport since before the Civil War and one of the world's major international ports by 1900. On that Tuesday morning in February 1930, West Street teemed with trucks ready to transport the barrels, crates, and pallets full of cargo that was soon to arrive, for the shipping news that filled page after page of a dozen New York dailies had announced the names of no fewer than seventeen liners due into port. Pictures from the 1930s offer glimpses of what the morning of February 11, 1930, may have looked like. Covered piers fanned out like fingers around the edge of Manhattan—a "horizontal city" that extended over the water, spreading like reflections of the skyscrapers above that stretched skyward. Steamers, ferries, and tugboats pulling strings of barges behind them created rush-hour traffic on a laneless thoroughfare. Although no one in the harbor that day could have heard the change coming above the harbor's busy hum, the wave of waterfront industry on Manhattan's shores was already beginning to crest. Within decades, it would vanish.

Steaming north up the west side of Manhattan, the *Muenchen* entered a major hub of maritime trade, the center of commercial shipping. En route to Pier 42, the ship passed crowded freight piers operated by a multitude of railroads. Typical of most transatlantic-steamship terminals of the time, the North German Lloyd Line's pier shed was built on a platform supported by a field of wooden piles driven one hundred feet into Hudson River mud. On this dais stood an ornate two-story building supported by exposed steel framing with catwalks, which extended above the shed's peaked roofline, serving as hoisting towers for loading and unloading. Clad in a skin of tin or copper sheeting, the building had large wooden cargo-bay doors along the lower level, while the upper level housed a long, open hall for passengers, with skylights that ran the length of the ceiling.

As the *Muenchen* approached, the longshoremen were waiting. Having read about offloading jobs in the papers the day before the ship pulled in, hordes of dockworkers had assembled on the streets near the piers, dipping now and then into local saloons to take shelter from the cold. The lucky ones whom the bosses had picked for work braced themselves for what would be a grueling day, well aware that hundreds of men stood ready to take their place should they falter.

Whenever a ship pulled in, the longshoremen worked for days on end with little more than a meal break. They labored in sweltering ship holds in summer, navigated rain-slicked gangways in spring, and on winter days like February 11, 1930, skidded across icy docks, all while hefting up to three-hundred-plus-pound loads. A worker was expected to move one ton each hour. It's no surprise they suffered three times as many injuries as construction workers and eight times those suffered in manufacturing. Brutal as it was, the work paid better than anything else readily available to a blue-collar worker without a high school education.

When the *Muenchen* came into view, the first crew of longshoremen, specially picked for preparations, kicked into gear. They opened pier doors and readied gangways, lines, and fenders. After the fleet of helper tugs nudged the *Muenchen* into the slip, the unloading race began—for people and cargo alike. At 9:10 a.m. the first passengers went ashore. First-class passengers disembarked first, of course—the notables among them posing for pictures that would run in the evening papers. In 1930, ship dockings still made news.

For the next hour offloading gangs rigged the deck, readied the slings, nets, and trucks, and started uncovering the ship's cargo hatches. Hollers and whistles erupted as men heaved sacks onto platforms, snagged carton edges with sinister-looking wood-handled steel hooks, and rolled wood barrels up steep planks. Movement of most goods demanded sheer brute force. Though offloading had begun, there was still no sign of the fire.

The dock was soon covered with a jumble of paper cartons and wooden casks and crates. Five cases of umbrella cloth, thirty-seven tubs of cheese, forty-three cases of harmonicas, and twenty cases of bronze wire—these items and hundreds more, stowed in a single cargo hold, had been loaded into place by hand. Efficient shipping depended on filling every inch of usable space, so dockworkers in Bremen had crammed cargo into compartments with little regard for what items might not keep good company. That's the way things were done. And such imprudence kept New York City's fireboats in business.

✦ ✦ ✦

When pilot John Harvey rounded up on the south side of Pier 42 at 11:30 a.m., he maneuvered fireboat *Thomas Willett* into position off the starboard quarter of the *Muenchen*, adjacent to Hold Six. As fire-fighters on board readied the deck guns to spray water, Harvey held the boat on station just a few feet from the burning liner. Just then, a tremendous blast erupted.

Showers of glass flew off the *Muenchen* as the ship's portholes shattered. A large steel plate shot into the sky and landed inches from a firefighter, who froze in his tracks. The 263 crew members still aboard the ship scurried like insects, sliding down ropes and jumping to the decks of nearby barges and small craft.

Captain Bruenings rushed to his cabin to snatch up the ship's papers and the logbook. Discovering he was trapped inside, he chopped through a wood partition with an ax, then slid down a mooring line to the pier to escape.

Three more explosions followed in quick succession, blowing the bottom out of the aft end of the ship. The river rushed into the lower hold as her ragged flanks settled into the mud. Despite the flooding, the ship continued to burn from the inside out, the fire feeding on cargo and the woodwork in the cabins.

Meanwhile, the International Association of Fire Chiefs, which happened to be holding a two-day conference at the Hotel Pennsylvania, suspended the day's sessions to stand on the roof and watch the inferno.

✦ ✦ ✦

A year after the *Muenchen* fire, a rivet gang, at the foot of Twenty-third Street in Brooklyn's Gowanus Bay, set to work fitting steel. Crews were building, under New York City contract, the largest, most powerful fireboat the world had ever seen. At 130 feet long and twenty-eight feet wide, she would pump eighteen thousand gallons of water per minute—as much as twenty fire trucks. The rest of the FDNY Marine Division's boats ran on steam; this was to be the first powered by internal combustion. With five engines that generated direct-current electricity to run the propeller motors, she would run 18 miles per hour, and only slightly slower while pumping.

On June 23, Fire Commissioner John Dorman drove the first rivet into the first hull frame. By October, a mere four months later, the boat, dressed in ribbons and bunting, slid down the shipway, with what *must* have been sparkling cider still dripping off her bow—champagne would have been illegal, with Prohibition still in effect. Mayor Jimmy Walker attended, as did the commissioner and his daughter, clutching several dozen roses in her gloved hands. When the boat was put into service that December, it was said to be the "last word" in marine firefighting apparatus. The model of modern fireboat engineering, the *John J. Harvey*, designated Engine 57, would set the standard for all fireboats to come.

Fireboat *John J. Harvey* showing off on December 17, 1931, near the George Washington Bridge. *(Photo by United Press International, from the collection of Tim Ivory)*

Meanwhile, at the corner of Thirty-fourth Street and Fifth Avenue, another crew of ironworkers threw up steel, still warm from Pennsylvania mills, at the staggering pace of four-and-a-half stories per week. Though lingering on the cusp of the Great Depression, America was still expanding. Four-man rivet gangs perched on wooden planks balanced hundreds of feet above the street. The "heater" would fling a red-hot, mushroom-shaped nugget up to the "sticker-in," who would catch the rivet in a metal can, pluck it out with tongs, and jam it into an empty hole. Next the "bucker-up" would fit a dolly bar over the mushroom cap–like button-head to brace the still-hot rivet. Then, with a deafening clatter, the "gunman," or riveter, drove the protruding stem with an air hammer called a rivet gun. The gangs moved at a record clip, because there was money at stake. Not just the cash-filled envelopes the bosses handed them on payday, but also the coins and bills they'd tossed into the hat as a wager that their trade's gang would beat out all the other trades' gangs in the sky-high race to build the Empire State Building, a symbol of American engineering prowess that could be seen from miles away.

I caught my first glimpse of the Hudson River from an office in the Empire State Building. The river, like the building, has long since transformed from an industrial site into a tourist attraction. Today, standing in the belly of the fireboat that was born in the wake of steamship *Muenchen*'s demise, I look through the engine-room portholes at the meager few finger piers that still remain. I register the gaps, like empty spaces between the teeth of a broken comb.

North River piers, Manhattan, circa 1930. *(Courtesy NYC Municipal Archives)*

Buoyed by history, I consider how the past informs the present. The Hudson is known as the river that flows two ways, its waters a brackish mix of seawater from tides pushing upstream and fresh mountain runoff pushing down. I know what it's like to feel pulled in two directions at once. I oscillate between worlds: white- and blue-collar, virtual and physical, human and machine, preservation and obsolescence, land and water. My days on the Hudson transport me through the past to the present, granting me uncommon access to the lasting lessons of history that somehow, as they likely have through time immeasurable, feel more important today than ever before.

Chapter Two

Girl Meets Boat

∽

ON MY FIRST day at the fireboat controls in April 2001, I have an audience of men. Never before has a woman run these engines. The pedestal was designed for someone six feet tall, and I'm five foot five, so the leverage is all wrong. Whenever the captain, Bob Lenney, signals Full Ahead, I need two hands to move the control lever into position, and have to stand on my toes to swing the telegraph pointer all the way up.

Props at 100 rpm for slow, 200 for half, 300-plus for full. Huntley Gill, one of the boat's original investors, had thrown all these numbers at me in a five-minute rundown, his cavalier tone only exacerbating my nervousness. He was the one who had offered me the chance to try my hand at engineering. "I don't know anything," I'd said, giving him a chance to back out.

"You don't have to," he'd replied. "A trained monkey could do it."

In his khaki shorts, oval, wire-rimmed glasses, and brown leather boat shoes, Huntley seemed to belong on decks of gleaming white, or varnished wood, not rusted steel. A construction manager with a degree in historic preservation from Columbia University, he keeps the *Harvey* moving by writing grants, scheduling trips, keeping the books, as well as steering whenever Bob can't be there. He has also rallied a contingent of friends who lend their support to the boat's not-for-profit in various ways.

Don't let the amps climb past 1,350. Run each engine at eleven hundred. "All set?" Huntley asked, then headed back up the stairs, leaving me alone at the stand.

On a bell boat like this one, the pilot can't directly control the propellers, so he signals down to the engine room from where he stands in the wheelhouse. By moving a red pointer on a telegraph—a brass dial marked with Slow, Half, and Full, in two directions, Ahead and Astern—he indicates which direction and how fast he wants to go. Today the movement of the propellers will depend on me. I have to read the commands, then shift the levers that move the boat and regulate its speed, in a harbor full of other vessels. Though I can't see the boats from where I stand, I know they're out there. It's the first warm Saturday of the season.

As I stand searching for answers in the gauges, sucking in short, tight breaths, the sun stops spilling down the stairs for a split second. I turn around and watch a pair of work boots begin their descent. It's Tim Ivory, the supervisor and mastermind of the boat's restoration, who is also in charge of everyday operations. A New Jersey native, he started washing trucks for an oil company at age thirteen and began fixing them two years later. After a long stint as a diesel mechanic at UPS, he went into the marine repair business, and by the time he started working on the fireboat in 1999, he had already earned a reputation around the harbor as someone who could fix anything. "That Timmy kid can make a piece of shit run," as someone once put it. It has since become his tagline, and when the time comes, he says, those words will be etched on his tombstone. Tim's mechanical and diagnostic abilities have found a perfect home on this 1931 diesel-electric boat that is always in need of repair. It was Tim, in fact, who first got the boat running again, shortly after its purchase at a scrap auction. One of the new owners, a real estate broker named Chase Wells, had asked him, "When do you think we could take the boat for a ride?"

Tim's answer was, "Do you have running lights?"—a response that basically translates to, "How about now?"

All I know at this moment, however, is that this is Tim's engine room and he seems none too pleased about me being there. Apparently, no one had asked him before inviting me to try out. With an unsmiling nod, Tim heads toward the back. I hear the chug of an engine trying to catch. Then another. Each *hrumph* rumbles in my chest and I feel a sudden urge to pee. Tim starts the engines, one by one, while I stand in one spot, hands limp at my sides. How did I get here? I wonder as the space roars to life. When Tim returns, I wave him over, leaning in toward his muffed ear and yelling, "I don't know how to pump water." Water displays are a regular part of each trip, and Huntley hadn't mentioned anything about how to start the pumps.

"That's later," Tim snorts. "You think we'd just leave you down here by yourself?"

"Uh . . . no?" I stammer, my shoulders tight, the soles of my feet tingling, semi-numb from being planted so firmly.

The engines ring out like a siren call, and a bunch of guys, one wielding a video camera, come down the stairs to watch me pull the boat off the dock. Sweat pools, sticky where the plastic earmuffs rest on my cheeks, beading up and running over my temples, trickling off my jaw. I don't dare take my hands off the prop levers to wipe away the drips. I stand at attention, my body rigid, my head full of numbers.

The first signal rings down: Slow Ahead. I lean my weight into the brass lever and it click-clicks stiffly forward. I watch the needle on the propeller gauge, and when it creeps past one hundred—too fast—my heart lurches and I yank the lever back. I don't look at the faces around me. I convince myself that the video camera is just another set of eyes. My own eyes dart across the control panel's gauges, reading the words: jacket water, lube oil, fuel. But their meanings don't register.

Another clang from the wheelhouse. Slow Astern on the left side, this time. It seems counterintuitive to go in two directions at once. I falter and Tim jumps in from behind. Without a word, he grabs the lever, folding his whole huge hand around my white knuckles, and jerks it into position. "Sorry," I mouth. He steps back and I feel the blood rush to my head. Some monkey.

But at the end of the trip, I sit with the crew, sipping a Brooklyn Brown Ale. The pilot, Bob, shakes my hand. "Very responsive," he says, which means everything coming from this man of few words. A graduate of the U.S. Merchant Marine Academy at King's Point, Bob had sailed the seas before landing a job with the fire department and working his way into the Marine Division. He first piloted the

Harvey in 1963 and steered her full-time from 1979 until 1994, the year the fire department placed the boat on reserve status. When she retired, so did he. Reunited in their respective retirements, there's no question that when it comes down to it, all paperwork aside, this is Bob's boat.

The glass beer bottle in my hand drips condensate onto the steel deck, and I poke at the puddle with my sneakered toe. I hang quietly in the background, listening to the boat banter as the sun dips lower in the sky and a breeze kicks up off the river. This is the first of many nights I will find myself skipping city cocktails in favor of beers on the boat to hear the salts swap stories.

◆ ◆ ◆

A few weeks earlier, I still had my dot-com job. I was working at a desk wedged into a corner of the Empire State Building's Suite 5809. My big, fat title—director of content and site development—conveyed the self-inflated grandeur of the dot-com era. I was twenty-seven years old. So was the CEO. My dad had been bragging to people back home that his daughter worked in the Empire State Building. "The Lady gazes up at *her*," he'd say, referring to the Statue of Liberty. Really I was gazing down, in wonder, at the blur of activity below.

At eight or nine o'clock at night, when hunger finally commandeered my concentration, I'd microwave a frozen vegetable potpie and bring it back to my desk. Crust crumbs and sauce drips would land on papers while my attention strayed out the window. This self-centered city defied sunset with all manner of electric light. Between buildings a dark smear on the cityscape was the only thing not all lit up and zooming—the river. I had only ever seen the Hudson from a distance, through windows.

My company had sublet the office space from an Irishman named David Beatty, who owned a dot-com incubator and was—along with Huntley, Chase, and a few others—another of the fireboat's original purchasers. One fall day he invited the whole office to join him on a "leaf-peeping" trip to Bear Mountain on a fireboat. I'd never heard of Bear Mountain, and had no idea what he meant by "fireboat," so I replied with a polite no.

His next invitation came in February 2001. David announced the boat was hosting a volunteer workday. "Come down and get dirty!" he said.

I had been driving a desk for years, but my dad had taught me a long time ago about what kinds of work mattered. "Pushing papers" was not included in his list. People in offices didn't really *do* anything. Here I was making Web sites—things you can't even hold in your hands. This time when David invited me, I said yes.

That Saturday, I walked west along Twenty-third Street, watching to make sure the numbers of the avenues I crossed were going up. The directions sounded simple enough: Take Twenty-third Street west until it reaches the river. But at that time, even though I had lived in New York City a whole year, I'd hardly spent any time navigating Manhattan geography except for the occasional networking party. Working twelve to fourteen hours a day, then taking late-night taxicabs back to Brooklyn, hadn't given me much chance to get my city bearings.

Twenty-third Street ended in a parking lot. This did not give me confidence. But I crossed the West Side Highway, reassured by the sign for Chelsea Piers, which David had mentioned was a landmark anyone would know, and the entrance to Basketball City, where a swarm of kids dribbled their way up the steps to the door.

It seems so obvious to me now that when you're looking for a boat, you have to find water, but that thought didn't occur to me then. The last time I'd been on a boat, when I was nine or ten, my dad had taken me on a whale-watching cruise in rough seas off Gloucester, Massachusetts, and I'd thrown up my fake-crabmeat sandwich. A long time passed before I could eat seafood salad again. Or think of boarding another boat.

As I rounded the corner of the Basketball City building, I spotted a big red-and-white vessel with a tower on the back. It was rusty. Really rusty. Everywhere, on every surface, buckling pockmarks of metal peeled away from itself in layers.

David, Huntley, Chase, and a handful of others had purchased the boat at auction from New York City in 1999 on little more than a whim, instigated by a character named John Krevey. The Fire Department's Marine Division had given up on the boat as too expensive to maintain, but the group had pooled their resources to buy it because they thought it would be cool to have a fire yacht. Their bid of $28,010 beat the next highest bidder, whose intention was to chop up the boat for scrap. Yet, here she was, two years later, hosting her first crew of volunteer workers determined to get her back into shape. Today the boat is cared for by a nonprofit that relies entirely on donations. But on this, its first volunteer day, the boat is beginning her latest transition. She had gone from working fireboat to outdated hulk to a platform for beer barbecues, and now is becoming a more serious restoration and preservation project.

At 130 feet long and twenty-eight feet wide, with two decks and a fifteen-foot tower on the stern, the boat was too big and daunting for me to take in all at once, so I scanned around for David, my only point of reference. I found him on the upper deck and called out to him from the pier.

"Oh, hel-*loh*!" he chirped in his high-pitched brogue. "Come on aboard."

But just as quickly as David said hello, he said good-bye. "I can't stay, but don't worry, Tim will tell you what needs doing. Come on, I'll introduce you."

It was after noon and the workday was already in full swing, so I followed David down some stairs to a room full of machinery: pipes and wires and five massive engines—each one seemingly as large as a Volkswagen Beetle. All the equipment was painted the same peeling gray.

We found Tim squatting to offer instructions to a worker whose torso was sticking out from a hole in the floor. When he stood up, I had to tip my head back to meet his eyes. I shook his mitt of a hand and tried to ignore what looked like a smirk when I caught him checking out my green Vans sneakers and eyeballing the barrette in my short, gel-slicked red hair.

"Here, help these guys," Tim said, casting me off to work with three men who were cutting out old, unused heating pipe with a power saw. My job was to carry the lengths up the stairs to the deck. But before long, the pile was gone and I was lobbying for a new assignment. I approached one of the guys, recently retired from the NYPD, whose name was Lew.

"So, um, would you trust me with that Sawzall?" I asked. Lew looked down at me and I braced myself for his answer. When I was little, my dad had used a Sawzall to cut the top off the pumpkin so we could carve it for Halloween. I'd seen the tool in action, and I figured I could handle it.

"Sure I would, Jessica," Lew replied. I was surprised he remembered my name after such a fleeting introduction, but that would happen to me a lot in the coming years. As I would learn, it's just part of being the only girl in a boys' world: Everybody knows your name. Lew handed over the saw with a smile that I couldn't interpret, and someone happened to snap a picture just a few moments later.

Years later I would see how clueless I was, sitting on top of a five-foot-high diesel, my head cocked back, with the two-foot power saw in the crook of my elbow, the six-inch blade gnawing through brass pipes above my head. The fingertips of the work gloves somebody lent me are at least an inch too long, the ends flat and empty. I'm squinting, my lips pulled in tight, my chin jutting out. To someone as green as I was then, I look tough. But to anyone who knows anything—my little brother, for instance—the photo reveals my naïveté. "You're working above your head with no eye protection? Jesus, Jess. You don't get a second chance with that stuff," scolded Josh, four years my junior, when I showed him the photo. "I never want to see a picture like that again." Today I see what he means, but tempering my retrospective cringe is a rush of warmth for the person I was then: gung-ho, innocent, ready.

In another photo someone took near the end of the workday, I'm standing next to Lew, who's got a fuzzy stars-and-stripes hat perched on his white head. He's grinning below his white mustache. My head comes up only to his shoulders, and I look like a club kid in the brown UPS-type work jacket I'd bought in a thrift store in San Francisco. Embroidered in yellow where the name should go, the letters spell out "Hot," in cursive, with a capital H. My hands are stuffed in my pockets, but I remember how the skin on my right hand, between my thumb and forefinger, was raw and red. I fingered the warmth of the still-forming blisters like a happy secret. Though I'd offered the camera nothing more than a closed-lip smile, hiding my grin, I made sure to write my name and e-mail address on the volunteer list.

Before we dispersed, Tim invited everyone to come out on the trip planned for eleven o'clock that night. He laughed when he said it. The offer was sincere, but he didn't expect many takers, since the forecast called for a drop into the teens. I had plans to have drinks with a radio producer friend who was in from out of town. Anyway, February was no time for boat rides.

✦ ✦ ✦

That night, having stepped out of a bar in Chelsea, I stood alone on the street corner. My friend had bailed early. Between the Ketel One and the conversation, I was a little disoriented, so I looked to the street signs for direction: Twenty-third Street and Eighth Avenue. Then I checked my watch: 10:55. A flashbulb popped in my head. Just then a cab rolled up. I waved spastically at the driver, and slid into the backseat. "Quick! Chelsea Piers! I have to catch a boat!"

We made the three blocks in no time.

Before I could see the boat, I could smell it. The exhaust billowed white in the cold, pouring a diesel fog into the parking lot in front of Basketball City. It was hard to run up the wooden ramp in heeled boots; ice was already beginning to form. When I made it to the pier edge, a tall man in a tan blizzard suit stood on deck. It was Tim, whose blue knit hat was pulled so tight over his head that only his earlobes poked out. His green eyes squinted at me from above his high, chiseled cheekbones, skin red with the cold.

"I was here earlier today," I said, like it was a question.

He offered me a gloved hand. I took it and stepped over the gap and onto the boat. Tim pointed me to the wheelhouse, where the captain steers, and I climbed the steps. At the top of the stairs, I could see the lights pouring off the far shore in New Jersey. Long, distorted beams shimmered on the river, warbling in the current. The boat stretched for an eternity behind me. An array of water guns pointed skyward, some on this deck, some on a tall metal tower toward the back.

The wooden door at the back of the wheelhouse swung heavy in my hand. I said hello to the man at the helm, who turned, nodded, and without speaking, shrugged at the brown pleather swivel chair behind him. The Jersey lights shone through the front windows behind his head. He was wrapped head to toe, just his fogged-up glasses peeking through an opening in his full-face ski mask. That's when the cold began to register. My thin leather jacket was great for bars but not for February boat rides. I was the only passenger and the only one not dressed for the occasion.

The boat slipped off the dock and out into the black river, but I hardly noticed the water. The city lights had me mesmerized. Wind blasted through gaps in the doorjamb and window frames. The steel walls sucked in cold, hoarding it like an icebox. The lights skimmed by, and I flipped up my collar, zipped together my thighs in their thin dress pants, pulled my shoulders up to my ears, and began to wonder if my toes were still attached. And where were we going exactly? And for how long? Just then a guy named Billy came up the stairs from the deck. I'd met him that afternoon. He was probably in his twenties, and I'd listened to him complain/brag about his hangover.

"You still here?" I asked. When I watched the slow recognition come over his round, freckled face, I realized how pathetic I must look, all folded in on myself.

"You must be freezing," he said, eyes wide beneath bushy reddish eyebrows.

"Yeah, well, I wasn't planning on coming. It's just that I came out of the bar, and I was right on Twenty-third Street, and then the cab was right there . . ."

"Here. Put this on," he said, peeling off one of three jackets.

"No, I'm not going to take your coat 'cause I was too dumb to wear something warmer." I worried about the price of his chivalry, but he insisted, and the grip of the cold was making it hard to breathe. I let him help pull the thick, brown work coat around me. The residual warmth poured through my own flimsy coat, and I was struck by the raw humanity in that transfer of heat.

Billy went back out on deck and I huddled in the corner, watching the man at the wheel, who I later learned was John Doswell. He wasn't the regular pilot, but just filling in. Other than Tim, the whole crew was temporary that night, which in retrospect made the whole trip that much more surreal. John maneuvered the boat, taking position in front of a waterfront restaurant. Some bigwig lawyer was having a party inside, and had paid for the water display that brought these fireboat people out on this frigid night.

Suddenly the rumble of the engines quieted. Then a great roar trembled up from someplace down low. The roar shook louder; then came an enormous whoosh of air. In an instant the whole deck exploded with water. The sky had opened up, only upside down. Water peeled through the big guns on the towers with mind-boggling force. Spray flicked off in all directions, cast aloft by the columns of water plunging into the river.

That night the water cannons pumped water in celebration, but for over a century fireboats and their deck guns have played a crucial protective role in port cities like New York. For an island edged with wooden finger piers, fireboats like the *Harvey* were the city's most critical defense against the spread of a fire from the water's edge inland. Powerful enough to blast through a concrete wall, the spray from these boats unleashed an endless supply of river water to quench harbor blazes. Even with no concrete wall in sight, I was awestruck— transfixed by the volume of water shooting into the sky then crashing through the river's surface.

A blast of cold air interrupted my trance. Tim had swung open the wheelhouse door. He was laughing. "It's going up water and coming down hail," he said. "I just got hit." Ice crystals glistened on curls of dark hair that poked out beneath his hat. He must have felt my stare because he turned, looked at me, and then said, "Come on, I'll take you to the warmest spot on the boat." Without waiting for a response, he yanked a pair of plastic earmuffs off the railing and tossed them in my direction.

I had no toes. They'd died in my boots. So when I tottered down the stairs behind Tim, I had to look to be sure I placed a foot on each step. The stairs ended in a bunk room. Four beds stood in stacks of two on the right-hand side. On the left, a metal table was piled with anonymous junk. It didn't look like anyone had slept here in a long time. I followed Tim as he headed for an open door, toward the light and the noise.

When I passed though the hatchway, I couldn't stop blinking. The engine room had come alive. I'd been here in daylight, with the boat dockside, gently swaying, the only noise a low, whirring hum. Now the whole space was aglow and trembling. The bellow of the engines vibrated in my chest. An oily exhaust smell scratched at the back of my throat. I looked left, then right, trying to take in all the dripping, shaking, spinning parts. There was the engine I'd perched on just hours ago. It had sat there asleep while I'd steadied myself on top. Now it was a throbbing, living thing.

Tim gestured me to a spot toward the back between two running engines, and left me there. Slowly, warmth crept through the thin fabric of my pants, blessing the skin on my thighs. When I tipped my head up to blow life back into my fingertips I spied a man eyeballing me from the center of the room. I gave a nod. I'd had no idea he'd been down here all this time. I was going to say hello, but my attention was stolen first by the control panel, then by the maze of wires on the ceiling. I tried to trace a section of braided cable—several clusters seemed to feed into an electric panel with open, Frankenstein knife switches—but my eyes got lost. The growling engines. The power. The diesel stink. I shook my head, dumbfounded that anyone could comprehend this technology.

The man at the panel kept watching me, and when he returned my smile, I approached. "I was here earlier," I shouted, thinking he would hear me. He just looked at me and blinked. I pointed toward the empty brackets near the ceiling and shouted, "I cut out the pipes."

After a moment, he leaned into my right ear, peeling the plastic muff from my cheek, and shouted back, in a thick Ukrainian accent, "You like it, old boat?"

"Yes," I said, nodding. "Yes, I do."

At some point I found my way back to the wheelhouse. As we approached the pier after what seemed like hours since our departure, a mad ringing of bells started up. The pilot was struggling to shimmy the boat back to its spot, yanking levers back and forth and swinging the wheel left and right. Everything he did seemed to elicit more mysterious bells. But none of it brought the boat any closer to the pier. I tried to pay attention, to understand what he was doing, but it was too cold to think. I was bone cold—the kind of cold that dry furnace heat can't fix. The kind you have to thaw with a hot bath. Outside I could see Billy and Tim on the icy deck. A flurry of thick ropes, half frozen, flew through the air.

Across the pier, a line was forming on the ramp leading to the doorway of another old boat, even bigger than this one—a lightship called *Frying Pan* that was being used as a floating dance club. Twentysomethings lined up in skimpy outfits waiting for the bouncer to let them in. They were as ill prepared for this weather as I was.

It wasn't until I was sitting in the backseat of the cab on my way home that I noticed that the odor of the boat was still with me. Then I realized it *was* me. The diesel fumes had seeped into my clothes. I didn't know then how that smell would invade my life. It makes a stink that defies repeated washings. Months later, I'd have to establish a separate drawer, and then a whole dresser, for my fireboat clothes.

Back in Brooklyn, I showered, then shivered under a pile of covers for a solid hour. I could still feel the throb of the engines. The intense physicality of the day was unlike anything I'd ever experienced. For years to come, my first time aboard would seem fantastical, otherworldly, like returning to someplace after you've seen it in a dream. But that night a single thought echoed: I need to get back on that boat. It came on with such force that, at the time, I didn't dare question why.

✦ ✦ ✦

My four siblings and I grew up with cows in our backyard and an ever-growing collection of abandoned vehicles languishing among the loosestrife and long grasses—one of them the Volkswagen bus that my parents drove across country in the late 1960s. They left as a couple and returned as a family, my mom carrying my big sister in her belly. I suppose the bus is a memento of sorts. Every day it sinks a little deeper into the swamp at the edge of the property, but no one in the family dares call it a lost cause. With two and a half acres of land, my parents are among the last homesteader holdouts in a Massachusetts town that transformed, during my lifetime, from farm country into a Boston bedroom community. There's some excuse for cars in your backyard when your dad's a mechanic (which doesn't mean the neighbors approve) because at some point the day will come to make right these rusting relics.

Growing up surrounded by wasting metal must have something to do with my passion for industrial decay. I have always been intrigued by complex mazes of industry. Even while driving I have caught myself veering toward the guardrail as the glitter of a power plant twinkling in the night captures my attention, stealing my eyes away from the road. The shiny tanks . . . the looping strings of piping, conduit, wires, and tubes creating a whole sparkling city that sucks me in with an unmitigated, visceral response.

It's not just shiny new industry that fascinates me. Once, driving in wine country outside San Francisco, I wandered onto the shoulder, drawn toward a rusty tractor that stood tangled in the tall grasses it once mowed, its seat-fluff strewn about where nesting creatures had commandeered the cushion. Left where it quit, the steel was slowly breaking down into its raw elements, becoming part of the earth once more. These things appealed to me aesthetically, yes. But it was more than that—less passive, more an active desire to engage with the machinery around me.

Days I spent as a kid in my dad's shop set the stage for my love of power tools, my lust for machinery, my awe of his ability to tear down a sick engine, rebuild it, and make it sing. But I never thought that kind of work was something *I* could do. I didn't think I was capable. In school, I caught grief for being the dorky redhead with glasses who always did her homework. My grades helped me obtain scholarships to attend Phillips Exeter Academy and Stanford University, but they didn't mean I could fix things when they broke. They didn't mean I'd ever be as mighty as my dad.

He's the one who taught me that material culture matters—that form and function are inextricably linked. Following in his footsteps, I spend more and more time working with hand tools, and appreciating the elegance of machines constructed with the goal of longevity and an eye for craft. Now hands-on work reminds me that even digital data has to live somewhere. Even the tiniest microchip occupies physical space. The more screen-focused our lives become, the more I fear we'll lose our grip on the matter that defines us and everything we hold dear.

Turning wrenches in the engine room of fireboat *John J. Harvey* gives me time to think, and I find questions about the country's future crystallizing in my mind: What are we sacrificing as we stop practicing craftsmanship? What will we lose as a culture, a nation, if we continue to devalue production and manufacturing? What constitutes real work in an economy that hinges less on making things than on selling and service? How do we find meaning in an increasingly virtual existence, in a society that divorces us from the physicality of the land and water, from face-to-face communication, from working with our hands?

✦ ✦ ✦

Months before my first fireboat ride, I had stood in the hallway of the Empire State Building's fifty-eighth floor, waiting for the elevator. It was 10:30 p.m., and I had just completed some finishing touches on what my company had been calling the Ten-Day Miracle Site. My team had been cranking nonstop to produce the impossible: a complete wellness Web site custom-branded for a new client in just ten days. We'd done it, and would each receive a $1,000 bonus for on-time completion. But the money was not what was on my mind while I stood staring with burning, bloodshot eyes at the glowing Down button beside the elevator door. I thought, I love my job—immediately followed by, What are you, nuts?

My two heads needed to justify themselves to each other, and I listened to them duke it out. Words like "exhaustion," "no life," and "neck spasm" battled with "satisfaction," "camaraderie," "building from scratch," and "making it work." I had encountered this internal parley before, in San Francisco, where I lived while finishing college—completing my last semester at the age of twenty-six. Throughout my "eight-year-degree plan," I had repeatedly taken time away from school to do something that felt "real." I worked off and on as a line cook in a natural cuisine restaurant, managed the kitchen of a brewpub, and earned my certification to teach preschool, before going back to college.

After graduation, I built spreadsheets that mapped health-plan benefits at an insurance brokerage and took a few magazine-writing gigs on the side before getting swept up in the dot-com bubble—the zeitgeist of the age—that finally brought me to my office in the Empire State Building.

Part of me did love my dot-com job. It was like running my own magazine, but with the bonus of online interactivity. Multimedia Web work felt so, well, cutting-edge. At twenty-seven I was leading a team of both technical and nontechnical people in crafting a comprehensive fitness tool. We shot video on location, recorded voice-overs for animation, designed the back-end matrix to feed the programming. We utilized new technologies to build something useful. Something new.

Our work kept pace with the pulse of the new economy—the frenetic bubble that rallied Wall Street and worried brick-and-mortar executives about how their comfortable corporate structures just might get undermined by groups of haughty young upstarts determined to overturn the basic tenets of business.

I lived off a buzzy cocktail of coffee and adrenaline. My coworker Bill's motto was "I'll sleep when I'm dead."

Mine was "Tired? Take a liquid nap."

We thrummed along, caught up in the right now. From my spot high up in the Empire State Building, after finishing the Ten-Day Miracle Site, how could I not feel like we were on top of the world?

Then, after the Miracle Site push and my first fireboat ride, a technical glitch and an accounts-payable disaster caused us to lose access, in an instant, to six months of work—the matrix, the data, the animation, the video. Snap. Gone, just like that. I was more woeful and incredulous than angry. How could that much work simply disappear? The CEO said we'd find a way to fix things, to get it back, but for me, the damage had been done. The virtual world I'd been feeding off had suddenly left me sucking air. That night I realized what was missing: the feeling of holding your work in your hands. The realest thing I'd done in weeks had been cutting pipes on the fireboat.

One way love is blind is that sometimes you don't even notice you're falling. When I stumbled onto the fireboat, I found a taste of home I hadn't realized I'd been missing. That newfound awareness left me and my virtual life struggling with irreconcilable differences.

Then, in April 2001, my theoretical-versus-practical dilemma became moot. The secret was out: There was no money to be made in Web content. The angel investors from the Philippines had grown impatient. My company was in the first throes of its protracted death, and I was the first casualty. The CEO summoned me into the conference room at the back of the office, away from my desk, my team, my river view. His eyes were ringed with red as he announced that my position had been eliminated. I blinked but managed not to flinch. Then I grabbed my bag, told my team I was leaving for the day, and hit the street, stepping into the current of the Herald Square throng. I was pushed along for a full block before I realized, Wait. I can just stop. At the corner of Sixth Avenue and Thirty-fourth Street, I slid out of the crush of the crowd, ducking under a section of scaffolding. Then I waited to see what I would do next. It was like watching a movie of my life—the menagerie of quick-stepping pedestrians became a diverse cast of everyman extras hired just for the occasion. I told my brain the news. This was the first time since I was fifteen that I didn't have at least one job. I felt unhinged, rattled, floating, certain I could fly.

✦ ✦ ✦

Two weeks later, at the next volunteer workday on the fireboat, Huntley pulled me aside to invite me to try out in the engine room. In the office David had mentioned that Huntley had gushed over that picture of me with the Sawzall. "He's your new biggest fan," David said. Apparently, Huntley liked the idea of women wielding power tools. His invitation caught me totally off guard, but saying no never crossed my mind.

Chapter Three

A Tale of Two Voyages

∽

"As soon as we finish singing, start the water." These were David's instructions, and Bob was all too happy to comply. David had invited his choral group for a summer evening cruise around the harbor, and when the boat stopped in front of the Statue of Liberty, he gathered everyone at the stern deck for a rendition of the national anthem. Thirty-odd singers stood openmouthed on deck, harmonizing. "O'er the land of the free," they belted out, warming up to a rousing finish. "And the hoooome of the braaaave." Then the deck exploded with water, dousing the entire group where they stood in their matching baby-blue "Bach on Board" Choral Society of Grace Church/Fireboat *John J. Harvey* T-shirts, which David had made up for the occasion. To this day it remains a mystery whose idea it was to soak the singers: Bob, David, or the wind.

Of course, I didn't see the soaking; I only heard about it after the fact. Though I'm the one who had engaged the pumps, I did so blindly, following Bob's orders. While passengers take in the salt air, I hide in the bowels of the boat like Oz behind the curtain, standing at my post in the engine room the whole time the boat is under way.

I'm beginning to sweat diesel. It's been three months since my first day at the controls, and the hours I've logged show in my callused palms and the muscles in my arms. The beauty of this old technology is how physical it is. As I swing the levers, I imagine my body memorizing the precise electrical code that triggers the correct contractions for each movement. But, of course, what we think of as muscle memory actually takes place in the brain.

During my first stints at the stand, I had to consider each and every response to the pilot's telegraph orders before complying. Now I don't think, I act—the commands hum straight into the brain regions that control automatic actions: the motor cortex, basal ganglia, and cerebellum. Just like a monkey, I presume. "If you use your body in a physical way year after year, the body speaks back not only in terms of sore muscles or swollen legs but also out of know-how," writes Janet Zandy in *Hands: Physical Labor, Class, and Cultural Work*. This is how it went with me.

I'm faster now, because of not just the repetition but also my new-found height. At the end of my first trip at the controls back in April, Tim pulled me aside. "Don't take this the wrong way," he began, hesitating, choosing his words carefully, "but I think it would be a lot easier if you had something to stand on." He figured I'd be insulted, so it surprised him when I showed up early for the next trip and went digging through the tool room. I found a wooden crate, which I turned upside down on the floor between the control levers.

That foot of extra height extended my range of motion, making it easier to swing the levers that open and close multiple sets of electrical contacts below the deck plates of the engine-room floor. The buzz of the vibrating engines traveled through the box, into the soles of my steel-toed boots and up my feet, which swelled with the heat.

On the Monday after my first time at the stand, Don Van Holt, the retired firefighter who'd held the video camera, sent me an e-mail: "You made the front page today!" he wrote, and included a link to the Web site he runs: www.nyfd.com (The Unofficial Home Page of FDNY). Attached was a still from the video he had posted online. There I was, standing between the telegraphs, my hands on the levers, my face shadowed below the brim of my black cap. I worried that everyone who looked at Don's front page would see what I did in my expression: a concentrated mix of nausea and fear.

Huntley e-mailed me too: "I have to say that one of the most surprising and rewarding things about Jessica-dom is the fact that these Old Guys adore a woman running the boat. Who would have guessed????????"

I quickly became the fastest operator on the *Harvey*'s crew. I can't explain how, exactly. I just immersed myself in the task. Whenever the

boat was called to navigate tight quarters, Bob said he wanted me at
the controls. He first piloted this boat in 1963. "I've been through lots
of engineers," he told me. "I can count on two hands the ones I could
trust." With no direct control of the propellers from the wheelhouse,
the hardest part of steering has always been telegraph coordination.
As Bob puts it, "You can stop this boat, but it takes two people—the
one up here and the one down there." (Only "there" sounds more like
"they-ah" coming from Bob, who grew up in Connecticut and now
splits his time between Long Island and Brooklyn's Breezy Point, aka
the Irish Riviera.) I was beginning to realize running these engines
demanded more than a trained-monkey mind-set.

At the engine-room control pedestal. *(Photo by Richard Andrian)*

These days I land each command as the signal comes down, pushing the prop levers quickly and smoothly. When I stand on my box
at the pedestal in the center of the engine room, the brass telegraphs
hang like clock faces on either side of my head. Painted lines represent speed and direction for each prop motor. Red pointers controlled
by the pilot issue the commands, and once I move the prop control
levers into position, I reply by swinging my own set of black pointers
to mirror those of the pilot, showing that I've followed his orders.

The engines have a particular drone at eleven hundred rpms. An occasional higher-pitched whine tells me that the Number Five engine, the one with the worn-out governor, has dipped to ten hundred. I nudge up the throttle and settle back into the hum of balance. Any bounce tells me to even out power to the two propellers so they stop fighting each other. I take the swoop and tilt of the boat's movement at the hips.

I could just stay in my spot at the pedestal, but I'm hungry to understand the power plant's complex systems. So whenever we're Full Ahead, running down the middle of the river, I pore over an electricity textbook, trying to wrap my head around diesel-electric propulsion, one concept at a time. I read and collect my questions while we're under way. Then, at the end of each trip, after twisting shut the sea cocks—valves that feed raw water to each engine—I stand in the baking, semidark engine room, holding a flashlight and talking shop with Tim, who patiently explains the mysteries of motors and magnetism using images and analogies that anyone could grasp: "To understand how a motor works, you have to think back to what you learned as a little kid—that one magnet can push or pull another magnet," he begins, then leans over to draw soapstone diagrams on the floor or a generator housing. He explains how air activates a clutch to engage the water pumps: "Picture blowing up an inner tube. The air fills up an inner tube, and as it expands, the two shafts connect." He opens engine covers to let me see the air inlet ports on a cylinder: "The ports are cut at an angle. When the air rushes in, it creates a swirling effect like little cyclones." He walks through the routine conversion from ship's power to shore power—again, because I still don't get it.

During the summer of 2001, I run the engines three or four times a week. The fact that I make a little money on these trips helps justify all the time I'm spending, and before long I start getting paid for repair work too. Kicked out of the comfortable nest of salaried employment, I decide to use the cushion of unemployment checks and fireboat pay to try my hand at freelancing. Friends help me score my first newspaper assignments, and before long I begin writing for national magazines, splitting my time between rounding up writing work and running the engines.

The boat trips are a mix of joyride cruises to nowhere and narrated tours aimed at teaching adults and kids about the New York City waterfront and FDNY Marine Division history. On weekends, the boat attends waterfront festivals, offering free trips to the public. On weeknights, owners take groups of friends on evening cruises. And when the foreign and U.S. military ships arrive for Fleet Week, we run out to greet them. Any excuse for a boat ride.

Content to stand among the droning diesels, studying (between the pilot's commands) the Fairbanks Morse engine manual and the textbooks Tim lent me, I come up for air once in a while and have to ask where we are, even though we haven't left the harbor. From down below, it's hard for me to keep track. My low-lying landmarks, the bottom edges of things, leave a confusing kaleidoscope of images shape-shifting in my head. Like a fish suddenly hungry for a bird's-eye view of the bowl in which it's been swimming, I want some perspective. The fireboat's first trip upriver offers a taste.

✦ ✦ ✦

At twenty minutes to seven on a Friday morning in August, I'm zipping across the Manhattan Bridge in the backseat of a cab, heading to the boat. I splurged on the taxi, because my backpack and duffel are just too big to schlep on a crowded subway. We are going to be on board for five days, but I have overpacked. I have no idea what to expect, so it was hard to decide what to cram into my luggage.

To soothe my nervous stomach, I look through the bridge rails at the water sparkling in the sunlight. Directly below me is the East River, but around the bend, at the tip of Manhattan, I can see the point where the Hudson, my river, begins.

I call it my river, but I'm not alone. Four hundred years ago, the Dutch claimed it for themselves, naming it River Mauritius, after the prince who led a rebellion against Spain. Before that, Henry Hudson, the English explorer employed by the Dutch whose reports enticed the first Europeans to settle here, had dubbed it "Great River of the Mountaynes." And long before he arrived, Algonquin-speaking tribes who lived along the river dubbed it the *Muhheakunnuk*, meaning "great waters in constant motion" or more loosely, "river that flows two ways." Today mariners, ever the traditionalists, call the south-ernmost portion of the Hudson the North River, harking back to the days when it and the South River (now the Delaware) defined the borders of the Dutch territory, framing the picture of a burgeoning new world just coming into focus.

The cabbie lets me off in the parking lot at the foot of Twenty-third Street, and I huff and puff up the ramp to the pier. The August heat keeps pace with the sun as it rises higher in the sky. The fore-cast has called for eighty-six degrees, which promises to push the engine room to one hundred-plus by midday. *Can I survive five days in the engine room during the hottest days of summer?* I have no way to gauge whether work that has been fun in short doses will still be fun over the long haul, once we have traveled 127 nautical miles upriver to the town of Troy and back.

Scanning the boat for familiar faces, I spot Tim on the main deck adjusting lines, then Bob on the deck above him. More than a dozen others—deck crew, boat regulars, and some folks I don't recognize—move gear and supplies around at the stern. I can see by the amount of stuff that they have brought that I wasn't the only one who suffered from packing angst while trying to prepare for our first boat camp-ing trip. As an operational crew member, I get dibs on a bunk in the crew's quarters, but others will be roughing it on deck. With no functional plumbing aboard (beyond a single toilet that flushes into a tiny holding tank designed for a few firefighters, not a boatload of campers), showering will consist of river swimming or an improvised contraption on the aft deck.

"All right, we can go now," Bob hollers out to Tim, loud enough for me to hear. "The last third is here." My chest floods with warmth.

As I clamber over the caprail—the ledge that runs around the outer edge of the whole boat—Tim reaches out and hefts the duffel effortlessly, though it's stuffed with heavy Carhartt work pants and the T-shirts I've come to refer to as "permadirty" since they will never again come clean of the grease, rust, and diesel stink.

"We were beginning to wonder if you were coming," he says.

✦ ✦ ✦

Bob Lenney, Jessica DuLong, and Tim Ivory. *(Photo by Eric Weisler)*

When I was fifteen my parents dropped me off for my first year at boarding school in Exeter, New Hampshire. The empty, industrial-white dorm room still smelled of the latex paint workers had used to erase any last trace of the previous occupant. My mom made up the bed. "You'll feel better once the bed is made," she said, as much to herself as to me. I waited until they pulled the car from the curb before crumpling, head between my palms, elbows digging into the hard white windowsill. *I have no business being at this school. How could I possibly have thought this would be a good idea? Why did I push so hard to come?* Any attempt at saving face was lost when my new roommate and her parents walked through the door and I had to introduce myself through sobs. "Sorry," I choked. "My parents just left."

That was thirteen years ago. First thing after stuffing my bags in my new locker on the fireboat, I make up my bunk, claiming the one on the bottom because the ledge on the inside will be perfect to hold my glasses case at night. Because my third-grade scars run that deep, my brain actually registers an insecure worry about being seen four-eyed between evening removal and morning reinsertion of my contact lenses, before my nose crinkles with self-disgust and I dismiss it. But before I left my apartment this morning, I made sure to remove the gold polish from my toenails, lest my crewmates think me soft.

Engine-room startup procedures are the same whether the trip is long or short, but today I pay special attention as I haul the hose across the floor to fill the freshwater tanks, spin open the hand wheels for the sea-cock valves that feed river water to cool the engines, and wipe clean each dipstick before reinserting it into the crankcase to get an accurate reading of lube-oil levels. We're used to two-hour trips around New York harbor, but at an average of 10 knots (11.5 miles per hour), it will take at least seven hours to reach our first overnight stop: Kingston, New York, seventy-five nautical miles upriver.

Just as I'm finishing my prep, Tim calls me up to the deck, where everyone is gathering for a photograph to document our first fire-boat camping trip. More than a dozen people have shown up for this first leg of our maiden voyage. In addition to the usuals (Bob, Tim, Huntley, David, me, and a deckhand named Tomas Cavallaro), Pamela Hepburn, who broke into the tug industry in 1976 and in 1985 became one of New York harbor's first female tug captains, has come to lend a hand in the wheelhouse, reading the charts and granting Bob the benefit of her experience with Hudson River landmarks. She's brought along her ten-year-old daughter, Alice, and their two tiny, yappy dogs (whose names, we decide, should be Underfoot One and Underfoot Two). David, meanwhile, has invited his brother, Andrew, and his parents, who've flown over from Ireland to be here. We squish together, laughing and joking about how we should book-end the trip with before-and-after shots. "Sure, we're all smiles now," I say. "But I wonder if we'll even be willing to stand next to each other after five days of all this togetherness."

The idea for this Albany trip developed after Huntley, Tim, and David had taken a road trip to Albany in the fall of 2000. I like making Tim tell the story because it inevitably includes his admission that, naive Jersey boy that he was at the time, he'd panicked about traveling alone in a car with two gay guys. "There was a learning curve," he concedes, now able to laugh at his stereotypical assumptions. No passes were made, and in fact, it turned out to be Tim who had a secret agenda.

"I'd found out about this boat that was diesel-electric like the fireboat," he explains. "I heard they wanted to get it running and might need a guy like me." That boat was the USS *Slater*, a 306-foot gray warship berthed in the Port of Albany—the last remaining destroyer escort afloat in the United States. A group of retired sailors had set up a not-for-profit to run it as a dockside museum, and some of the old navy men seemed to be withholding their last breaths until they could finally see the ship move, once more, under her own power.

Tim became fascinated from afar with the ship's four 16-cylinder Cleveland diesels that ran four 525-volt DC generators. He couldn't wait to see the power plant. But when they pulled off the freeway into the *Slater* parking lot, they discovered that the museum was closed for the day. David decided to see if they'd make an exception. He walked over toward a man on the ship. "I couldn't hear what they were saying, but I could see the guy shaking his head," says Tim. When David returned, defeated, Huntley decided to try his luck, figuring, They have a boat. We have a boat. They've got to let us on, recalls Tim. But Huntley returned, dismissed. By this point, the *Slater* rep whom they later came to know as Raph had walked to the parking-lot side of the gangway in an effort to shoo away the interlopers. This time, Tim approached him. "Listen, we run a fireboat that's diesel-electric too. I heard that you guys might need some help getting the engines running. Can I see your engine room?" That was all it took. The idea of someone helping to get the ship under way was too much for Raph to pass up. He took the three of them on a tour. "It's all here," Tim told him. "Everything is intact. You guys could be running this boat." Ecstatic, Raph called some board members down to hear what Tim had to say. Thus began the relationship between destroyer escort *Slater* and fireboat *John J. Harvey*.

From that point on, every time anyone expressed ennui about doing our usual loop around New York harbor (Pier 63, Statue, South Street Seaport, Pier 63), Tim would suggest going to Albany. By mid-July 2001, the Albany trip had become reality. David had one of his company's staffers check a map of the Hudson River shoreline between New York and Albany, then put calls in to see which towns could accommodate us. Enough towns with deep-draft waterfront access said yes, so David sent out press releases announcing the boat's arrival and advertising public tours all the way up the river.

Clearly this whole fireboat thing was too cool not to share. Unlike most historic exhibits, this museum could move, could take you on a boat ride, could get you wet.

✦ ✦ ✦

As soon as we pull the boat off the dock, Bob signals less and less frequently. I can see through the portholes that the boat is running up the middle of the river, and with both telegraph pointers at Full Ahead, I figure I have at least a few minutes before the next command rings down. I step down off my box, pick up a broom, and start sweeping up down below. When Tim descends the stairs and spots the broom, he peels the muff off my left ear: "What are you, nesting?"

"No," I say, a little huffy about the mother-hen reference. "I just figured if we're going to be down here for five days, I'd make it a little cleaner."

Forty minutes later, through the portholes on the starboard side, I catch a glimpse of the Little Red Lighthouse, which perches at the base of the George Washington Bridge. Looking every bit like the cartoon character in *The Little Red Lighthouse and the Great Gray Bridge*, the children's book by Hildegarde H. Swift, it has a jaunty white cap, windows all around, and a metal ball at the top like a pom-pom. This is my landmark. I've never been on the boat farther north than this bridge. And here's fireboat *Harvey*, gliding her way into the big river beyond. As the great gray bridge moves over us, the whole engine room is cast in shadow.

When the George Washington Bridge opened to traffic on October 25, 1931, just days after this boat was launched on October 6, its main span, measuring 3,500 feet, was the longest in the world. The engineer, Othmar H. Ammann, originally designed it to have granite-clad, Gothic-style towers, similar to those on the Brooklyn Bridge, rather than its distinctive latticework of criss-crossed bracing, but cost considerations and praise for the look of the exposed steel gave us the bridge we see today.

I don't know anything about the river outside New York harbor, and with my porthole view I can't see the Hudson opening its wide jaws with the Palisades, New Jersey's tall cliffs, on our left. Still, it's hard not to feel mythic as the fireboat pushes through the river toward the unknown.

Within minutes I have swept all I can sweep without straying too far from the stand. Though I might wait an hour before the next command, I have to stick close to the pedestal to be ready when it comes. Between bells I monitor the engines.

Two feet in front of me, the control panel stands nearly eight feet high, littered with levers, switches, and alarm indicator lights. It looked pretty daunting when I first saw it, but slowly the components began to identify themselves the way strangers in a room gradually transform into individuals with distinct faces and personalities after you've watched them interact. Needles inside the round gauges, painted red, yellow, green, and blue, bounce between marked ranges that indicate health or sickness in each engine. An engraved steel tag between the throttle levers lists the proper pressures and temperatures for lube oil, starting air, fuel oil, and jacket water, and I watch the bouncing needles for any dramatic changes. Like the computer system that runs today's cars, I evaluate inputs and make changes, as needed, to protect the machines.

The pause between Bob's signals gives me time to think. It's been four months since I lost my desk job and I'm surprised to realize I don't miss it. When I first moved to New York, I cut a tiny quote out of the newspaper, which I reinforced with a strip of Scotch tape and left on my dresser: "In this city you have to be known as being the best at something." One of the most intolerable parts of living here is that 7,999,999 people stand between me and anything I want to accomplish. Usually when I say this, I'm complaining about the subway or crowded sidewalks, but it applies, I find, to everything.

In this city of strivers, networking is capital. Scoring my next writing assignments depends on it, so I sip pink cosmopolitans at schmoozy parties where editors bemoan being trapped in the "pink ghetto" of women's magazines. I attend "job mixers." I even pick up flyers for library classes like "Turning Interviews into Job Offers," but never go. Green is the color I use in my calendar to code freelancing gigs and events. Red is for fireboat trips and volunteer days. As time passes, I find red rivaling green.

As we head farther upriver, I catch sight of something I've never seen in the portholes: greenery. Rolling lawns glide by, as do narrow, sandy shorelines with tree roots dangling, exposed, where the soil in which they had made their homes has been stolen by the river. Little waterfront houses stand free rather than shoulder to shoulder like the buildings in New York City. Snippets of parkland. Little floating docks. Clusters of tall trees. All the open space and green lift the city's weight off my chest.

From my Empire State Building window, the thin black ribbon of river had promised quiet stillness, but up close, the water is in constant motion. The Hudson is not actually a river, but a tidal estuary where fresh water from the mountains mixes with salt water from the sea. For half of each day the Hudson does what most rivers do: It flows downstream. But every six hours, the water switches direction, shifting with Atlantic Ocean tides. First the flood tide pushes more water to the north, raising the level an average of 4.6 feet, then the ebb tide drains the river back down. Sometimes the river flows in two directions at once, when the waters at the surface begin to push north, even as the deep water continues moving south.

Gouged out by glaciers beginning more than a hundred million years ago, the Hudson River Valley is what geologists call a fjord, or "drowned river." Unlike some rivers that tumble down mountains, the Hudson stretches flat and low from the tip of Manhattan to Troy, its bottom below sea level. With a mean gradient of just five feet, no waterfalls disrupt the traffic of boats, which can skate along either north or south in a fair tide, depending on the time of day. In the past when moving anything heavy was best done over water, these characteristics determined the Hudson's destiny to become a crucial commercial corridor.

Today, aboard fireboat *Harvey*, we are reaping the benefit of the flood tide, which pushes the boat north at an average of more than 12 knots—2 knots greater than our average speed based on prop power alone. Five hours after we set out from Pier 63, we reach Pough-keepsie. The sun goes dark for an instant as we pass under the Mid-Hudson Bridge before pulling into the town dock. From the bottom of the stairs, I watch through the engine-room door on deck as the girders of the bridge's underside slip behind us. This peculiar view reminds me of what I love about riding trains: the chance to see the backs of places and the things people stash by the tracks, out of view from the road.

Then a clang jostles me out of my reverie, and a volley of wheel-house commands directs me to shift our position for docking. The pier grows in the portholes, and I spy an array of feet—some big, some little—waiting on the dock's wood planks. A rich tar smell rushes in from the pilings infused with creosote, a brown goo derived from coal tar that's used as a wood preservative. Bob finally rings down Finished With Engines, and I shut everything down and head up the stairs.

On deck, I stop short. The hillside is dotted with townsfolk. They've all come down to the river to greet us. "It's like a Western when they all run out to meet the stagecoach," I say to Tim, who's sitting on the caprail. He grins, absentmindedly peeling rust from the underside of the rail with his fingers.

I find a spot in the shade while David leads tours. His chirpy voice echoes up from the steaming engine room: "There are three ways we can kill you on board this boat . . . ," he begins, before passing out of earshot. I already know the ways, and have resigned myself to the fact that the ugliest deaths take place in the engine room. Look back at any maritime disaster. If casualties are listed, chances are the engineer (or oiler, machinist, electrician, or anyone else who works in the belly of the boat with the machinery) is among the dead. With all the equipment shut down, the engine room is safe for visitors, but that's not the case while we're under way. This boat was built long before modern safety precautions became the norm. David is walking these visitors back in time to an age when workers' common sense was all that protected them from their equipment—when technological realities demanded that people remain far more aware of their physical surroundings than is often required today.

✦ ✦ ✦

On this, the *John J. Harvey*'s maiden voyage upriver, I can't help but think of Henry Hudson, who took his own pioneering toe-dip into the river that would come to bear his name on September 11, 1609. He sailed his three-masted ship the *Halve Maen*, or *Half Moon*, into what his first mate, Robert Juet, called "a very good Harbour for all windes," and then up a river wide and salty enough to hold out promise as a passage to Asia, a bridge between seas.

To trace Hudson's path, historians look to the log Juet kept of his captain's third failed attempt to find a northern route to the East. (This was the same Juet who in June 1611, during another attempt, led a mutiny of Hudson's starving crew, casting the captain, his teenage son, John, and seven others adrift in a small, open boat in what became Canada's Hudson Bay—never to be seen again.) Hudson's own logbook has been lost to time. Some say it was auctioned off, after which it disappeared. Others say it was sold as scrap paper. In any event, Hudson had been hired by the Verenigde Oostindische Compagnie (VOC), or Dutch East India Company, to find a shorter ocean route from Europe to China and Japan. The company's charter granted it a monopoly on all Asian trade carried out on southern routes, but to protect its territory, the VOC wanted to be first to discover a passage to the north and a backdoor to Asia, so that no rival could undercut the company's trade in silk, spices, and dyes.

Hudson hoped that an opening in the land north of the area known as Virginia might just be the passage he was after. So, after spending a night off in the "soft Ozie ground" where, as Juet described, the "banke is Sand," on what is now New Jersey's Sandy Hook, the *Half Moon*'s crew of sixteen to twenty Dutchmen and Englishmen weighed anchor, and set sail through the Narrows, a 0.3-mile strait between eastern Staten Island and western Brooklyn, toward what is now called the Upper Bay. Built of pine and oak and painted in bright colors with geometric motifs, the eighty-five-foot-long *Half Moon* rode high in the water, despite its eighty tons. The crew coexisted in tight quarters under rough conditions, though not altogether peacefully. They grumbled about their freewheeling captain (who habitually chose his own routes for exploration, despite explicit orders from the company), fought among themselves (in spite of not speaking each other's languages), and periodically threatened to mutiny.

✦ ✦ ✦

After stopping for tours in Poughkeepsie, fireboat *Harvey* continues cruising up the middle of the river. Deeply immersed in a chapter on DC electricity, I jump when all of a sudden Bob calls down with All Stop, then Finished With Engines. This has to be a mistake. Maybe the pointers need adjusting. *Did he mean to point a little farther along on the dial, to Slow Astern?* That doesn't make any sense either. Whenever Bob went from Full Ahead to Astern in the harbor, it was to avoid colliding with some sailboat that had crossed our bow, or a kayak that had pulled some boneheaded maneuver, not realizing how much momentum a 268-gross-ton boat has, and how long it takes to slow her down. But something like that would call not for Slow Astern but Full Astern, the emergency gear, the hydraulic brakes, so to speak.

I slide the levers into their full upright position to All Stop and wait, watching for Tim's work boots to appear on the top step. As soon as I can see his head, I nod at the telegraphs with a questioning look. He laughs and reaches around me to idle down engines. The diesel growl softens a bit, and he leans in to explain. "Float and swim," he says. "Let 'em cool to two hundred, then let's shut them down." I stare at him. How could it possibly be a good idea to shut down all power in the middle of the river? But I do as I'm told.

By the time I make it up on deck, someone has slung a wooden ladder over the side and tied off a life ring on a string. Three or four heads bob in the current. "Come on in, Jess," Pamela hollers from the water. She must have instigated the float-swim. She had mentioned they did this sort of thing when she was still running tugs. Among the other bobbing heads is Pam's daughter, Alice, who was raised until age nine aboard the *Pegasus*, the 1907 Standard Oil tug that Pam bought for her business, Hepburn Marine Towing, in 1987.

"You've got to go in," says Huntley. "You need it more than any of us." My T-shirt is wet with sweat from roasting in the engine room all these hours.

"How long do we have?"

"Long as you want."

When I come back up from changing into shorts, Huntley shouts, "Ah! Snipe legs!" making fun of my lily-white skin. ("Snipe" is a navy term for engineer, stemming, supposedly from an officer named John Snipes who had demanded improved conditions for engine crews. When Snipes called for sleeping accommodations and food that equaled those of deck gangs, the captain just laughed. In retaliation, Snipes instructed his men to quench the boiler fires, cutting off power to the ship. Deck crews got the message loud and clear, and thereafter engineers became known as Snipes's men, or simply snipes.) Huntley's comment gets me in the water faster. I climb onto the caprail, hold my nose, and jump.

Gliding back to the surface in what seems like slow motion, I feel the diesel heat drain away, drawn from my body by the coolness of the river. Air bubbles tickle my skin on their way up to the sky. When my face breaks through to the air, I wipe my eyes and mouth. *Wow. The water is fresh here.* We're far enough north that the runoff from the mountains has dominion over the salt from the sea. I won't say I'm not worried about whether the water is clean enough for swimming, but now that I'm in it, the river is delicious, irresistible. As I look around at my fellow swimmers, my crew, I shake my head, grinning.

✦ ✦ ✦

By the time we park the boat at Kingston, I'm more than ready for a beer. While those who have spent the day relaxing on deck cook dinner on the barbecue, I sit with my feet up, looking out over the still, black water. My workday is over. The diesels are silent. Heat skips up the engine-room stairs, promising a cooler start to tomorrow, and New York City seems a long way away.

The town dock is on Kingston's Rondout Creek, right where Broadway dead-ends at a park with picnic benches. After dinner the crew lounges on the caprail, leaning against the bitts—cylindrical posts used for fastening ropes that secure the boat to shore—and laughing loudly late into the night. We entertain summertime strollers taking their evening promenades along the creek, drawn to the boisterous, jolly crew.

The next morning, we make the *Poughkeepsie Journal*'s front page: "Historic Fireboat Visits City: Floating Museum en Route to Albany."

Huntley bought the paper on his way back from the bed-and-breakfast where he stayed, because Huntleys do not sleep on board. He says he needs a hot shower daily, and we don't hesitate to chide him for being precious.

David leads tours for the more than two hundred people who show up at the Kingston Town Dock, while Bob, Tim, and I gather in the wheelhouse. Every half hour or so, we hear David's voice warbling from the crew's quarters below, signaling that another tour group will be wandering up any second for a session with Bob, our gruff pilot. Huntley calls Bob's native tongue "Fireman"—a language of grunts, punctuated by the few single-syllable utterances that manage to sum up the whole matter at hand.

When Huntley does his Bob impression, he stiffens his arms, holding them out to his sides, and shakes his shoulders back and forth, chin tucked in, grumbling throaty nonsense words before issuing some example of a two-word pronouncement that explains everything perfectly. This mock grunting is particularly amusing coming from Huntley, a man who says, "See you around the campus" instead of "Good-bye," and uses contrived accents whenever he says a place-name like, "Boleeevyah" for Bolivia or "Nawfuk" for Norfolk. We all have our quirks, and if there's one thing we can count on as part of this crew, it's that someone will lay them bare, opening us up to merciless teasing.

Tim gets teased for his spelling and his hearing, both of which I like to refer to as "creative." Each time he has to write the name of his title, chief engineer, he asks me, which comes in first in "chief," the i or the e? But spelling is nothing more than mechanics, and many of the crew have also commented on how poetic his writing is over e-mail, which I think comes from his keen eye for visual detail. Because Tim has a genetic hearing loss that has only been exacerbated by his lifelong exposure to loud engines, I make him repeat back to me anything I've said that's particularly important, lest he end up nodding in agreement with what he thinks he heard, not what I've actually said.

In return, Tim likes to remind me daily that I'm short. I also get razzed for the way I eat: no meat, lots of vegetables, or as Bob calls anything that looks too threateningly green or whole grain, "Jessica food."

Before long, Huntley warns the guests that have boarded for tours that if they don't intend to join us for the twenty-two-nautical-mile trip to Hudson, they'd best disembark now.

Three hours later, Tim comes down below to let me know we'll be docking soon. Bob plans to spray water to herald our arrival, so it's time to open the two sea chests—the huge mouths at the bottom of the boat that open to feed river water to the pumps.

When Bob swings both telegraph dials back and forth, ringing down for water, I drop the engines to an idle, then flip the switches to engage the air flex clutches that connect the engines' drive shafts to the driven shafts in the pumps. I slowly raise the throttles, in sync, until they reach the proper pumping rpm of 900, sending a whoosh of air blasting out of the deck guns, followed by a cascade of water.

Outside, the slope of land at the river's edge is overgrown with lush green vegetation. Through the portholes I watch the broad, flat leaves bend beneath the spray. Beyond the column of white water, I can see people onshore, waiting in an open dirt lot. Now that he has an audience, Bob is going to put on a show. It's a hot day, the water is fresh, so why not give everyone a nice little cooldown? "I'm playing with inches here," Bob likes to say about his choreography of water displays. As the mist approaches them, the visitors step into it with upturned palms, grinning.

For maximum effect, Bob waits until the last possible second before signaling me to shut down water. This means I have to scramble to disengage the pumps before swinging through his rapid-fire docking commands. He likes to throw a little challenge in there to keep things interesting. "If it stops being fun, we'll stop doing it," he says.

Each stop on this trip offers the thrill of newness. I climb the stairs to the deck having no idea what I'll find. Blinking in the sunlight, I see that we've parked for the night in an industrial yard owned by a company called St. Lawrence Cement, whose lot shows vestiges of old industry ripe for exploration.

While David leads tours for locals enticed by the newspaper coverage that's been tracing our progress north, I savor the privilege of being off duty and jump onto land for a stroll around the yard. I wander over to a concrete slab by the water's edge to peek upriver at the pleasure boats tied up in the marina. Huntley calls these little runabouts LSPBs (little shitty plastic boats) to distinguish them from workboats, which, like the huge hunk of steel for which I've fallen so completely, occupy a whole different world.

The next day we head to Albany, where the USS *Slater* gang will be waiting, arriving around noon. Tim steps halfway down the engine-room stairs to give me the hand signal for docking, as usual, before heading back on deck to handle lines. His grin is contagious. We've finally made it. Bob rings the bells that instruct me to saw the boat back and forth through the water as he tries to line up the fireboat's port side against the *Slater*'s starboard without scratching any paint. All I can see through the portholes is the hull's endless gray. Even before Bob rings Finished With Engines, Tim bounces back down the stairs, juts a thumb toward the deck, and steps into my place at the control pedestal so I don't have to wait any longer before sneaking a peek at the ship.

As I step around the corner of the deckhouse, a sea of faces greets me. Old sailors wearing navy caps and button-down uniform shirts—some light blue, some beige—peer down at me from the edge of the *Slater*'s rail, well above us. I'm still wearing my earmuffs, so it's clear I've just come from down below, and my permadirty brown T-shirt seems to be causing some confusion. I came up to look, but instead I feel looked at, awkward, onstage. So I scurry back down into my engine hole. This trip is the first time I've really interacted in my engineering role with people from the outside world. With my boat mates, I'm just crew. But other people are not necessarily as comfortable with a girl running a fireboat.

Back down below, I shake off the weird, watched feeling, shut down engines, and then follow Tim onto the *Slater*, into one of its engine compartments in order to go over the diesels. He wants to check for stuck injectors to see how run-ready this ship really is. A couple of *Slater* volunteers, an elderly man and his son, both in navy-blue jumpsuits, join us and offer their help. Tim directs us to pull off engine covers so we can make sure the fuel racks slide freely. I still know so little about engines all I can do is mimic what he shows me, but before he climbs the ladder to check out the engine in a second compartment, he tells the guys that if they have any questions, to ask me. Fortunately, they don't take me up on it, though they do enlist

Fireboat *John J. Harvey* alongside USS *Slater*, from left to right: Tim Ivory, Jessica DuLong, Pamela Hepburn, Alice Hepburn, Bob Cunningham (below), Tomas Cavallaro, Carley Scott, Alex Weisler, Bonnie Weisler, Marjorie Beatty, Bob Lenney, Eric Weisler (below), Huntley Gill (below), Andrew Beatty, John Doswell, Jean Preece, David Beatty, Wallace Beatty. *(Photo by RACTO'C Photography)*

Fireboat *John J. Harvey* honors USS *Slater* with an eight-deck-gun salute in Albany. *(Photo by Richard Andrian)*

my help each time they drop a wrench in the bilge. By the third time I have to pull up the deck plates to clamber over grimy piping and retrieve a lost tool, I begin to wonder if, instead of shaky hands causing all these dropped wrenches, it's their amusement at watching me climb around.

Later that night, after a barbecue with the *Slater* crew (who turn out to be a warm, hospitable, and friendly bunch), a few of us sit on the aft deck sipping the Irish whiskey and snacking on the Cadbury chocolates David's parents brought over with them. David's brother Andrew tries to strike up a conversation with me: "So what got you interested in engines?" Suddenly all eyes are on me. It's an innocent-enough question, but I freeze, then reply with some quip that diverts the conversation elsewhere. My growing love for the boat still feels too new, too private to share. Fortunately, there's a long tradition of quiet engineers, so my tendency to clam up rather than talk about myself has found a suitable new home.

✦ ✦ ✦

Considering the scenery that greeted him, it's no wonder Henry Hudson held out hope of finding a passage to the East. The Palisades' dramatic geology—its cliff face of giant teeth—suggested not just a river but a strait between seas. Farther north he entered the Tappan Zee (its name derived from a mash-up of the moniker of a local Indian tribe and the Dutch word *zee*, meaning "sea"), where the water widens into a bay three miles across. Even when he reached the river's narrowest part, which sailors later dubbed World's End, Hudson would have kept the faith based on the soundings his men had taken. Here the river floor drops to depths of up to 177 feet, which surely meant he was gaining on the sea.

But alas, it wasn't to be. Eleven days after it began, Hudson's push north came to a disappointing end. "This night, at ten of the clocke," wrote Juet, "our boat returned in a showre of raine from sounding of the Riuer; and found it to bee at an end for shipping to goe in." "Vnconstant soundings" had revealed shallow waters north of what is now Albany. This waterway did not lead to Asia. Hudson turned the *Half Moon* around in defeat and headed back downriver toward the sea.

Our downriver journey is much happier than Hudson's. At six o'clock on Tuesday morning, we depart Albany for a straight shot to New York City, the passengers placing bets on how long it will take. Bob and Tim are disqualified, since they know too much and could control the outcome, but I'm allowed a bet, since even though my hands are on the levers that control the propellers, I still don't know enough to worry the judges.

✦ ✦ ✦

As Huntley and David spoke with more and more reporters throughout the trip, the fireboat's mission became ever clearer. A Poughkeepsie newspaper article explained that the boat was "making a tour of the Hudson River in hopes of encouraging the state to invest in boat-friendly piers and subsidize the docking of historic vessels at Hudson River Park in Manhattan, now under construction." The *Troy Record* explained that the mission was to raise awareness of historic boats. "These boats and ships have played such an important part in the creation and growth of New York City and the Hudson," Huntley told reporters. "It's important that they are preserved and that people appreciate their historic importance in the growth of the region."

For Bob, though, the mission is more personal: "I am so excited. This is my baby," the paper quotes him saying. "I never thought I'd see it again once I retired. When these guys bought it, it was one of the best days of my life."

The return trip takes ten hours, and the winner of the betting pool decides to donate the pot back to the boat. Tied up at the pier, a handful of us linger on board, not wanting to leave the unexpected joy of newfound family. When I finally make it back onto solid ground, my legs wobble like I've had too much to drink. Now that I've gotten my sea legs, my land legs have gone missing. Suddenly it's the landlubber world that feels strange—unnatural, unreal.

Chapter Four

FIREBOAT *JOHN J. HARVEY* SERVES AGAIN

〜

AT 7:30 A.M. ON September 11, 2001, I checked my e-mail and enjoyed a warm reminder of our first Hudson River trip—a newsletter from the USS *Slater* that touted our August visit as their month's "big event." The fireboat season showed no signs of letting up, and the *Harvey* was lolling easy in her berth.

Then two planes changed everything.

A few minutes after 8:46 a.m., FDNY firefighter Tom Sullivan, stationed with his company at Pier 53, the "Tiltin' Hilton" at the foot of Bloomfield Street on the West Side, got the call. He jumped on board fireboat *John D. McKean* and shot south toward Lower Manhattan. As the boat nosed in to the seawall just south of North Cove, less than a block away from the Twin Towers where the World Financial Center meets the Hudson, he heard a roar. "We looked to our right, and just over the Statue of Liberty, here came another plane," he remembers.

The panic had already begun. "People are coming out . . . burnt, cut up. People are helping each other, carrying other people. They're coming to us for help," Tom recalls. While the *McKean* crew struggled to tie up the boat, people started jumping onto the deck from the concrete seawall. "It was low tide, so they had to jump down about ten feet," Tom explains. "They're not waiting for assistance . . . as they're jumping on, they're breaking their legs."

Two women who jumped had landed in the water, and firefighters pulled them out. Mothers, or maybe nannies, passed down their babies, recalls Tom. "We were catching the infants. We had about four or five of them wrapped in little blankets. We stuck them down in the crew's quarters. I had four of them lined up in a bunk, like little peanuts." It was 9:02 a.m. and the *McKean* was the first FDNY boat to arrive at what the media would soon dub Ground Zero. Retired fireboat *John J. Harvey* arrived just after 10:30.

A message from the Coast Guard crackled out over the marine radios all across the harbor, summoning "all available boats" to evacuate people stranded in Lower Manhattan. Tugboats, ferries, tour boats, dinner boats, go-fast boats, and private recreational vessels all charged toward the scene. Suddenly the harbor was as busy as it had been in its heyday, white wakes zigzagging across the river as vessels of all kinds darted about the Hudson. Hundreds of shoes lay piled on the seawall, discarded as people plunged into the water to try to escape the torrent of ash. That day, 300,000 people evacuated Manhattan by boat.

By the time the *Harvey* arrived, both towers had collapsed and the whole area was choked with dust, soot, and smoke. The shoreline was mobbed with people, and the crew prepared to take on passengers. "We pulled up and said, 'We're here to take you out of here,' " remembers Tim. "They said, 'Well, where are you going?' 'We're going to New Jersey.' And nobody would get on the boat," he says, shaking his head with a touch of Jersey-boy resentment. "Finally, when we offered to take them uptown, people poured on." With about 150 people on board, the boat set out for Pier 40, less than two miles to the north.

Meanwhile, FDNY lieutenant (now retired captain) Tommy Whyte had arrived at Ground Zero just after the second collapse. When he headed inland to where the buildings had come down, a flood of injured firefighters, eyes wide and many of them banged up and bleeding, filed past him. There was no water anywhere. The mains had burst when the towers came down; the hydrants were dry. Buses, cars, fire trucks, and buildings were still blazing all around. What was needed, urgently, was a way to tap the river.

Company members from the *McKean* rigged up a number of hose lines, but they weren't enough. So Tommy radioed the *McKean*'s pilot asking him to call the *Harvey* to put forward the crucial question: Can you still pump water? The answer to Tommy's question was yes. Antique *John J. Harvey*, removed from regular service back in 1995, auctioned off by the city for scrap in 1999, could still pump water.

Tommy rallied a group of men to help him gather equipment to supply the *Harvey* when she returned from offloading passengers. "There was a whole crew of people," he recalls, "office guys in white shirts who worked in the building and hadn't left the site, carpenters, firemen, two chiefs, just a whole mishmash. I had them strip all of these rigs that were smashed down." He told the engineers on the *McKean* to collect extra hoses and fittings that weren't being used—everything necessary to run lines from the boat. Tommy was waiting onshore when the *Harvey* returned.

"I was standing there on the boat with a line in my hands, trying to figure out where I was going to tie to," recalls Tim. "Tommy said, 'Do your pumps work?' I gave him a thumbs-up. He said, 'Can you take hose lines?' I said, 'Yeah.'" Because there were no cleats or bollards to use, securing the boat required stretching ropes across the walkway, tying them to trees. "Tom's third question was, 'What do you need to make this work?' I said, 'I've got about three hundred gallons of fuel. I can pump for about an hour.' And I watched him deflate. But he got on the radio and said, '*Harvey* needs fuel, critical.'" Before long an Army Corps of Engineers boat arrived with diesel.

The fireboats couldn't use their deck guns to fight fires directly because the blazes were too far inland. Instead, they served as massive pumping stations, able to provide limitless volumes of river water, supplying hoses for firefighters working on land. The *McKean*'s crew had been able to hook up hoses to the on-board valves that tapped into their boat's water-main system. But *Harvey*'s seventy-year-old valves were seized shut, so Tim figured out how to connect the hoses directly to the deck guns. In order to maximize the pressure through the hoses, stretched as far as they were inland, he plugged the ends of the unused deck guns with plastic spring-water bottles.

Thus fireboat *John J. Harvey*, led by her civilian chief engineer, was able to serve the city she had been built to protect one final, crucial time.

✦ ✦ ✦

On the morning of the twelfth, I call Huntley's cell phone and Tim answers.

"Where are you?" I ask.

"Where do you think we are?" he says. My head begins to spin. I had spent all day Tuesday in Brooklyn, wandering around the way so many New Yorkers had, trying unsuccessfully to donate blood, asking police officers if there was any way to help. "They don't even know what to do with *us*," one officer replied. It hadn't even occurred to me that the boat would be down there.

I want to help, but I have no idea how to get to the fireboat, since subway service is shut down and the bridges and tunnels are all still closed. Tim passes the phone to Bob, who has just arrived, having caught a boat at FDNY Marine Division headquarters in the Brooklyn Navy Yard. He tells me that's my best bet.

I just go.

Will my *John J. Harvey* crew shirt—with its line drawing of the boat on the front and "Crew (Really)" printed on the back—be proof enough that I'm actually an engineer? It is. An FDNY lieutenant escorts me to a boat where three men in fatigues, merchant marines, are eating lunch. When the lieutenant gives them their assignment, they throw down their sandwiches, all charged up, ready to take me over.

They don their life vests, toss me a spare, and direct me to the "best seat in the house" in front of the steering station of a small open-decked pontoon boat that looks something like a golf cart on water. When I see that the crew remains standing, I stand too. As the boat picks up speed, I steady myself first with one hand, then two, against the slap of the bow on the water. The life jacket zipped up the middle of my chest was last worn by someone much bigger. It flaps in the wind, an apt metaphor for how I feel cruising into this situation: ill-equipped.

A pillow of white smoke rises above Lower Manhattan from between the remaining buildings, ascending quietly, gently, in that clear blue sky. At about eleven o'clock on Wednesday morning, more than twenty-four hours after both towers have collapsed, Ground Zero is still ablaze. No one knows yet that firefighters will work for months to extinguish the last fires, or that ironworkers cutting away at the pile will pull up sections of steel beam, only to watch the nearly molten ends flare up when exposed to a fresh burst of air.

As we swing around the tip of Manhattan, the caustic smell grows stronger and more bitter, the distinctive acrid mix of ash, heat, concrete, steel, and death.

Just south of North Cove, I spot the unpolished bronze nozzles of the *John J. Harvey*'s deck guns, and a wave of love consumes me.

One deck gun at the stern sends water back into the river, showing me that the pumps are operating and that the boat is actively feeding Hudson River water to the hoses on land. For the first time I see the boat pumping water with a purpose, doing the important work for which she was built.

The merchant marine at the helm of my transport ducks the boat into North Cove, and I climb onto the ladder of a police boat, then a wooden dock before reaching solid ground. A day after the collapse, the search-and-rescue effort is operating in full swing. Everyone moves purposefully, the medical people in their scrubs and white coats, construction workers in their hard hats, firefighters with their turnout gear. Even on this first day after, when controls on who can enter the site are considerably looser than they will be by the time I leave on Friday, everybody seems to have a uniform.

The seawall is lined with boats. Tugs, with their big rubber bow fenders, nose into the concrete, while the fireboats rest alongside. The first person I see on board is Huntley. "You're always late," he says, and I struggle with how to respond, explaining that I was stuck in the wrong borough. I've walked fresh into the apocalypse, and though I understand the quip is a coping mechanism, it is all the more disconcerting coming from a member of my newfound family.

Next I see Tim, who tells me the Number Four pump needs to be repacked. After pumping all night at a much higher pressure than usual, the seal broke, sending water spraying all over the engine room, filling up the bilge. Tim has swapped pumping operations over to the Number Five engine, so now is the right time to address the Number Four. I've done this job once before, so I gratefully take it on, gathering my tools and heading down alone.

But once I'm in the engine room, a job that should take me thirty minutes takes two hours because I keep putting parts together backward. In the engine room it feels like I could be anywhere. The low roar of the one engine that's still pumping cloisters me from all other sound, cutting me off from the rest of the universe. Normally I'd rather be on this boat, in this engine room, than anywhere else on the planet. But today I want to help in a bigger way. And I don't want to work alone.

Seeing how long it takes me to perform this one simple task, Tim realizes how jarring it was for me to dive straight into an engine-room repair without first grasping my surroundings. "Come on," he says. "Let's take a walk."

The boat is stationed at the mouth of a treacherous scene. We walk up a ramp to where rows of mangled cars, many of whose drivers won't be going home, sit neatly in their parking spots.

What I see on this late summer day is snow. The powdery ash and concrete dust have settled on every surface. The trees—those yanked up by their roots by the collapse and those still standing—are strewn with paper, plastic bags, and debris. It looks like some kind of per-verted Christmas. The constant movement of rescue workers in hard hats, coveralls, turnout coats, and blue and green scrubs makes no sense in the middle of a blizzard.

I follow closely behind Tim. With each footfall my black work boots sink into the slurry of soot and water from the hoses and emerge coated in a gray film. Tim steps across puddles that I have to slosh through. I feel dwarfed by all the huge men made enormous in their fire gear, hard hats, and tool belts. Closer to the river, every window has been blown out of the otherwise intact buildings, but farther in, any trace of New York City has been reduced to rubble and ruin—all of it coated with the same penetrating, powdery dust. And paper. Reams upon reams of paper. Some crumpled. Some burned. Some perfectly flat and unmarred. Single sheets continue to fly out of shattered windows and the holes in the sides of buildings, darting like butterflies in the wind before reaching the ground.

I pick up a few sheets at my feet. Memos, financial reports, e-mails, a newborn's identification card with tiny inked footprints. In spite of the heat of the fires, all this paper survived. Each floor of the two 110-story buildings occupied the equivalent of an acre of land. Out of all those acres of offices, with their mazes of cubicles, their coffeemakers, bulletin boards, Xerox machines, framed family photos, desk trinkets, and watercoolers, not a single chair, desk, telephone, file cabinet, or computer survived. Only paper tumbles through the dust.

Each step brings me closer and closer to huge fields of crumpled steel—the raw, jagged edges jutting out in all directions—where the world has lapsed into black and white. The only color is yellow—the stripes of reflective tape on the black bunker gear the firefighters wear as they clamber over the pile.

Back on the boat, we worry about Bob, who served the FDNY for decades. As civilians we recognize we can never properly understand a piece of this tragedy because we aren't part of the fire, or police, department families that have suffered so many losses. Bob knows men who are missing—sons and fathers, family friends, neighbors from Breezy Point, where he and his family spend summers. Mostly he just stands quietly in the wheelhouse, with the FDNY radio that Tommy Whyte has issued to the boat strapped across his chest. A small TV hums in the background, the volume turned down low. Footage loops. Planes crash into buildings, over and over again.

Bob wants to sleep in the wheelhouse, the proper place for the pilot to sleep, especially while the boat is on station, because he wants to be easy to find. But the bed that was once up there has long since been torn out, and he took home the cot he had used during the Hudson River trip. I go out on land to look for a bed of some sort.

At a medical triage station in front of Two World Financial Center, where I head first, a doctor stands outside, her stethoscope hanging limply around her neck, beside a row of empty hospital beds. I tell her I'm looking for a cot for my captain and she directs me inside, saying I can take a stretcher that's there against the wall.

I step into the lobby and stop short, some confusion having overtaken me while I stood outside. For a moment, I've forgotten where I am and somehow expect, when I walk through the doors, to find myself in a medical facility. Instead I enter a lobby blanketed with that pervasive powder. The room is dark, the escalator frozen and silent. My throat tightens up. I snap to, collect the stretcher, and then maneuver my way back to the boat.

Walking down the ramp toward the pier means turning my back to the outstretched claws of remaining tower facades that still stand defiantly—their narrow archways blasted clear of their glass, like the ruins of a Gothic cathedral. I turn to face the sparkling river and catch sight of a sunset that is almost unbearably beautiful—peach and pink and orange swirling low on the horizon. Against that backdrop the boat that I love bobs a little with the current, tugging lightly on the lines, while the Statue of Liberty stands her ground on her island off to the left.

When I reach the boat and show Bob the "bed" I've procured, he recoils. "I'm not sleeping on that," he says. Only then do I realize the stretcher's grim implications.

"You can have my bunk," I offer, knowing his knees aren't up for an upper bunk.

As the sun drops out of the sky, Bob, Tim, and I gather in the wheelhouse, not saying much, just sitting. So much weight and solidarity stitches itself between us in the wordless sharing of this silence.

Eventually we decide to try to sleep, or close our eyes, or at least lie still in the dark. Tim has set up a hammock on deck, determined to be reachable at a moment's notice. Bob takes my bunk, and I set up a mattress on a table in the crew's quarters. I lie there, boots, clothes, and glasses on. The generator rattles its tinny roar and one engine, still pumping, thrums along with a lower-pitched rumble.

Sleep does not come. The door to the engine room swings open, and I turn my head toward the sound. Tim steps into the crew's quarters. "You okay?" he asks.

"Yeah," I lie. "You?"

"Yeah." Then he walks back up the stairs to the deck and his hammock.

✦ ✦ ✦

On Thursday I get antsy. It's frustrating to have been granted the opportunity to be here, but I feel like I'm contributing nothing. Once the pumps are engaged, they're capable of running with minimal attention. Meanwhile the crew hovers in hurry-up-and-wait mode. I can't stand my empty hands.

By this point the nation has rallied into the kind of generous action that we do best: respond to a crisis with stuff. In a kind of reenactment of the mishmash break-bulk cargo shipping of days gone by, cases upon cases of mixed goods arrive at the World Trade Center site by boat. Volunteers pile giant cardboard boxes and trash bags in the plaza near the water's edge, directly in front of the boats. Workers go digging through a perplexing mix of irrelevant wares to find something useful—a pair of gloves, a flashlight, a hard hat.

Heartfelt generosity has produced a nightmare, and I want to help make things better. "Tim, listen," I say. "If you need me blow the horn and I will come running, but I need to go on land and do something." Then I climb off the boat. I can tell by his expression that he's not happy about my leaving, but he doesn't stop me.

The chain of boxes stretches from the waterfront up the long ramp to the edge of the World Financial Center. I read the dispatches traced into the dust on the windows: "Revenge is sweet." "Goodness will prevail." "It doesn't matter how you died, it only matters where you go." "You woke a sleeping giant." Among them is the word *Invictus*. Latin for *unconquerable*, it's the title of a poem by William Ernest Henley, published in 1875, that begins: "Out of the night that covers me,/Black as the Pit from pole to pole,/I thank whatever gods may be/For my unconquerable soul."

Other messages are more practical than poetic: "Go to Stuyvesant High School to sleep," and "Lt. John Crisci call home." I just assume that particular personal instruction is directed at one of these rescuers here on site—a message conveyed in dust because cell service has been shut down for so long. Only later will I read John Crisci's name on a list of the Fire Department dead.

In the chaos of the effort, people create jobs for themselves. One young man with dirty, matted hair dashes back and forth, mouth agape, from the front lines to the supply area to bring the diggers what they need. The masking tape across his chest says "Runner," and his open flannel shirt flaps behind him as he goes.

Standing next to a sign for "Luxury Yachting and Dining Afloat" I'm trying to grasp the best approach to dealing with the boxes when two hands grip my shoulders from behind. I hear a voice at the back of my neck: "Can you help?" For three days I've been waiting to hear those three words. A woman in a hard hat and a paper mask points at the hill of boxes and bags. "We need to make some order."

The ubiquitous dust has crept into the bags and boxes, and donated goods are spilling out from where people have burrowed through them. Garbage has ended up on top of usable goods that arrived in black plastic bags. So a group of us set about matching like items and separating the useful from the absurdly out of place. Workers come over saying, "I need a flashlight," or "I need a hard hat," or "I need a respirator," and we give them what we can find.

But it's impossible to keep up with the deliveries. For an hour I turn away people looking for flashlights without knowing that two cases are hidden at the bottom of the pile. Boxes of saline, eyewash, Band-Aids, batteries, Advil, face wash, anti-itch cream, peroxide, gauze, face masks, filters, used shoes and boots, jeans, TGIFriday's hats, a box of new *Miracle on 34th Street* T-shirts. It just keeps coming.

Men and women in National Guard camouflage approach the boxes asking for civilian clothes. Ironworkers wearing union T-shirts hunt for batteries. Firefighters with dust caked in their hair request bottled water. There is no singularity to the faces, all ashy and grayed-out except where rivulets of wet have traced clean lines on their skin. The rescuers are, as songwriter Kate Fenner describes, "covered in and breathing in the ones they're looking for."

I can see a dozen bucket brigades from where I stand sorting goods—workers are stretched in long lines passing buckets full of debris, and occasionally remains, off the pile. The buckets travel hand-over-hand either to waiting trucks or to fire chiefs and others on morgue duty.

Suddenly voices swell up from somewhere deep in the pile. Then people are running past me, heading toward the river. I dart out from behind the row of boxes and jump into the mob, picking up words that explain the mad rush—a building is coming down. Another collapse. We scramble to the river that promises escape.

People plow into me as I run. Ahead of me I watch an overweight man stumble and hit the ground. Many tromp right over him, but finally a couple of men stop and help him to his feet.

I dash toward fireboat *Harvey*. At the river, some people hook a left and keep moving, but their sprinting slows to a jog once they encounter the tangle of ropes and hose lines stretched across the walkway. Having forgotten its maritime roots, this Manhattan waterfront park doesn't have a single cleat, bollard, or other proper fixture for tying up a large boat—every single boat has been forced to tie up to trees. People holler out, "Watch the ropes! Watch the lines!" to try to help those behind them. But everyone stalls in the bottleneck.

I scramble over the awkward railing (built with no openings— another large-boat impediment) and climb down the seawall (built with no ladders) to the *Harvey*. Just as they did on Tuesday, people begin spilling onto the boats. One man, in full firefighting gear, jumps into the water. When the wooden ladder leading down to the *Harvey* gets clogged with people, they pile over the railings, skidding down the seawall to the caprail on the boat. I stand at the edge, catching the hard hats, helmets, and bunker gear people pass to me. People on board start yelling at us to pull away, "Go! Let's go!"

I look up at Bob, who just stands outside the back door of the pilothouse watching. He sees me look up at him, keeps his mouth closed, and looks away. Tim, standing between us, looks at Bob too. A moment goes by and Bob turns to Tim, giving just a slight nod of his head. Tim turns to me and points a finger toward the engine-room door. I bolt down the stairs and fire up the engines.

I act fast, but it still takes time. Tim stays up on deck, preparing to free hoses and lines. Once all the engines are running, I stand at my post, my heart hammering at the inside of my chest. Staying still with the surge of adrenaline in my bloodstream makes my limbs ache. But, at the same time, standing at the center of this space filled with throbbing diesels gives me an overwhelming sense of relief. No questions remain about where I should be or what I should be doing. I belong right here, standing in this spot, hands on the brass levers, watching the gauges. This is something I know how to do.

I wait with visions of an approaching dust cloud so thick it will stuff itself like a rag down my throat. Bracing myself, I eyeball the telegraphs, hunting for any itch of movement that will allow me to kick into gear.

Then I see the shadow as Tim steps slowly, calmly down the stairs. He slashes at the air with his hand, which I know means, "Shut down." Back on deck I learn there was no collapse, just a false alarm. Now I understand why Tim was angry at me for going ashore. My job is here. I stick close to the boat for the rest of the day.

✦ ✦ ✦

The next day, Tommy Whyte tells us that the water mains have been restored. We've completed our mission and the boat is free to go. Just shy of her seventieth birthday, the *Harvey* has performed honorably, casting off the specter of uselessness implicit in her close call with the scrap heap. As we ready to leave, Tommy comes up to the wheelhouse with a few firefighters from fireboat *John D. McKean* and passes out small plastic cups. Into each he pours a couple inches of Celtic Crossing, an Irish liqueur with a ship on the bottle, and offers a toast of appreciation.

Over the past three days fireboats provided the only water available at the World Trade Center site. When firefighters on land bent over their hoses to rinse the ash from their faces, they spit and sputtered in surprise, tasting the salt of the Hudson.

Before we can go, an Army Corps tug called the *Gelberman* ties up alongside the *Harvey* to pick up rescue workers and deliver them across the river to New Jersey's Exchange Point. Firefighters crowd the whole back deck of the tug, ready for their workday to end, but before the boat can drop lines and head out, an announcement comes out over the marine radio. The president is due to arrive any minute, so as a security measure, the harbor has been shut down completely.

I stand with Tommy on the bow of the *Harvey* as the fading sun lights up the whole sky with a rose glow. The haggard firefighters slouch against every flat surface on the back deck of the tug, silhouetted against the pink. I turn to Tommy. "You know, we have all this beer," I begin, explaining that there are cases left over from our Hudson River trip. "It's shitty. It's canned. It's warm. But do you think they'd like it?" I ask, gesturing to the guys on the boat.

Tommy doesn't hesitate. "I think they would absolutely love it."

So I open up the pantry and start handing over beer by the case, warning them it's warm. A huge hurrah rises up through the crowd, and for the first time since Tuesday, I grin a full-face grin. Then one guy calls over, "Don't you have any ice?"

"I'm sorry, I don't have any ice."

Then two or three of them chime in at once: "We'll find ice!" They step over the caprails from the tug to the fireboat, then climb the seawall. When they return, with a barrelful, another great hurrah erupts. This tiny transaction offers a moment of camaraderie. Some of the ways we help can seem so trivial, but doing something—anything— matters.

Fireboat *John J. Harvey* and the World Trade Center towers, still under construction, in the early 1970s. *(Collection of Bob Lenney)*

Part II

∾

ABOVE AND BELOW DECKS

A New Purpose

Gowanus Bay, March 23, 2002.

Mark Peckham

Chapter Five

APPRENTICESHIP

"Make Yourself Useful"

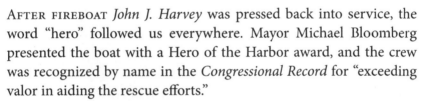

AFTER FIREBOAT *John J. Harvey* was pressed back into service, the word "hero" followed us everywhere. Mayor Michael Bloomberg presented the boat with a Hero of the Harbor award, and the crew was recognized by name in the *Congressional Record* for "exceeding valor in aiding the rescue efforts."

During our time at Ground Zero, I experienced firsthand the work for which this fireboat had been built. So many people had ached to contribute something during those first days, and by some miraculous accident, I had been thrust into a world of workers with useful skills. Like others who worked down there, I was consumed by guilt about not doing enough, but kept telling myself that a little bit was all any of us had to give—like the tiny buckets transporting debris off the pile, one by one.

In the aftermath of the attacks, the dichotomy between hands-on and hands-off work played out in stark relief. As blue-collar tradespeople swarmed over the pile, the earth seemed to have shifted on its axis. For months afterward, Americans flocked to their local firehouses to volunteer. Suddenly an Ivy League education seemed far less useful than knowing how to use a cutting torch. My respect for the building blocks of the physical world was rekindled, and while everyday Americans discussed the maximum temperature of burning jet fuel and the melting point of steel beams, I immersed myself in learning how materials go together, and what happens when they come apart.

I wanted to work with my hands. Though I hadn't yet thought of it that way, I was undertaking an informal but very real apprenticeship in the engine room.

✦ ✦ ✦

On off evenings and Saturday afternoons volunteers come to get dirty doing work that offers a change of pace from their desk jobs. In good weather, nearly everyone opts to work on deck, but I stay in the engine room, wanting to learn everything about the machinery. Impatient, I already feel like I'm a lifetime behind. I curse my fancy education, wishing I'd taken shop classes instead. My vocabulary makes me self-conscious when I talk to the crew; I watch helplessly as ten-cent SAT words fly out of my mouth before I have time to order them back. *Why do I have to make everything sound so frickin' complicated?* At the same time, I struggle with boat lingo like it's a foreign tongue. Because I can't name the objects around me, my questions, like a child's, involve a lot of pointing. When the crew gathers on the pier to sip post–boat trip or post-workday beers, I open my ears to collect new words and phrases.

Early on, Tim had figured my interest was fleeting, but when I kept coming back, he started giving me simple engine jobs, handing me the tools I'd need, demonstrating the task at hand, then moving on to coach another volunteer. I'd follow his instructions as best I could, but would inevitably reach a stumbling block and slink back to ask for help. A lot of my initial difficulties stemmed from strength—or lack thereof. I hadn't yet learned how to manipulate tools to my advantage and got caught short without enough leverage to loosen rusty bolts or pry a part out of position. "Don't worry about it," Tim reassured me. "You can always find a gorilla to do the heavy work. What's more important is knowing what the problem is and how to fix it."

But size matters. And learning from someone six foot two and 225 pounds has both pros and cons. "Put some ass into it" is a common job-site refrain that translates to "Apply more brute force." Working

Heat-exchanger repairs on the Number Five engine. *(Photo by Sarah Lyon, www .sarahlyon.com. From* Female Mechanics Calendar 2009, *produced by Sarah Lyon)*

on engines taller than I am makes it painfully clear just how much ass I don't have. At times I have to stand on top of a wrench and bounce to crack free a bolt—the same bolt that Tim can crack holding the wrench in his hands. This, of course, means I can't just mimic his actions, monkey see, monkey do. I have to strategize. And, with an eye for leverage, Tim is always ready with ideas for mechanical solutions to compensate for my stature.

When he was eighteen, Tim volunteered with the Glen Rock Fire Department in New Jersey. What first attracted him, he admits, was the idea of violating traffic laws. "I was sitting at a red light when I saw a guy zoom through with a blue light on the dash," he says. "I thought, I want to do that." But what kept him with the department was the camaraderie, training, and equipment. He eventually took over as chief engineer, responsible for inspecting the rigs to ensure all the gear was in good working order. One day he watched a fellow fire-department volunteer struggle to start a chain saw because she lacked the arm strength to yank the cord. Tim saw her experiment until she discovered that crossing one arm over the other worked better. That started him thinking. When I arrived on the fireboat years later, he was ready to help me brainstorm new approaches.

I have to keep reminding myself that most guys aren't as big or strong as Tim, either. Everybody reaches the limits of his or her strength at some point, and if you can't figure out what to do next, what do you really have to offer? And sometimes, being small offers an advantage, especially when dealing with the *Harvey*'s rear electric panel.

Electricity both scares and enthralls me. I hold off as long as I can before facing the back panel. Littered with wheels, rheostats, gauges, and knife switches, it stands a foot or so taller than me, stretches fourteen feet across the back of the engine room, and extends about five feet deep. But the confrontation is inevitable. I have to learn the electrical system of the boat as well as the engines. My dad always told me electricity behaves just like water running through pipes, but that doesn't quell my trepidation. When visitors tour the engine room, we tell them that with our 625 volts of DC electricity at 1,000 amps we have enough power to run a New York City subway train. But all that power is invisible. And if you can't see it, how can you understand the cause and effect? How can you know what's safe to touch and what isn't?

These days, this kind of equipment would be tucked safely away behind insulated enclosures, but in this 1931 engine room, motors, generators, and circuit breakers stand out in the open. Designed four decades before the Occupational Safety and Health Administration even existed, this engine room has startlingly few safety protections beyond the occasional wood railing and signs that read "Danger, LIVE." Back in the day, workers' common sense was their only protection. And it wasn't always enough.

My common sense does not like the idea of me climbing inside that back panel, the distribution center for the DC electricity that powers the propellers, but when Tim notices that a buss bar inside has arced with too much voltage, leaving burned traces on the copper slab, we have to remove and clean it. There is no question about who will squeeze herself in to retrieve the piece. The boat sits silently in her berth. With no engines or generators running, there is no way the power could be live, but still . . . Just like the games you play as a kid, when you fall backward counting on a friend to catch you, I have to trust Tim's judgment.

I limbo past the wood guardrail, my hands curled around its surface, smooth like a ballet barre. Careful not to crush the fragile resistors at my feet, I tap gently with my toe in search of a clear spot for my foot to land, then stand up inside one of the two-foot-wide sections of the seven-section panel, the steel supports brushing each of my shoulders, my cropped hair dusting the top edge. I'm standing inside a three-dimensional subway map—a maze of copper bars.

From outside, peering through the wire mesh opening, Tim shines the flashlight and points out which bolts to pull. I have to turn around to reach the back bolts, which requires shrugging my shoulders and spinning slowly to clear the dividers. It feels like this space was designed just for me—like someone knew I was coming.

"The first engine I ever worked on was a lawn tractor," Tim tells me. "I was in sixth grade. My next project was my 1951 Buick Roadmaster—my Buick Road*monster*—that I bought from my grandmother for fifteen hundred dollars. I was in eighth grade. It took me five years to pay that off," he laughs. I wonder how far along I might be now if only I'd gotten an earlier start, but try to channel my frustration into focus. During big repairs, I content myself with handing Tim tools, holding the light, and saving my questions until the end so I don't distract him from the work. When we have the luxury of time, I attempt small jobs on my own. That's what generations of apprentices have done.

✦ ✦ ✦

In colonial America, an apprenticeship starting at age twelve or fourteen was a boy's best hope for a practical education. I restrict the conversation here to boys because, as William J. Rorabaugh points out in his book, *The Craft Apprentice,* formalized craft apprenticeships were considered a male institution. "Occasionally a woman practiced a craft that she had learned from her husband or father, but in all the first-person accounts I read and documents I examined, I never encountered a female craft apprentice," he writes. "Poor girls were 'apprenticed' to housewifery or sewing, but that sort of apprenticeship provided only legal guardianship and training in traditional female work rather than the learning of a craft." Despite the fact that sewing, quilting, cooking, canning, and other such "female work" constitute crafts that demand just as much mastery and experience over time as blacksmithing, carpentry, shoemaking, tailoring, and silversmithing, let us, for the sake of simplicity, follow Rorabaugh's narration of the arc of American apprenticeship as a male world.

The apprenticeship model, firmly entrenched in European societies since the Middle Ages, had followed colonists overseas. Codified into English law, the English system required parents to either provide for a boy's professional education or bind him by signing a seven-year indenture to learn a trade. The master craftsman who took on the apprentice was responsible for feeding, clothing, housing, and providing religious instruction for the boy until age twenty-one. In exchange, the apprentice offered up his labors, free of charge, for the duration. By twenty-one, the apprentice had learned enough to set out on his own as a journeyman, traveling the countryside searching out the best wages for his trade. Once he earned enough money to open up his own shop, he would establish himself as a master craftsman and take on his own apprentice.

Conditions in colonial America posed some unique challenges to the traditional system, rendering the American apprenticeship "considerably less vigorous," according to Rorabaugh. The colonies did not have the powerful guild system that kept tight control of numerous trades and craft wages high, by maintaining discipline, establishing quality standards, and restricting numbers of apprentices. "Vast distances, shortages of skilled labor, a largely agricultural population, and a poorly developed legal system all contributed" to the failure of guilds to develop in the colonies, Rorabaugh explains. Without this regulatory system, anyone in America could call himself a master craftsman and take on an apprentice. Having no guild to evaluate the apprentice's masterpiece—the work that demonstrated his skill had reached a master's level—opened the door to a cycle of shoddy workmanship.

Changing economic, political, and social factors also undermined the apprenticeship system. One famous apprentice, Benjamin Franklin, who was bonded to his brother James, a printer, at age twelve, embodied this New World attitude. After he eventually fled his obligations, his successes encouraged future generations of boys to follow his lead, abandoning their masters as well. By the close of the Civil War the system was nearly obsolete.

✦ ✦ ✦

A century later, my younger brother Josh happened upon his own modern-day apprenticeship. In 1997 he started training to become a machinist at J. H. Horne and Sons Company. For nearly 150 years, J. H. Horne, the longest continuously operated business in Lawrence, Massachusetts, built machines that milled paper—from pulp beaters to formers to the end-stage dryer stack units where wet paper serpentines through a series of heated rollers. When Josh started working there at age twenty, he was by far the youngest in the shop.

Youth is what got him the job in the first place. "Byron wanted to train a young kid with mechanical ability," he says, referring to Byron Cleveland III, Horne sales manager and great-great-great grandson of the company's founder, John H. Horne. "He saw that all of his skilled workers were older. They were all at least forty and some were over seventy." Josh walked into the shop cold: "I didn't even know what an end mill was."

For the first two weeks, Josh did nothing but sort tools, including end mills, which he learned were cutting tools similar to drill bits. The foreman had him label and fill a new set of cabinets with drills, taps, and other tools. At first Josh was disappointed, but he didn't complain. Later on he realized that sorting tools had provided an important benefit: Now when he was called upon to make a certain cut, he could picture the tools in his mind, matching their shapes to the job at hand. And he knew where to find what he needed. He was learning his first real trade.

His first month was intense—not only learning about machining, but also trying to find his place among his new coworkers. For years Horne had apprenticed youth from local vocational schools. "A lot of the kids were punks, whether they were sneaking up onto the roof and smoking dope or taking a nap in the corner or whatever it was."

So the guys prejudged him. "It was up to me to prove different. Those old bastards still can give me a hard time." Josh laughs. "It doesn't matter how old I am, I'm still just a kid to them." Some of those "old bastards" ended up becoming good friends.

Instrumental to Josh's education was Gordon Barlow, who worked in the Special Parts Department, a room with milling machines, grinders, and a small lathe. Gordon was paid a bit more for the effort of teaching. "He was my mentor. He's the best machinist I've ever seen." A proper gentleman from England who at one time made jet engines for Rolls-Royce, Gordon was about seventy when Josh started. His mastery inspired Josh, who speaks reverently about the man who "knew exactly what the metal was going to do before he did it," and almost effortlessly fashioned parts with accuracy that you could measure to dimensions finer than the width of a human hair.

Josh worked with Gordon for just over two years before the older man retired, leaving him in charge of Special Parts. Josh was ready for the challenge. "You'd get a print and the material and they'd say, 'Here you go.' I'd take raw material and some blueprints and give them the finished product. It got to the point where they didn't even check my work. I'd just put it in the box and they'd say 'All right, you all done?' and I'd say, 'Yup, there it is.'"

He had an aptitude for the work, clearly—maybe because for years he had worked alongside my father, fixing cars.

✦ ✦ ✦

Since before I was born, my father has worked on German machines. That's how he explains it. Most people use "machines" as a generic term to describe things that clack and whir and slap their metal parts together for some mechanical purpose. My father uses it to mean cars, specifically Porsches, Audis, and Volkswagens. He got his start as a mechanic by fixing his own vehicles. "When I realized you can't trust anyone else to do it right, I learned to do it myself," he says. Plus, managing his own repairs was a good skill to have for a hippie bent on cross-country adventures in a Volkswagen bus.

Dad's particular affection for German vehicles stemmed from not just Volkswagen's hippie icon status, but also his heritage. His mother, Margot, told him it was in his blood. Some years after she boarded an ocean liner in Bremen on November 30, 1948, as a war bride joining her new husband—my grandfather, Frederick, a career army man—Margot's mother, two sisters, and their husbands immigrated to the States, too. So growing up, my dad was surrounded by Germans—his aunts, uncles, and grandmother—all of whom spoke with a thick accent like his mother. Just before World War II broke out, Volkswagen had established Die Autostadt in Wolfsburg, northeast of Hanover, where my grandmother's family came from. So, for them, Volkswagens offered a taste of home—especially since Margot's father had been among the factory's initial investors. Years after Margot arrived in the States, a Volkswagen representative called her to offer her the chance to run one of the first of its dealerships in this country. She turned him down, but the tradition lived on in her son.

Our house on Hancock Street in Stoneham, Massachusetts, just outside Boston, belonged to my father's parents before we moved in. The blue-collar neighborhood was filled with the starter homes of people with middle-class aspirations. White with dark green shutters, our house, like all the other houses on the block, had a metal screen door that squeaked when the rod slipped through the piston that kept it from slamming.

I told my first lie on the sidewalk in front of that house. A group of kids from the neighborhood stood around, one-upping each other. "My father's stronger than your father," one of them started. I pointed to a green VW, a customer's car, parked in front of the house. "My dad's a mechanic and he can pick up this car with his bare hands. He does it all the time." I'd never seen him pick up a car without a jack, but it didn't seem so far-fetched to me, really. He was my father. And though he stood only five feet, seven inches tall, to me he was larger than life.

Every day that I was home when my dad left for work, I begged him to take me with him. He occupied some foreign land and I wanted to be part of it. Sometimes he let me tag along. I remember those shop days as a slinging of names I couldn't keep track of—words for vehicles, customers, parts stores, tools. There's a running joke in my family that when Bridget, Josh, and I went to the shop, my dad would have us girls—ages seven and ten—sorting nuts and bolts while the boy—age three—helped him fix cars. "Here. Make yourself useful," he'd tell us. He denies it now, shaking his head, laughing as his defense crumbles under the unified front of two stubborn sisters.

To this day, Josh and Dad work together on cars. Whenever I did anything mechanical with my dad, he seemed to start his explanations in the middle, instead of the beginning, and I could never catch up. I wouldn't understand, he'd get frustrated, and I couldn't find a way past his impatient anger. If I'd had the push of societal expectation that said girls could fix things just as well as boys, would I have kept trying? Impossible to say. Instead I took solace in what I was already good at: school.

In seventh grade some scheduling fluke placed me in a shop class. I remember splicing wire. But what stood out most was a classroom discussion about internal combustion that made a tingle skip around under my skin. Here was a teacher explaining the principles, and some of it started to make sense.

That night, between forkfuls of Mom's famous rice with cheese sauce, I told my dad about the class, prodding for more information. From his place at the round wood table that he had built himself, my dad launched into his own explanation of the mechanics of engines. "First, the spark ignites the gasoline, causing an explosion—therefore the name: internal combustion. Then the pressure of the explosion pushes the piston down in the cylinder." I was with him so far, but then he lost me in the language, which became all rod journals and crankshafts. He must have seen my confusion. So, to facilitate his explanation of how the crankshaft converts lateral into rotary motion, he wrapped one grease-stained palm around the food end of his fork, the other around the handle, and bent it to show how the position of the crank affects the position of the connecting rod. "Four strokes: intake, compression, power, exhaust."

It wasn't like a flashbulb went off, exactly. More like a dimmer switch nudged slightly brighter. But it was a start. For years thereafter the bent fork sat with the others in the olive green plastic utensil tray, always the last one left in the drawer. "Ha, ha, you got the crankshaft fork," we'd tease whichever kid ended up with it.

✦ ✦ ✦

Time after time, while I stood at my post in the engine room, I imagined my dad climbing down the narrow metal staircase from the deck. Though he's never been on a fireboat, I knew he'd recognize the components of each engine, from the fuel lines to the flywheel. He'd understand the concept of throttling down before engaging the air flex clutch. He's a mechanic. I'm not . . . yet.

When he finally pays a visit to the boat and sees the kind of work I've been doing, my father nearly bursts with pride. I feel a twinge of nervousness as I walk him through the paces. I describe how the engines produce the electricity that powers the two propulsion motors. I show him the redundancy of the system—how we can operate with fewer engines by swapping over to auxiliary generators. I explain that the only things running direct-drive off the diesels are the water pumps. He punctuates each of my explanations with one of his signature phrases: "Wow." "That's ace." "That's dynamite." Though he's a gasoline-engine mechanic who doesn't think much of diesel, he knows which questions to ask.

Later, after I pry him out of the engine room and the family heads to dinner, my father asks me about the fuel system. He was puzzling over the open drip-cups that collect unburned fuel oil.

"The runoff ends up in the sump tank below the deck plates," I explain.

"Nah. Nah. Nah. It can't be like that," he insists. "There's no opening in the system."

"It's not a closed loop," I maintain, while the rest of the family looks on. "The sump tank catches the excess and we have to pump it back into the main tanks."

I remember the night of the crankshaft fork and how desperately I wanted his makeshift visual aid to etch a comprehensible, working model into my head—to carve out understanding that would stay. Then I flash back to that unmistakable *I don't get it* feeling. It makes me falter. "I dunno," I say, even though I've emptied the sump tanks myself—fuel oil sloshing from the bucket onto my pant leg. "I dunno. Maybe I misunderstood."

The next day I check with Tim.

"You're right," he says. "It's an open loop."

✦ ✦ ✦

I was Tim's apprentice. And I was learning. One of my first major trials came, literally, by fire.

In the engine room, any quick change in light makes me nervous—I've often spun my head around on alert when a person above decks walks past the engine-room door and momentarily blocks the sunlight from pouring down the stairs. Here, in the rush of noise and vibration, noticing any slight fluctuation is key. Tim and I joke about being hypervigilant, but belowdecks, surrounded by the pounding conversion of heat into work, combustion into power, our hypervigilance isn't paranoia. It's prevention.

In late October 2001, the fireboat set out for the annual Fall Leaf Trip with a deck full of passengers excited about the brilliant weather, which was perfect for an all-day boat ride. The plan was to cruise north for three hours, see the colorful foliage, and then head back to the city.

In the engine room, we were excited about starting up the Number One engine after a complete rebuild. Tim had enlisted me to reinstall some of the last components to ready the engine for service on this long trip, but when we had started it up, cooling water from the water jacket had shot out the side of the engine. One of the cylinder adapters I'd been charged with resealing had leaked. We pulled off the dock, running just four engines instead of five, and I was standing in my usual spot at the control pedestal, kicking myself that Tim had to fix my mistake. "It's no big deal," he told me, and the repair took him only minutes. He fired up the engine again and my eyes bounced over the dials—scavenging air above three, lube oil pressure above twenty psi, starting air steady at two hundred pounds.

A loud pop disrupted my brooding. A light flashed under the deck plates to my left. You can't really hear a pop over the whine of five 8-cylinder diesels. But an impact with enough force transfers sound at its most elemental level: You *feel* it hit.

My mind raced with the flash. No way that was caused by sunlight.

A yellow-orange glow reflected off thick water mains below the floor. The spark lit up parts of the bilge I'd never seen before. The small tornado of white smoke that followed the pop ricocheted my heart against my rib cage.

I couldn't find Tim. I'd never used the panic button he had half-jokingly installed, but I reached for it now. You have to hold the button down for three seconds before it makes a sound, but right then, half a second felt too long. There's definitely a design flaw in a panic button that expects you to remain calm for three seconds, waiting.

Craning my neck around the Number Two engine, I saw Tim walking toward me. My wide eyes communicated my alarm, and my outstretched finger gave direction. We peered over the edge of a deck plate into the gap beside the Number Five pump.

I saw fire.

Tim yanked the port prop control lever into neutral. I followed his lead and pulled the starboard lever to a stop. Then, at his single-gestured instruction, I slammed all the throttles to idle and signaled the wheelhouse: Full Stop.

When he reached for a long screwdriver, I understood his plan to pull up the deck plate. As he dug the flat metal tip into the corner to catch the underside, I yanked the fire extinguisher off its bent metal bracket and set it within reach. Together we pried up the plate.

Flames shot up from below. I tried not to focus on the slick of fuel oil and lube oil sloshing in the bilge.

I handed Tim the extinguisher. He pulled the pin, squeezed the trigger, and with a few short sweeps the foam suffocated the blaze.

For a moment, everything stopped. The engine room seemed suddenly suspended. There was no noise.

The Full Stop had aroused concern in the wheelhouse, so Don, one of the retired firefighters who volunteers on the boat, came down to the engine room. He nearly fell into the bilge where we had removed the deck plate.

Tim waved him to get out.

So Don swung over to my side. I pushed him back, both my palms pressed flat against his chest. Tim had told me just the week before that my first job in a crisis was to kick everybody out.

"The captain wants to know what's going on," he shouted, peeling the plastic earmuff from my sweaty cheek so I could hear. The boat was in the middle of the busy Hudson, and Bob had nothing but manual control of the rudder.

"Tell him we had a fire, but it's out," I shouted back, and Don made his way forward again.

Tim headed aft to the back electrical panel to cut off the power to the whole port side. He shut down the Number Five engine, then signaled to me to throttle the others back up. Starboard-side power was better than none at all.

As Tim leaned over to reach the scorched contactor cover, swiping at the extinguisher foam with a rag, I knew to help him lift and slide the cover up and out of the way. Effortlessly we navigated together in this space. For more than six months I'd been hawkeyed, watching him work. Now, I could almost predict each step, even in this completely new situation.

Down on his belly, Tim reached below the contactor with his rag. Before I could see it, I smelled the source of the flames: a jet of fuel oil shooting from the pipe that supplies the engines.

"I need a hose clamp and a piece of rubber," Tim shouted at me. Maybe I actually heard him say this. It's equally possible I only read his lips.

I dug out two clamps and a stretch of hose from a box at the back of the engine room. Back at the stand, I yanked the SwissTool off my belt and split the hose down the middle. "This big?" I asked silently, forming a circle over the rubber with my thumb and forefinger.

The patch fit, but the port-side electrical system had been damaged. We called off the day's voyage and limped back to the pier on two engines. Knowing Bob had minimal maneuverability, I concentrated on zero-second response time, keeping my hands on the controls. Between commands, the brass control levers heated up in my grip. We landed at the pier with hardly a bump.

The fire, we discovered, had resulted from salt water splashing up from the bilge onto a badly insulated splice of a wire in what is charmingly called the "suicide circuit." Printed on the schematic beside that particular circuit is a little heart with a lightning bolt through it. When he first saw the graphic, Tim worried that the name implied significant hazards posed by dealing with this particular circuit. But no. "Its whole job is to destroy the magnetic field to get the prop motor to stop," Tim explained. "Suicide for the motor, not the operator."

Back at the dock, I played apprentice to Tim's master mechanic, and before long we had the wire replaced and the fuel pipe mended. The passengers had missed the fall leaves, settling instead for shrimp and hot dogs, pier-side.

✦ ✦ ✦

Just as my own personal mission solidified following our work at Ground Zero, the boat's larger purpose took shape as well. We, the crew, appeared as characters—with our real names and recognizable illustrations—in a children's book by *New Yorker* illustrator Maira Kalman called *FIREBOAT: The Heroic Adventures of the* John J. Harvey. Schoolchildren wrote us letters, and the wheelhouse filled up with stacks of children's drawings and thank-you cards.

In the years since, thousands of kids have come for boat rides, some of them running down the pier, calling to me by name, since I'm recognizable as the only woman on the crew. I love watching their excitement as the boat they've read about comes to life. Although the personal attention can be uncomfortable, I've been grateful that the boat's fame has encouraged the donations upon which we depend to continue restoration work. Over the next few years, our May to October seasons become a blur of trips, sometimes three a day while we're in the city, as well as our growing list of annual extended voyages upriver—two weeks every August and weekend overnights, including the Fall Leaf Trip.

✦ ✦ ✦

On a Thursday morning in July 2003, I'm the first crew member to arrive at the pier for a scheduled trip, so I take my time, stealing some quiet on this boat that has become a home.

I click open the padlock on the engine-room door, then bang on the levers, called "dogs," with the palm of my hand to swing the latch free. I brace myself for the blast, as forceful as the hot exhaust that shoots from the back vent of a city bus. Roasted diesel air wraps itself around me as I descend the metal-grating steps—the heat a kind of invitation, readying me for firing up these engines that will only make it hotter. At least when the engines are running, the air moves around. At 130 degrees, the movement of air—1,324 cubic feet of displacement for each engine running at eleven hundred rpm—means the difference between hot and intolerable.

At nine thirty in the morning there's more than enough light for me to navigate the engine room without firing up the 2-71 generator for ship's power. A relief, because its piercing whine would disturb the peacefulness of the gentle slosh of bilgewater beneath the deck plates and the creaking of the lines that slack out and tighten rhythmically every time a boat going by throws its wake. I ready the engines for startup, addressing each of their five basic needs: compressed air, lube oil, fuel oil, fresh water, and raw (river) water. Once I open the sea cocks, fill the fresh water, top off the diesel day tank, check the oil, and click on the compressors so they produce starting air, I head up to find a shady spot on the deck to wait.

By now Bob and Tim have arrived, as have the PAL kids, swarming in matching fluorescent green T-shirts. The kids are summer campers from the Police Athletic League, a youth organization that "inspires and supports New York City youth challenged by the highest risk factors to overcome obstacles and realize their full individual potential as productive members of society." Many of these kids had lived their whole lives on Manhattan Island without ever being out on the water. In this, they're not unlike legions of adults, privileged and underprivileged alike.

When a round-faced little girl with white baubles on the ends of her pigtails looks up, eyes wide, and bubbles over with, "I'm finally going to realize how big the ocean is!" the boat's mission rings true. After all, what good is preserving a taste of maritime history if we can't share it? This boat is a living museum, a way to connect people to the river of American history. People who set foot on her decks get a visceral sense that this antique technology was cutting edge at one time. They feel the rumble of the engines beneath their feet and feel the whoosh of water escaping the deck guns. And out on the river, they can see their city in an entirely different way. As we share this piece of history, we introduce New Yorkers to the river in their own backyard that so many have somehow never before noticed.

Tim and I start the engines, and when he's confident that everything is running smoothly, he heads up to the wheelhouse to keep Bob company and shoot the shit with Karl. A new addition to our operating crew, Karl Schuman has become a trusted deckhand. During trips like these, one of his most important jobs (after making sure passengers are safe and Bob has everything he needs) is to prevent the rear end of any wet kid from plopping down on Bob's new bunk. He does this by making sure his own skinny butt occupies the spot. These days Bob likes to camp out in the wheelhouse overnight sometimes, even when the boat's in the city, and a wet bed is no fun.

Later, when Tim comes down to the engine room to spell me, I head up on deck. A group of kids sits clustered on the bow listening to a lesson on charts and navigation, while others gather on the stern, practicing knot tying and learning about how a 268-gross-ton steel vessel can float. But, really, what the kids are waiting for is the chance to get wet.

As I step into the wheelhouse, I hear a boy ask Bob, "When are you going to sparkle water?" Bob turns around and looks at me with a grin.

"I dunno," he replies, pointing a thumb in my direction. "You'd better ask Jessica."

"As soon as the captain tells me to, I'll sparkle water," I say. "I guess I'd better get down there so I can turn on the pumps, huh?" And the boy nods his head.

When I do engage the pumps, I can almost hear the kids squealing as they dance and splash and play. These moments give new meaning to all that I'm investing in my grease-monkey apprenticeship on fireboat *John J. Harvey.*

Chapter Six

RED SKIES IN MORNING

∽

IT'S DECEMBER 1, 2004, and Bob, Huntley, Tim, Karl, and I are aboard a sixty-five-foot tugboat that's getting bashed by waves in the Chesapeake Bay off Windmill Point, Virginia. All I ate for breakfast was a slice of toast, and this stroke of luck is helping me pass more quickly through vomiting and into endless dry heaves. Though I don't usually count dry heaves as a blessing, in this case the less my retching produces, the less it interferes with my doing my job: helping this tugboat—my newest charge—and her crew—my fireboat friends—reach land safely.

I blame Tim. Without his scheming I never would have found myself here, in the middle of an angry sea, wedged against the railing of a boat that threatens to shake me off like a petulant pony, worrying that my crew will never forgive me. But the truth is that I fought for this boat of my own accord. I fell for her the instant I saw her.

✦ ✦ ✦

A few years into my job on the fireboat, I had started daydreaming about owning a tugboat. This was a safe enough fantasy, since there was no way I could afford one. But when I mentioned it to the *Harvey* crew, they latched on to the idea. Huntley kept saying, "Oh, don't worry, we'll find you a boat." Telling them that boat ownership was beyond my budget fell on deaf ears. By now I had a good sense of how much maintaining a boat could cost. Still, Huntley kept talking about it. Then Tim started in. And his prodding was much more dangerous: He actually formulated a plan.

Tim happened across the perfect boat in September 2004. He'd been hired to go tug hunting with a prospective buyer named Rick Batchelder. From his time volunteering on the fireboat, Rick knew that Tim was a good person to have scope out a potential boat purchase. So the two of them drove down to Norfolk, Virginia, to look at a 1956 retired army tug that had been sold at a surplus auction in 2000, and had since changed hands a couple of times. The deal soured when Rick and the boat's owner couldn't come to terms on a price. Once it was clear that Rick had walked away from it, Tim called me, raving, "Oh, this is the perfect Jessica-sized boat."

I cut him off right away. "Stop. I don't want to hear it. I don't want to know. I can't afford a tugboat and you know it, so don't torture me."

"But this boat is in such great shape. Everything works. Everything. And all the drawings are here too."

I begged off the call.

The next time the fireboat went out, he couldn't stop talking about the tug. Built for the army in Fort Everglades, Florida, it was called an ST, for small tug (as opposed to LT, for large tug). At sixty-five feet long and nineteen and a half feet across, it certainly qualified as small, but still offered plenty of boat. "It's in really good shape. There's practically no rust. The thing got shipped back and forth overseas in a box. It's got very little run time." I tried not to listen. Without a winning lottery ticket, there was nothing to discuss.

My defenses fell apart when Tim hatched a plan after meeting Robert Iannucci, an attorney who had done well in real estate. Rob told Tim he wanted to own a boat but didn't want the responsibility of being a boat owner. His situation was the perfect complement to my own, and Tim couldn't help instigating this partnership of convenience. So Rob and I brokered a trade—sweat for money. He'd pay, I'd work, and I'd get full boat privileges in exchange. Rob and the tug's seller had agreed on a price over the phone. Now I just had to make the buy on behalf of Rob's corporation. Rob set me up with the papers and the check, and since Tim had previously dealt with the seller, he volunteered to join me on the trip to serve as a go-between. We drove the seven hours south to Norfolk (which we soon came to rename Norfuck for how the place treated us). The tug lived in a salvage yard not far from the Campostella Bridge, the rounded arch that curves up above the Elizabeth River to accommodate the big ships that move in and out of Norfolk harbor. We pulled behind a Hardee's parking lot onto a mud road gouged with tire tracks that led into a dirt lot. Tim pointed to an opening in the fence, and I swallowed hard. Through the gate, a jumble of derelicts half sunk into the muck—cranes, old ropes, piping, chain, stripped engines, unidentifiable machinery—formed an unnatural topography. Junkyards intrigue me, but this place just reeked of destruction.

The owner—we'll call him Bill—wasn't around, so we talked to his underling, "Butch." Tim took the lead, since he'd met Butch when he was down here the first time. "So we're here to buy the boat," he explained. "Our guy talked to your guy on the phone. She's got the check and the paperwork right here." Meanwhile, I kept peeking over Butch's shoulder. Between piles of junk I could make out a patch of gray. I tried not to look, but couldn't help myself. "Can I show it to her?" Tim asked. And with Butch's consent we headed off toward the tug.

Stepping through the sludge of poisons that had bled out from the crunched carcasses of so many machines, I kept telling myself, Don't love it. Don't love it. Fat chance. The model-bow tug sitting in the filthy creek, filled with bobbing detritus, had classic lines—the epitome of tugboat, with its rounded wheelhouse, swooped-up nose, and low-profile stern that squatted down low in the water. This little tug was scrappy—with patches of mismatched, peeling paint and black scars on the forward deck where the owner had burned off her anchor winch and small lifting davits.

I stepped onto the caprail, then swung open the heavy steel door to look inside. It wasn't hard to see past the clutter—empty buckets, strewn papers, dirty clothes—to know that this was the perfect little tug. Given the boat's overall dimensions, the living quarters were remarkably spacious. Two separate crew's quarters below the galley housed bunks for a (crowded) ten, and the irregularly shaped galley table could seat a cozy five or six.

The equipment in the engine room, on the other hand, occupied every inch of usable space. At the center stood one big, fat diesel, an Atlas Imperial of a type they've long since stopped making. Though it began below floor level, the Atlas stood more than a foot taller than me. Auxiliary equipment had been packed in tightly around it, floor to ceiling. Anyone taller than five-five would have to duck to make it under the steering motor, but I could circle the whole engine without bending over. And in the pilothouse, which is where I intended to spend my time on this boat, the wheel stood at just the right height. This tug was indeed Jessica-sized. Hard as I tried to shore up my defenses, the boat snagged me. The poor, forlorn little thing just *had* to come home with me. But first I had to get the bill of sale signed for Rob and pass his check to the seller.

Another of Bill's minions, his engineer—we'll call him Fred— boarded the boat, offering to fire up the Atlas. Fred looked like a gnome with a mullet. He fit down in the engine room just fine, but that didn't mean he knew how to run the engine. One of the two air compressors was broken, so it took an eternity for the working compressor to generate enough starting air. Then, even after the air had built up, Fred cranked and cranked and still couldn't get the thing to fire. Every start attempt used up air, which meant that after a certain number of tries, he had to stop and wait for the compressor to build more.

"Let's leave him alone," Tim said, knowing how much fun it isn't to have people watch you work. So we went into the galley to flip through the stack of manuals that the army had compiled for the boat. Seeing all the documentation sent me off into a reverie of bringing this boat back to life. I'd clean it out, sort all the spare parts, set it up with the basics—a coffeemaker, a camp stove—for simple, efficient comfort. I'd use the boat as my hideaway. I'd take charge of the project, jump in armed with manuals, and figure out how to do repairs on my own. This would be different from the fireboat. After four years of whistle-stop tours up the Hudson where I'd pop up, pale and sweaty, after we'd already arrived wherever it was we were going, I was thirsting for a wheelhouse view. I wanted to finally see the way the winding river connects the towns to each other, and to their shared history. This boat could offer me that chance.

Just then Fred came into the galley making excuses for why the engine wouldn't start. "I know *you* would probably use ether, but *I* don't use that stuff. It's a drug." The way he pronounced that last word reminded me of a televised public service announcement from the '80s. By ether he meant starting fluid, which is often used to help start stubborn engines. We use it on the fireboat all the time.

As I stepped back into the yard, I could hear yelling, but couldn't make out the words. The first man I saw had straight black hair and an oval-shaped face, and wore a filthy red sweater. He seemed to be at the receiving end of the tirade. Squishing through the mud, and stepping around the carcass of a crane, I spotted the haranguer, the guy who must be Bill, with his prominent brow jutting out over wide-set eyes. I held my breath and steeled myself for the coming interaction. He looked right past me, recognizing Tim, who was walking a few paces behind me. "You're back," he said.

"Yes. But this time I'm not here for that other guy," Tim replied. Things had not gone well in negotiations between Bill and Rick, and Tim was careful to draw the distinction.

I stepped forward and stuck out my hand. "Hi, I'm Jessica."

But instead of shaking, Bill threw up his own hands, turned his back, and walked away. "I don't have time to deal with this now," he screamed, suddenly spastic, arms flailing.

I turned to Tim, hoping his previous Bill experience might offer some direction. "Listen, we're not here to bother you," he said. "We understand you've got things to do. She's got the paperwork right here and the check. You go ahead and get things settled in here first. We'll just go wait in the truck. Come find us when you're ready."

I followed Tim out through the gate. We sat in the cab of Tim's pickup, watching Bill lurch around the shimmering muck of his empire, hunched over, his arms swinging by his sides as he ripped into his minions, then tore through the air-box covers of a doomed 6-71 Detroit diesel engine with the jaws of an excavator. I shuddered at the snap of the steel between the machine's merciless teeth. "This man has no respect for equipment," said Tim.

An hour passed and my legs started to twitch. "I can't sit here anymore," I pleaded. "What should we do?" Just then, Bill and Butch walked past the truck. Tim and I opened the doors and stepped out. I held a legal-sized manila envelope and a pen at the ready.

"Time to eat. Come on, if you want," said Butch.

The restaurant was a home-style barbecue place. My singular focus on getting the signature made it easier to overlook the inconvenience of the all-meat menu. I hunted for side dishes, like collard greens and yams, figuring I could pick out the pork bits. The last thing I wanted to do was draw attention to my eating habits.

A minute later, the waitress blew my cover. "What kind of meat you want with that?" she asked when I ordered. "No meat?" she asked again when I said no, certain she couldn't have heard me right.

I knew from conversations with Huntley, whose family claimed some Southern roots, about the genteel tradition of lunches that skirted around any mention of business. We were in Virginia after all. So I tried not to get too concerned about how topics skipped about, lighting upon everything but the sale of the tugboat. One particularly bleak subject arose when Tim mentioned the fireboat's Fairbanks engines and how he was hunting for spares now that parts were getting harder and harder to find.

"I know where you can find some of those," said Bill, with two fists wrapped around a rack of ribs, a glob of sauce dripping down his chin. "They're under 160 feet of water off the coast of Florida where I sank them," he cackled.

In addition to scrapping machinery, Bill was in the business of reefing boats. He told us he'd bought the small army tug to tow some tugboats he planned to sink off the coast of New Jersey, for which the fisheries department would pay him. "So you want to reef the boats first," I said. "Why don't we just make an agreement to take the boat off your hands once you're done?" Bill changed the subject.

We followed him back to the yard with the bill of sale still unsigned. He'd barely pulled into the driveway when he started hollering again at the workers he referred to as "my Mexicans." Tim and I stood by the truck as he walked by. "Come back tomorrow," he said.

"Okay," I answered, deflated but trying to disguise it. "What time?" He didn't respond. Just picked up yelling where he left off.

The next morning, Tim offered to fix the tugboat's malfunctioning compressor, hoping it would show a gesture of good faith toward Bill's reefing job and encourage him to sign. Fred piped up in protestation, "You don't need two compressors on that boat. I thought you were some big-shot *New York* engineer. I thought you *knew* about boats." *I thought you knew about boats* quickly became the refrain of our Norfuck stay.

While Tim worked on the compressor, I staked out the parking lot, waiting for Bill to deign to deal with me. I waited. Bill cursed out "his" Mexicans. I cleaned the garbage out of Tim's truck. I changed settings on my cell phone. Bill chomped more equipment with the excavator. I got hungry and went to fetch Tim so we could get some lunch. Returning to the parking lot, we could see the dust kicked up by Bill's truck tires.

A few minutes later Butch came over to tell us that Bill had just left for Boston and wouldn't be back for at least a few days. When he said it, he shook his head in what was either sympathy or an Oscar-worthy performance of feigned solicitude. Tim and I drove back to New York, defeated.

Back at the fireboat, as we prepared to set out for the annual Fall Leaf Trip, I stood in the wheelhouse with Bob. Tim had arrived early and recounted the saga. Bob wrapped an arm around my shoulders and gave me a squeeze. "I'm sorry," he said.

"It's all right," I said, shrugging it off. But it wasn't all right. And it wasn't over.

✦ ✦ ✦

People like tugboats. Everyone I talk to agrees, but no one can explain exactly why. I don't mean just boat people, *everybody* seems to have a fondness for the stocky little boats with nice lines that move huge ships and barges. "Hardworking and cute, what's not to like?" I've heard laypeople say. Or, "I love tugboats. They've got such character."

Then there are the "professional" aficionados: Members of the Tugboat Enthusiasts Society reach a whole new level of buff-dom. "Dedicated to the history, technology, and culture of tugboating in the Americas," the society publishes a quarterly magazine and organizes annual meetings where members share photos and talk about tugs.

A tugboat captain I know named Ann Loeding says tug aesthetics capture people's affection. "The older boats have this nice little rounded belly and this cute little stack. The shape is just very under-standable and somewhat anthropomorphic. There's also the appeal of this valiant little boat doing all this hard work."

Tugboats seem to hook into a childlike curiosity. So many people stop, ogle, and wonder, What goes on aboard those boats?

John Callahan banks on that curiosity every year when he plans his annual Tugboat Roundup in Waterford at the convergence of the Erie and Champlain canals. With a regular turnout of fifty thousand people, he's never disappointed. Sure, maybe some people come only for the fried dough or custom-airbrushed T-shirts, but most seem drawn to the tugboats that arrive each year from all over the region to gather along the seawall.

Nostalgia and romance play a part in people's affection for tug-boats, John says, explaining that from the house he grew up in, just a few blocks away from the Erie Canal's Lock Two, he could hear the lock gates opening and closing. "You hear that metallic ringing of the gears, sometimes in the middle of the night, at two o'clock, three o'clock. It's like hearing a train coming through. People like the idea that in the middle of the night, while most of the world is sleep-ing, there are people out there moving things back and forth that are absolutely necessary for you to go on with your life."

I knew exactly what John meant. And I was starting to feel like get-ting my hands on this army tug was necessary for me to go on with my life.

✦ ✦ ✦

Two weeks after the Fall Leaf Trip, Tim returned to Norfolk to look over another boat for Rick—this one an army LT, large tug, owned by someone other than Bill, but berthed less than a hundred yards away from Bill's yard. Rick and the LT's owner were hashing out terms when Fred appeared, looking for Tim. "Bill wants to sell the tug," he said. "Right now. Come over." Since Tim was there on Rick's dime, to represent Rick's interests, this put him in a difficult spot. But once the LT deal closed, Tim headed over and Bill confirmed he was ready to make the sale.

So a few days later, I was back in Norfuck, waiting. Again. After another full day of goose chasing, I sat in Bill's lawyer's office at the agreed-upon hour, but Bill was still nowhere to be found. Finally the lawyer reached him on the phone, secured authorization to sign on his behalf, and finally pressed the necessary ink to the paper.

Sold! Now what? Reality began to set in.

The little army tug needed repairs before we could head north. The toilet, the freshwater pump, the ship's-power generator and electrical panel all needed work, as did the main engine. All systems had to be made operational before we could go, and it was impossible to gauge how long this would take.

Pushing to move as quickly as possible, Tim and I divided tasks based on skill. I still had nowhere near enough experience to tackle a foreign engine room on my own, so, much as it frustrated me, my most important contribution would be research. While Tim learned his way around the engine room, I called around for parts, and located a diver (since the insurance company required an underwater survey of the tug). I put all my reporter's diligence to work, filling notebooks with estimates, phone numbers, specs, and referrals. This was important work—something I was good at. But division of labor sucked. I wanted to be in the engine room, but I hadn't yet learned how to apply my growing marine diesel knowledge to this new and different machinery.

After a grueling four weeks outfitting the boat in a town legendarily inhospitable to mariners (for a time Norfolk residents supposedly posted signs on their front lawns that read "Dogs and Sailors: Keep Off the Grass"), the time had come to bring the tug to its new home in the Brooklyn Navy Yard. We'd made the repairs, rounded up all the requisite safety equipment, and stocked the boat with food. The rest of the crew—Bob, Huntley, and Karl—drove down, and we planned to set out the next morning.

✦ ✦ ✦

"Red skies at night, sailors' delight; red skies in morning, sailors take warning" goes the old sea adage. Here it is five o'clock in the morning on the first day of December, and Huntley is looking at the blazing blood-red sky. "Do you see that, Cap?" he says.

"It doesn't always mean that," Bob barks back. I hope Bob's right.

Five hours into our journey I finally manage to sit down. Eventually I plan to be the one at the helm of this boat, but today there is still too much to do in the engine room, and the wheelhouse is crowded enough with two people who have the kind of steering expertise I still only dream about. Sitting on the cushioned vinyl bench that wraps around the galley table, I breathe for what seems like the first time in a month, relishing that sense of closure you get when you arrive at the airport before a trip—when what's packed is packed and it's clear that any task you neglected to take care of before departure will just have to wait until your return.

So far, the engine is running well. The bay is choppy and the wind has picked up, so we're bouncing around but still making headway. After a particularly rough wave that rocks the boat left and right before slamming it back to center, I ask Tim, "Is this boat designed for this?"

"Sure," he says. Since I don't realize he's lying, and because I can't control the sea, I feel my shoulders soften and the flush in my face begin to cool. I lean my head back against the wall and close my eyes for just a second.

Just then, the door swings open and Huntley bursts in. "There's a white cloud pouring out of the engine room," he says. I snap back to attention and bolt for the door.

A geyser of water is spewing from the engine. I race through the thick white fog of steam that engulfs the whole space and shoot down the engine-room stairs. Tim reaches the controls first and slams the lever into the Off position. Then he swings around to the other side to cup his palm around the heat exchanger, feeling for temperature. He snaps it back, recoiling, hot metal burning his hand. A normal, healthy temperature range varies between 140 and 160 degrees. This gauge reads 220, which means the cooling water isn't circulating.

Running an engine this hot can cause severe damage. The geyser has resulted from the water in the engine boiling over like a pot on the stove. Instead of keeping the engine cool, the water is turning to vapor, causing stubborn steam pockets to accumulate in the engine, which is boiling in its own skin. If we don't find a way to cool it down, the heat might seize the valves or crack the cylinder heads. The engine could destroy itself and leave us stranded in the Chesapeake Bay. If we can't get the water flowing with the engine running, the only real solution is to shut it down and let it cool. Given the seas, this isn't an option for long.

With the engine temporarily silenced, we get a taste of how treacherous it would be to ride out these waves in a boat without power. The instant the propeller stops pushing the tug through the water, the boat bobs like a cork, rocking and pitching. This tossing back and forth wrecks my insides. I bolt back up the stairs and race to the head.

All morning, as the seas had kicked up, I kept looking out a porthole, focusing my eyes on the horizon to calm the roiling in my gut. I tried to chalk up my churning stomach to anything but seasickness, hoping that by refusing to name it, I could will it away. But I also swallowed the Dramamine pills I had tucked in my bag just in case. At this moment, while the bay heaves up, tossing the tug like a plastic bath toy, the Dramamine fails me. Behind the closed door of the tiny toilet closet, I petition the universe for a little help.

Before I head back to the engine room, I grab a Tupperware bowl from the galley so at least I'll be more mobile in my misery and can try to keep working.

I stumble back to the engine room, where Tim is still formulating a diagnosis. When he sees my slate-gray complexion and the container I'm carrying, he tries to shoo me out. But I refuse to leave him down here by himself while waves knock the boat around, sending us both banging into equipment. Useless as I am for more than keeping an eye out, I sit down in the most out-of-the-way spot I can find, tucked in beside a circuit-breaker box. When my stomach spasms, I try to retch discreetly. My body is shutting down right when I need it most. I need to remain alert and functional, but my eyes keep closing, and my head falls forward, then snaps back as I try to will myself awake. I can't understand how, despite every urgency demanding my attention, I could be falling asleep.

As I sit in the corner, Tim checks to see if the sea strainers have clogged. He cranks open a valve that essentially opens a gate for the bay to enter the boat, and a gush of water pours in, washing Tim to the back of the engine room. "Shut the valve! Shut the valve!" he yells as he slides. My body clicks into a slow-motion dash toward the strainer valve. Despite my weakness and the boat's rocking, I manage to spin the wheel closed.

There is nothing left to do but restart the engine. Since its own equipment has failed, our only hope is to rig up some alternative cooling system. We have 770 gallons of fresh water on board. Discharging the boiling engine water into the bilge and replacing it with cool fresh water from the boat's supply tanks could buy us some time.

This whole time Bob and Huntley have stood together in the wheelhouse, slamming into each other in the small space every time the sea drops out from under the boat in one wave trough after another. Bob grips the tug's wooden wheel, steering as best he can to soften the blows. Huntley keeps his eye on the charts and the GPS. Once Tim restarts the engine, the boat limps along at idle speed, 3 or 4 knots, tops. When Bob, man of so few words, utters, "This is bullshit," Huntley grasps the gravity of our situation and pores over the charts, attempting to locate the nearest land with water deep enough to accommodate the tug's nine feet of underwater draft.

Even the pauses between waves batter us as the boat drops into the troughs between six-footers. Early that morning the weather report had predicted twenty- to twenty-five-mile-an-hour winds. But by ten o'clock the forecast had worsened, calling for winds from the west gusting forty-five. Winds over thirty-two qualify as gale-force.

Sick or not, I have to climb to the boat deck to do my part in making up the engine's stopgap cooling system. There are two ways to get there, and both involve going outside. Green water pours over the bow every time the nose slams into a new wave, so I give up on taking the stairs at the front of the boat and head toward the back. I keep one hand on the railing to avoid getting tossed overboard, pulling myself inch by inch toward the ladder, careful not to drop the bowl I'm still carrying around just in case. By this point my hurling produces little more than dry heaves and bile, but somehow clinging to this container offers reassurance.

From the ladder, I crawl to the engine-room hatch, shaped like an A-frame skylight hinged at the top. It's tied open, and I check the rope before sticking my head under it. I peer through a quarter-sized opening to gauge the level in the day tank that feeds the engine fresh cooling water. The tug shakes like a bull trying to fling off its rider. So I lie on my belly, cramming the sole of my boot against the lip that runs along the edge of the deck.

Meanwhile, Tim is in the engine room, gradually discharging water from the bottom of the engine while I control the valve that refills it from up here, at the top. Together we become a makeshift heat exchanger. I squint through the opening at the top of the tank, looking for the reflection cast off the water inside. When the reflection fades, it's time to add water. Since the valve handle is broken, I use vise grips to turn the stem directly. Look, fill, wait, hurl, repeat.

Tim checks on me every now and then from inside the boat, on the other side of the hatch. When he sees me shivering, he pulls the hat off his head and hands it up. Although it's soaking wet, I put it on in hopes it will retain some heat. The wind roars and I can feel my core temperature drop. Before long, my vise-grip hand goes numb. I start shivering so hard I can hardly close my fingers around the tool to turn the valve. But being up here, I can focus on the horizon and breathe fresh, not diesel-ated, air, which I hope will ease my raw insides.

Huntley wobbles out of the wheelhouse, clutching the rail. "You okay?" he yells into the wind.

"Yeah," I answer, not sure if I believe it.

"We're headed for the closest deepwater port," he says. "At this speed we should be there in two hours."

My heart sinks. As I lie pinned on the deck, looking up at the sky, then down at the choppy gray sea, I have that meta sense of watching my own movie—of seeing myself as the protagonist in a film. Is she going to crumple? I wonder.

When I can no longer hold the vise grip to spin the valve, I have no choice but to put on more clothes. Stashed in my locker in the crew's quarters is a bright orange survival suit, which in addition to being warm is not a bad thing to have on at a time like this.

Slowly I bend my knees and push myself upright on the upper deck, digging my fingers into the bolt holes of an empty light bracket. Every move is calculated. I draw upon everything I've ever learned about physics—utilizing playground lessons about balance, calling forth techniques for staying vertical I acquired in the slam-dancing pits of my youth, summoning instructions from boxing coaches about how to center my weight. Once standing, I grab the rail with both hands and pull myself to the wheelhouse. Huntley opens the door a crack. "I'll be right back," I yell over the wind, before heading toward the front of the boat. I watch the action of the waves across the bow, waiting for a window between swells so I can make it down the stairs and around the starboard side to the galley door. I make my move, and teeter down the slick steps. Keeping one hand on the rail, I pull myself back toward the galley. Just as I swing open the door, a wave spits itself through the doorway, soaking me completely.

Karl is sitting at the galley table ashen-faced, his arms curled around the top of a five-gallon pail. Earlier, he had decided to go down and take a nap, not realizing what it might do to his inner ears. At least I'm not the only one aboard who can't hold on to their breakfast.

I find the suit and drag it up to the galley, where there's more room to try and pull it on. Made of flotation material like a life jacket, the fluorescent orange suit is designed to keep you afloat and warm should you land in the water. It's like a snowsuit filled with stiff foam. Pulling it on is no small feat, even on a level surface, and as the boat slams through the heaving seas, I struggle to get my feet in, then scooch it up my legs. When I finally pull the zipper up my chest, it's time to make my way back up to my post. As I travel forward along the side of the boat, I parcel out my stiff, clumsy snowsuit movements, trying to calculate each shift in weight, strategizing the safest, most controlled way to move my own mass to avoid losing my balance as the boat pitches and yaws.

I stop back at the wheelhouse to let Huntley and Bob know I've returned. "Look back every few minutes and make sure I'm still there, okay?"

I lie back down and check the water level through the narrow opening. The depth in the reservoir is deceiving, since even an eighth of an inch of water at the bottom of the tank reflects up with a reassuring shimmer. I second-guess my eyes, which are dry from so much puking. The bay continues to rise up, flinging rains of spray, but I'm warmer and protected in my suit. I settle in for the ride.

At three o'clock we finally reach land. Almost instantly, as we round the bend into Fair Port, Virginia, the sun comes out and the wind dies down, making this whole saga seem even more unreal and movielike.

We tie up at the end of a wooden pier, and a bearded man comes out to greet us, speaking so fast his words trip over each other on their way out. Huntley and Bob had talked with him on the radio on the way in. All they wanted was advice on where to find a safe place to tie up, but they were hit, instead, with a barrage of excited questions: "Is that an ST? What number is it? My friend Ed in Boston has one just like it. I have to call and tell him."

It turns out we couldn't have found a better place in all of Virginia to regroup and nurse our wounds. Scott the Pirate (he smiles coyly when we dub him that, though he's the most benevolent of pirates) is both thrilled to help and well equipped with a cache of supplies that he keeps stashed in boats, barges, and containers all around the inlet.

The next day he helps us make some repairs, gives and sells us some equipment, and chauffeurs us to the nearest grocery store in the back of his pickup to replenish our coolers (now that eating is once again possible). On our way back to the boat, Bob asks if there's a phone he can use to call his wife, since none of our cell phones have service. We stop at Scott's place—a yard overrun with things—a menagerie of machines and implements just waiting for their day of usefulness. After Bob speaks with Mama (as he calls his wife) I dial the number for my voice mail. "You have seventeen messages." I've been out of cell contact for less than twenty-four hours. This can't be good.

The first message is from the boat's insurance agent, Totch Hartge, a friend of the *Harvey*, with whom we'd had vague plans to meet for dinner the night before in St. Michael's, Maryland. When we hadn't called, he was worried, especially given the severity of the storm. The ensuing messages escalated in tone. By this morning we'd become an "overdue vessel" and Totch started dialing numbers. He called the tug's owner, Rob; the oil company where we'd purchased fuel; tug captain friends from the Norfolk area; even Bill, who apparently drove around to different spots where he could see the bay, looking for us. Message number seventeen, left an hour ago, is from the Coast Guard. Within the hour they plan to launch a search party.

"Huntley!" I holler out, and my crewmates, who have been poking around Scott's yard, turn around to look. "The Coast Guard is about to go out looking for us. You've got to call them right now." Since I don't have a Coast Guard license and since Bob's not a talker, Huntley is the best one to make the call.

✦ ✦ ✦

At five thirty the next morning, Tim crosses himself and I cross my fingers as we fire up the engine. With a new valve for bleeding trapped air out of the cooling system, which Scott the Pirate has welded on, we pray our overheating troubles are behind us.

We finally make it to St. Michael's for dinner with Totch, who

Storm-tossed tug *Gowanus Bay* arrives in St. Michaels, Maryland, December 2004. *(Photo by Totch Hartge)*

despite (or maybe because of) our harrowing adventure has decided to make the run with us the rest of the way to New York City. We set out the next morning, for the last leg of our journey. By midnight we make it through the Chesapeake and Delaware Canal and enter Delaware Bay, heading for the Atlantic. Huntley takes the wheel so Bob can get some sleep. Once we round the tip of Cape May, New Jersey, and head to the "outside," we're committed. There are few, if any, places for a deep-draft boat to pull into along the 120-mile stretch of open coast from Cape May to Sandy Hook.

That night Tim and I alternate engine-room shifts of three hours on, three hours off. A champion long-distance sleeper, I don't adjust well to these short naps. A low-grade nausea follows me throughout the rest of our run, despite the fact that the seas are calm. Unlike on the fireboat—where at least one person has to stay in the engine room at all times, since there are no wheelhouse controls—engineering duty on this boat involves regular tours down below to check temperature and pressure gauges, change filters, and fill the fuel as needed. Between tours, I stand in the galley, trying to stay awake, peering out the porthole at the dark sea.

Just before eight o'clock we pass Barnegat Lighthouse ("old Barney"), the second-tallest lighthouse in the country, which operated from 1859 to 1927. Stepping outside onto the aft deck to watch it pass, I see the sky ignite, a strip of orange rising at the horizon until an egg-yolk sun emerges from beneath the sea.

✦ ✦ ✦

Three hours later, I'm standing at the helm, my fingers curled around the wooden wheel, steering a boat for the first time. Not just any boat,

First time at the helm of tug *Gowanus Bay*, December 2004.
(Photo by Karl Schuman)

but a tugboat that is kind of, sort of, a little bit mine. At 1:00 p.m., we pass beneath the Verrazano-Narrows Bridge into New York harbor. From this vantage point the harbor looks nothing like it does from below. Though I've been plying these same waters for nearly four years, I feel like an immigrant aboard the *Muenchen*, seeing, for the first time, the port that was once the center of world trade.

As we pass through the anchorage in the Upper Bay, a tug pushing a barge heads toward me. "What do I do, Bob? What do I do?" I ask, despite the big, wide water all around.

"Just don't hit 'em," Bob says, and leaves it at that.

South of Pier 63, I turn the wheel back over to Bob. No way I'm ready for the challenge of docking just yet. As I watch him line up for the swing into the pier, I'm overwhelmed with gratitude. I give a prayer of thanks to Rob for bringing my tugboat dreams to fruition, to my crewmates for sticking it out with me, and for the fact that, standing in this wheelhouse, I will finally have the opportunity to see the full, wide, winding expanse of the Hudson, instead of just my strange, telescoped porthole view.

Safe Home: Tim, Jessica, Karl, Bob (top), Huntley, and Totch upon arrival in New York harbor. *(Photo by John Krevey)*

Chapter Seven

On the Hard

The Inevitable Decline of Old Things

~~~~~~

On a cold Saturday morning, just after New Year's 2005, Bob, Tim, and I meet on the fireboat at Pier 63, as we do most Saturdays, for fireboat repairs and restoration. Today's project is a huge undertaking—one we've saved for the off-season, when no boat-trip schedule will constrain the work.

On a trip late last season Tim noticed a noise in the Number Four pump. "Do you hear that?" he asked with a gesture that cut through the roar of the engines. With its compatriot, the Number Five pump (the "five" indicating the engine to which it is attached), the Number Four was busy blasting tremendous columns of water through the deck guns and into the sky. I leaned over, pressing the foam earmuff tight against my head to drown out the background noise, and nodded when I heard the heavy thunking, rattling sound that was vibrating the pump casing. Now that the season has ended, Tim has declared it time to open the Number Four and have a look.

Picture a walnut as big as a washing machine. Instead of shell halves, the pump has two housing halves, which are held together by bolts with three-inch hexagonal heads. To examine the pump's innards, we have to rattle off all twenty-two bolts with an air-powered impact gun and winch up the top half of the housing (which weighs probably eight hundred pounds) with a chain hoist hung from the ceiling. It's unlikely this pump has been taken apart for at least thirty years.

After spending half the day spinning off the monster bolts, now comes the moment of truth. I pull the hoist chain to open up the pump while Bob steadies the guide rope to keep the newly freed piece from swinging. The gasket between the two halves peels apart, revealing the guts. It looks kind of like a walnut on the inside, too—the steel housing has cavities like a shell, and the spaces where the nutmeat would be hold water. Even when the pump's not running, some water lies inside, which is one factor that has led to this pump's demise.

The steel housing has been eaten by electrolysis, a process of chemical decomposition caused by exposure to salt water. Over time, the binding elements of the metal have dissolved away, transforming the housing into crumbled granules, like bits of iron sand. A whole handful of what had once been solid steel breaks off in Tim's hand. He passes the chunk to me, and I feel its brittle weightlessness. The lump is porous and fragile like a piece of cooled lava I once held on Mount Etna in Sicily. Our pumps are turning to dust.

The Number Four pump is damaged beyond repair. It stares back at us, unblinking, unapologetic, unashamed, unfixable. Bob, Tim, and I toss feeble solutions back and forth—every one of them dropping limp and futile to the diamond-plate deck beneath our feet. This is the pump I resealed at Ground Zero. Though the Number Four is the only one we've opened to look at, they have all been subjected to the same seven decades of exposure to the same corrosive concoction: salt water from the Hudson River.

The ability to spray water is what distinguishes *John J. Harvey* from other boats, and the pump's disintegration seems like an assault on her very character. Though it lasted nearly seventy-five years, reflecting the ethos of principled craftsmanship that held sway at the time the boat was built, she is—we are—now down to only two functional pumps out of the original four. While we can still spray water through all the deck guns, the redundancy of the boat's systems has been further reduced.

The boat rocks a bit in her berth and the housing—dangling from a ring in the ceiling by a pair of yellow cloth straps—rocks too. We stand there, suspended like the piece itself, hovering in limbo—not wanting to concede the death of a component so crucial to this boat's operations, its life.

"We might have to take the boat out for a Viking funeral," says Tim.

I scold him. "You can talk shit about the people, just don't talk shit about the boat." This makes them both laugh, but I feel my throat tighten.

There's not much one can do after a death knell but register the information and keep plugging on. Tim finds out that the company that manufactured the pump has long since vanished, and along with it any patterns we might have used to cast a new piece. If money were no object, we could have a pattern made, but the boat's hand-to-mouth existence precludes anything like that. All trips on *John J. Harvey* are free, and dependent as we are on donations, we're in no position to fund this kind of replacement. Equipment has a life span—even something as overbuilt as the *Harvey*, finely crafted in an era before planned obsolescence became manufacturing's modus operandi.

✦ ✦ ✦

As it happens, the term "planned obsolescence" was born one year after the *John J. Harvey*, according to Giles Slade. The goal during that Depression year was to restructure society to "achieve an equilibrium of supply and demand that would eliminate technological unemployment," writes Slade in *Made to Break: Technology and Obsolescence in America*. He credits a Manhattan real estate broker named Bernard London with coining the phrase. During the summer of 1932, London published a pamphlet, called "Ending the Depression Through Planned Obsolescence," in which he proposed that the government "assign a lease of life to shoes and homes and machines, to all products of manufacture . . . when they are first created," after which time "these things would be legally 'dead' and would be controlled by the duly appointed governmental agency and destroyed if there is widespread unemployment."

These days, however, we don't need government to collect and throw away perfectly usable "dead" objects based on some arbitrary expiration date. Today, the goods we buy die of "natural" causes inherent in their making or get tossed because they have become outmoded. Automated assembly lines, as well as the plethora of plastics and other diverse, readily available materials, make it relatively easy to manufacture many everyday products cheaply. When we buy a low-cost product, it doesn't matter how long it will last, since a new one goes for peanuts. In this climate quality and craftsmanship become less and less relevant.

Technological one-upmanship is the other reason we keep buying. From iPods made with batteries so costly that they are not worth replacing to cell phones and computers whose features seem dated by the time they hit store shelves, high-tech gizmos live extremely short lives before they end up creating unmanageable amounts of waste filled with toxins that end up in the ground and air. In 2001 an estimated five to seven million tons of electronic waste entered America's landfills, according to the Silicon Valley Toxics Coalition. And by 2002, more than 130 million working cell phones were "retired" in the United States alone, writes Slade. Today, our ideas about quality in electronics are often determined not by longevity or craftsmanship but by possession of the most cutting-edge features—we are blinded by "a veneration of newness," according to Susan Strasser in *Waste and Want: A Social History of Trash.*

The shift toward intentionally producing goods with a limited life span became widespread in the Depression years, when manufacturers were desperate to find new ways of encouraging repetitive consumption. Though striking a balance between supply and demand has challenged makers and sellers since the dawn of the market economy, concern that America was "suffering from overproduction" began at least as early as 1876, when an anxious retailer wrote, "The warehouses of the world are filled with goods." But employing deliberate obsolescence as a solution "is a uniquely American invention. . . . Not only did Americans dream up disposable products, ranging from diapers to cameras to contact lenses," writes Slade, "we invented the very concept of disposability itself." Even back in the mid-nineteenth century, industry seized upon a variety of increasingly cheap materials to produce the first throwaway items. Among the earliest were invented right along the Hudson River—the detachable cuffs and collars that gave Troy the appellation "Collar City."

✦ ✦ ✦

Then, as now, the driving market forces were convenience and status. In 1827, household laundering burdened women with a weekly routine (often undertaken on "Blue Tuesday") of time-consuming, hard physical labor. There was no getting around it. The men needed clean, white, starched shirts, cuffs, and collars to wear to work in occupations that came to be known as white-collar jobs. But Hannah Montague of Troy wearied of having to wash her husband's shirts when only the collar was soiled. To ease her laundry burden, she decided to experiment. With the consent of her husband, Orlando, she snipped the collar off one of his shirts, laundered it, then sewed it back on, creating the world's first detachable collar.

Recognizing the business opportunity stemming from his wife's ingenuity, Orlando and a partner opened a factory overlooking the Hudson that produced collars, detached shirtfronts called dickeys, and separate cuffs. "By 1886 approximately thirty-three shirt, collar, and cuff factories in Troy employed more than eight thousand workers," writes Slade. Some were involved with making the latest innovation: disposable paper cuffs and collars that could be discarded after a single wear. In 1872 the U.S. produced 150 million paper shirt collars and cuffs—launching the trend of blue-collar labor making white-collar status symbols. Today, drowning in the detritus of our own disposable, consumerist culture, we have lost touch with the inherent value of things.

✦ ✦ ✦

Both my father and my brother remember the day that Josh first grasped the concept that some things were built to break. When he was eleven, Josh's two-stroke dirt bike was his most prized possession, and when the bolts attaching the chain sprocket to the wheel hub stripped out and broke, the damage seemed catastrophic. "Replacing that part would have cost more than what I paid for the bike," Josh recalls. When he sought help from our father, Dad explained that the bolts the manufacturer had used were too small and poorly made. So the two of them drilled and tapped new holes for larger bolts. The repair outlived the bike, but what lasted longest was the lesson.

My father still recalls Josh's disillusionment: "He asked me, 'Dad, wouldn't someone want to make something the best they can?' Because I had always told him, 'Do the best you can.' So I explained the idea of planned obsolescence. I told him about a boot maker in Maine whose boots would last for a lifetime. 'Now you'd think that if these boots were so well made that a customer would only ever need one pair, it would limit demand. But that's not the case,' I said. 'Because when people are pleased with the quality of a product, they tell other people, who become customers. And that's the right way.' " The other way to get repeat customers, he explained, was by making sure that your product would fail.

Like so many other people, my dad had wrongly believed that Henry Ford was the father of planned obsolescence when, in fact, it was his competitor, Alfred Sloan of General Motors. There's an oft-repeated myth that Ford had his workers hunt through junkyards to find out which components outlasted the useful life of his Model T automobiles, then made those parts out of cheaper materials. In actuality, Ford "stood steadfast against unnecessary obsolescence," maintains Slade, and represented an "ethic of quality and durability in manufactured goods." Instead Sloan's practice of "repackaging" last year's model as the next big thing hastened product extinction, before the word "packaging" even existed. Sloan's spin set a new standard for a style-focused version of planned obsolescence on a grand scale. In fact, his success with this strategy set the stage for General Motors' climb to become the largest automaker in the world, making its 2009 collapse the largest industrial failure in U.S. history.

✦ ✦ ✦

The death knell of the Number Four pump was just one symptom of how the fireboat was showing her age. Increasingly aware of all the work this fireboat needs, I was beginning to resign myself to the inevitable decline of old things when new hope appeared.

Because the *Harvey's* insurance policy requires an out-of-water survey every five years, we have to go into a shipyard in 2005 to haul out the boat. Though this will not fix the pump, it will afford us the opportunity to address many other repairs possible only while the boat is on dry land.

The timing for this work is perfect, since in May 2004 the fireboat was awarded a coveted $320,000 Environmental Protection Fund grant for boat restoration. While the grant offers a huge opportunity, it also poses a huge challenge, given the terms. Simply put, the grant says that if we can raise and spend $640,000 for restoration, the fund will reimburse us for half the dollars spent.

On May 13, 2005, we head for Derecktor Shipyards in Bridgeport, Connecticut. Home to Remington rifles, Singer sewing machines, and Bridgeport milling machines—as well as Phineas Taylor (P. T.) Barnum, showman, circus founder, and former mayor—Bridgeport was once among the great manufacturing centers in the United States. From out on Long Island Sound, the red-and-white-striped power plant chimney stack is the first far-off sign of the navigation channel into the city's harbor. I can make out the stack through the porthole, but from where I stand, I can't see the landscape's most prominent feature as we make our approach: the bright blue 600-metric-ton travel lift.

By the time I shut down engines and step onto the deck, Bob has nosed the boat into the slip that serves as the travel-lift pit. The lift, a monstrous, sixty-foot-tall, square metal frame on wheels, looms over us with its dangling marionette strings connected to three sets of straps already in position, submerged beneath the hull of the boat.

Once the boat is secure, we climb off onto the paved lot that will be the *Harvey*'s home for the next six weeks to watch the haul-out. Obie, the young guy running the lift, wears the controls slung from his shoulders, the yellow box sticking out like the trays that ballpark souvenir vendors wear. Tiny little joysticks control the massive beast—and Obie is its wireless puppet master. Over the next month I'll catch him dancing while rolling the thing through the yard, in a clear demonstration of how effortless technological advancements have made heavy lifting. Just a few little nudges with thumb and forefinger send fireboat *John J. Harvey* rising up out of the green water.

Workboats are like icebergs; much of the boat exists out of sight. Unlike motorboats, plastic runabouts, or even yachts, the hull of a fireboat runs deep and substantial below the waterline. I've only ever seen the boat's belly from the inside. Now she slides out

slowly—dripping, encrusted with barnacles, and coated with a gray-
ish slime.

The crew congregates in a little cluster, taking it all in. Our pilot,
Bob, who's been with this boat longer than any of us, stands there
grinning. Huntley does his Huntley dance: arms rounded out in front
of him, twisting his torso side to side, saying, "We have the best boat.
We have the best boat."

Tim says, "She looks like a pregnant guppy," because the hull bulges
out at the sides to accommodate the pump. Deckhand Karl watches,
too, although he doesn't know that this will be his last glimpse of
daylight for a month. Over the course of the next brutal weeks he'll
spend more time chipping away rust in the bilge than anyone—never
mind that he's just a tad younger than Bob.

Once Obie hoists the boat high enough to clear the ground, he sets
the lift into forward motion. Double sets of wheels—each one eight feet
tall—begin to roll forward. The boat dangles in the slings, cradled by the
three sets of yellow straps, and as the wheels move, the boat sways. The
travel lift has yanked this 268-gross-ton vessel as if the fireboat is a toy,
rocking back and forth. We've faced equipment failures, near collisions,
even the engine-room fire, but now, seeing the boat hovering over the
pavement, I'm overwhelmed with the sense of her vulnerability.

Fireboat *John J. Harvey* in the travel lift slings at Derecktor Shipyards
in Bridgeport, Connecticut, 2005. *(Photo by Jessica DuLong)*

After yard crews scrape off the marine growth and pressure-wash the hull, it's time for us to take soundings, which entails using an ultrasound gauge to measure the thickness of the boat's skin, identifying any thin spots in need of repair. I squirt conductivity gel onto the spots of bare metal where we've ground away the paint on the surface of the boat's belly, smearing it around to get a good signal with the stethoscope end. She scores remarkably well, considering, in lots of places. But in some places, the steel is just too thin. The boat will need patches.

For the first time, while the boat is "on the hard," I'm out of the engine room, crawling around spaces I've never seen before, becoming ever more connected with her physical substance. It becomes painfully clear to me how urgently this project needs to make preservation the first priority.

We've entered the yard with a budget of $80,000, largely from private donations, and the yard will get every cent we have. But we hope to take full advantage of our time on land by using as much volunteer labor as possible. The yard won't allow us to do our own welding, but we can save dollars by doing the prep work. Tim and I, charged with running the project, are the only paid crew. The rest are volunteers who, by lending their time, not only help us accomplish more during our time on the hard, but also offer credit toward our matching grant in the form of time tallied as in-kind donations.

The historic-vessels community is all about taking care of, instead of discarding, old things. But simply maintaining a large boat, never mind restoring it, costs an enormous amount of time and money. The biggest expense by far is the shipyard bill. Old boats usually run on a shoestring budget and are cared for by largely volunteer labor. Extensive shipyard repairs can sink a project. What would make a huge difference in the successful restoration of boats like *John J. Harvey* is a small not-for-profit yard where preservationists can fix their own historic vessels at minimal cost.

✦ ✦ ✦

The first person who explained to me how cool it would be to create an old-boat shipyard/museum was Steve Trueman, a salvage diver with a life-consuming habit of collecting old boats. I met Steve when the fireboat was in Kingston during the 2003 Hudson River trip and a whole troop of us visited his tugboat collection on the north shore of Rondout Creek.

At Steve's place, a wide ramp led up through the open door of a covered wooden railroad barge that was among the last few of its type remaining from the 1930s and '40s. In addition to the barge, Steve was caretaker for six tugboats—the oldest one a former New York Central Railroad tug from 1886—all of which were tied together along the creek's northern bank. Steve had saved boats that nobody else wanted to care for—some sunken, others abandoned—and he planned to restore and share them with the public as examples of fine craftsmanship from a bygone age.

Steve Trueman steers *Frances Turecamo* in Port Albany en route to the 2005 Waterford Tugboat Roundup. *(Photo by Jessica DuLong)*

Originally, he had wanted to get a single tug and run it from place to place, stopping in different towns and opening it up for tours. But soon Steve's vision expanded, his eyes bigger than either his day planner or his wallet could sustain. "We started feeling like we should build a tug museum to preserve all these machines that were going away." It would be a destination where visitors could learn about the history of tugs as well as see the evolution of marine engineering technology over time. More than just a static display of tugs, Steve dreamed of an interactive community program that would teach hands-on skills in shops that also served as exhibits for visitors who wanted to observe the work.

"We could have a little wood boatbuilding shop, where you can build a wooden tender like they had on the tugs. People could row it around, go fishing, take their kids out. They could put a steam engine in it. 'Wow, we can do that?' 'Yeah, we have a little shop. Pay us fifty dollars and you work with the old guys and you buy a kit and you put it together. We'll help you and you go away with a boat.' All of that. Then we'd have metal casting day, say the first Wednesday of every month. 'We'll show you how to make a casting pattern. Come over with your kids and we'll pour everybody's cast.'

"The museum would exhibit all the transitions from steam to internal combustion engines. Using a CAD program, I started to make a three-dimensional visual, like a cutaway to put in a kiosk that showed these engines running so I could point out the similarities and differences. I also wanted to compare different hull designs," he said, explaining that there were some spots in one of his boats, *K. Whittelsey*, a 1930 tug I would later come to know well, where you could see an example of almost every common riveting technique.

✦ ✦ ✦

The importance of preserving old technology, like the *K. Whittelsey* rivets, becomes clearer to me in the shipyard as I learn more about the fireboat and all that fixing her entails.

Standing in the service trailer with Tim, I watch as Charlie, the marine surveyor charged with overseeing the structural work on the boat, unrolls a shell expansion, a poster-sized diagram of the fireboat's hull construction. Leaning over, the sleeves of my insulated flannel shirt rolled up to make sure no grease smears the page, I trace the drawing's clear lines. The shell expansion is the Rosetta stone for the boat that I have been appreciating aesthetically for so long. Now I can see the engineering behind the placement of each rivet. I can grasp how designing and assembling this boat was like putting together a complex 3-D puzzle, where not only the positioning of pieces but the order of their placement mattered. Sections of flat plate had been fitted and curved precisely, their edges strategically sandwiched in between other sections.

For the first time I'm able to comprehend the artistry that went into designing this one-of-a-kind boat. No one makes boats like this anymore. No one knows how. And here, it seems, some of the ship-yard's welders don't seem to know how to repair them either.

Riveting, a precursor to welding, joins pieces of metal mechani-cally, while welding fuses metal chemically. Because riveting involves driving a fastener through overlapping plates instead of sealing plates together at the ends, the whole thought process is different. As I dis-cover in the yard, using the newer technology to repair a structure built with the older creates complications.

"You can't run in a whole continuous bead like this," I have to say, pointing out a seam the welder has made. I explain again (since it appears he didn't grasp the point the first time) that putting too much welding heat into a riveted hull can cause surrounding seams to split. The welder just shrugs. This riveting technology is out of date. A yard that catered to historic vessels would be good not only for preserving the boats but also for keeping alive old techniques, and the diversity of skills they require, simply by putting them to practical use.

✦ ✦ ✦

"The formation of rust is gradual; at first merely a brown discolor-ation, it becomes, later, a thin hard scale. Each new scale or layer adheres to the last, and in the course of time they form together a thick, brittle, slate-like mass." So reads *Practical Shipbuilding*, the 1918 treatise on the structural design and building of "modern" steel ves-sels by marine surveyor A. Campbell Holms. Rust, Holms explains, is the compound oxide of iron, resulting from the slow combination of iron with oxygen from the air.

Wearing double hearing protection, safety glasses, gloves, knee pads, and a respirator, I pretzel myself around the port-side water-pump piping in the engine room with a chain-saw-sized pneumatic air chisel to blast away hard scale. Once I've finished giving the vol-unteers their assignments—explaining the tasks and the tools, and handing out gloves, earplugs, and safety glasses—I can jump into the jobs on my own work list, primarily prepping steel for the yard's welders. Hunkered beneath a maze of pipes, I combat the hull steel's ugliest intrusions.

To arrest the disintegration of the boat's surfaces, we attack rust and scale with intense mechanical force, vibrating it off with tools that run on compressed air: big chisels like the one I'm using, which operate something like a one-handed jackhammer; smaller, pistol-sized chisels; and needle-scalers, which look something like a rolling pin with scores of little nails poking out the end that you push against the steel to rattle away the rust. Tim orders all these tools for this job from Harbor Freight, a discount tool store that has attained mythic status among the mechanically minded—not for quality, but for price. The trouble is, the tools keep breaking. Actually, just one part in all the air tools keeps breaking: a spring. The springs snap over and over, all day long, so Tim orders replacements. The tools themselves were, as Tim says, "stupid cheap." But if we started tallying the cost of not only the replacement springs, but the time lost in ordering the parts and fixing the tools, we'd perhaps calculate the real price differently.

In my twisted position, the vibrations that ripple off the air chisel rattle my brain. Sometimes in the midst of my work I catch myself wondering, Why are you here? Why do you like this job? Why do you put your life on hold, earning so little money restoring this hunk of wasted steel? But every time I try to reason through the questions, my heart blows me off with a snort, my head rallying to try to cover for my heart's insolence.

On a day in Brooklyn, however, a glimpse of answer comes to me while I'm speeding along the Brooklyn-Queens Expressway where construction crews toil in the wicked heat that flashes off the pavement, sucking on the exhaust fumes of passing cars. Despite all the differences between us, I feel a connection with these men. The work I do helps me understand the world around me, and where I come from. It delivers me back home in a way I was never home before.

When a manager at the shipyard who has been observing our work offers Tim and me jobs, it's like being handed a ticket for admission to a once-private affair.

✦ ✦ ✦

After six weeks in the yard, the pressure is on to finish our repairs. It's June 2005, the customary fireboating season has begun, and the *Harvey* is still sitting on dry land. In the race to get the boat back in the water, it's easy for anyone who hasn't been crawling around with us in her hidden spaces to forget that when it comes to deadlines, the fireboat is boss.

On a Friday afternoon, Obie picks up the boat, all shiny with its new cherry-red paint job, and gently splashes her back in the water. A swarm of us descends on the engine room to hunt for any holes that might have opened up during the sandblasting, or seams that could have split from the heat of welding. Everything looks good, so we fire up engines and prepare to head home. Bob calls down for Slow Astern, and we slide out toward the opening of the slip. A moment later, Tim races up the engine-room stairs without stopping to tell me what's up. When Bob rings for Slow Ahead, I realize we are not yet going home. We have a leak. A stream of water the diameter of a pencil shoots through the side of the hull behind the Number One engine. The boat isn't fixed. It's time to haul her out once again.

Obie is no longer dancing when he pulls the boat back out. It's after five on a Friday. The yard calls a welder back to work to survey the damage, and while he taps on the hull to listen for the *tink, tink* sound of thin plate, he sinks his chipping hammer right through the side of the boat. Ultimately the repair requires a five-by-five-foot patch of steel.

The next day, Tim writes an e-mail to the folks in New York: "We of the Hackensack River have always said, 'A bad day of boating is still better than a good day at work.' But then there are days like this. . . . Man once believed that the universe revolved around the earth. On Friday we were again reminded that it revolves around the sun. *Harvey* is in charge. We are the servants."

✦ ✦ ✦

A few days later, the boat is finally ready to return home to Pier 63. She muscles through the remainder of the summer season—birthday parties, wedding displays, a tour for a local historical society, PAL trips and outings for other kids, and, in August, a twelve-day Hudson River voyage.

And then, that winter, two months after our final trip of the year, Tim and I go aboard to drain down the engines in preparation for the first big freeze.

I shiver in the uncommon silence of the engine room. Few people get to see the old boat this way: quiet and gently lilting in her berth. A faint drip comes from some pipe low beneath the deck plates. The familiar huff of diesel scrapes at the back of my throat. By now I can tease apart the smell the way some people discern hints of oak, cherry, or chocolate in a fine wine—an exhaust-fume bouquet wedded with a richer base note of lube oil and a trace of bilge bacteria.

A thin light glints off the shiny brass of the starboard-side telegraph and flits across the gauges. Though it flickers lambently, like a campfire, the light is actually reflecting off the river water lapping at the portholes. There's something slightly sad and embarrassingly intimate about seeing the boat so still. In my head I list the repairs Tim and I hope to accomplish before spring: patching the mufflers, rebuilding the compressor motor, and rewiring some circuits in the back panel.

I try to see the control pedestal the way I did that first time—an incomprehensible collection of switches and dials. But after hundreds of trips, running my eyes over these gauges, my hands tugging at the levers and cupping black knobs to tweak throttles, it's hard to separate myself enough to see it anew. We're connected.

Chapter Eight

A View from the
Factory Floor

෴

THE WATERS OF the Hudson give the river a sense of substance, of mass. Depending on the sun and the shadows cast by clouds, the river can appear blue, or brown in patches like a calico cat. I've seen the river sparkle, and I've seen it chop rough enough to create little whitecaps. At these moments it almost looks as if the Atlantic seawater pulled north by the flood tide can't help but rise skyward to express its inner wave nature, trying with all its might to remain salty, setting about forming a million little seas.

On this clear, late-summer evening in 2005, as I stand in the wheelhouse of the tug, the Hudson shows a mottled face with distinct pockets that have their own currents, temperatures, and characters. One pocket has a shimmery black, mirror-smooth veneer that reflects the warbly outline of buildings on the Jersey shore. Beside it, another twinkles choppy, blue, and elongated, as if the force of the tide is dragging it along, beckoning it first north, then south.

Riverfront towns show different faces too. On the fireboat I've learned to recognize them by the pilings that support their docks. The creosote-soaked wood in Poughkeepsie emits a dank, oily tang. Catskill's beams grow a telltale green moss. And the rotten clusters at Peekskill's China Pier crumble at the slightest nudge.

For nearly five years my place in the fireboat's engine room has granted me only a subway-stop knowledge of the Hudson as I pop up from "underground" in a different neighborhood in every port of call. Without the chance to see how the districts fit together as a whole, my mental map is perforated, like Swiss cheese. Now, with the tug I'll finally learn all the twists and turns of the river I've taken to calling my own.

Since that first arrival beneath the Verrazano Bridge, I've been poking around New York harbor, savoring my newfound vantage point, while learning how to steer. Today I'm piloting the tug around the tip of Manhattan where the Hudson and East rivers meet, bound for a stretch of seawall in a derelict corner of the Brooklyn Navy Yard—this former army tug's new home. To avoid oversteering as I make the turn, I move the wheel to port just one click at a time, then wait to see how the boat responds. Continuing up the East River, I pass beneath the Brooklyn and Manhattan bridges, holding the wheel steady as the current swirls in little cyclones around the abutments. I've been steering as often as I can this summer—at first with adult supervision (Huntley's) and then on my own. The tug requires a minimum crew of three, typically Tim taking care of the engine room, Karl on deck duty, and me, now alone in the wheelhouse.

Across from a little bump of land in southeastern Manhattan that mariners call Corlears Hook, a power plant on the East River along the northwest shore of Brooklyn defines the entrance into Wallabout Bay, whose designation derives from the Dutch *Waalen Boogt*, meaning "Walloon's Curve," named for the area's original French-speaking settlers, the Walloons, who arrived in 1637. During the Revolution, as many as 11,000 American soldiers, merchants, and traders died on British prison ships in Wallabout Bay. That's almost triple the 4,435 Americans who died in battle. Eventually Wallabout Bay became the site of the Brooklyn Navy Yard, which, during World War II, operated twenty-four hours a day to build warships, employing 70,000 people, including many female mechanics.

As I nose the boat toward home, I announce my intentions over the radio: "Tug *Gowanus Bay* inbound for the Brooklyn Navy Yard," and steer into the cove toward GMD Shipyard's giant cranes. The boat's owner, Rob, chose the tug's name for its Brooklyn flavor. I like the name because Gowanus Bay is also the birthplace of the fireboat—the place where *John J. Harvey*'s riveted steel was pieced together at Todd

Shipyard on the Gowanus Canal, the man-made (and now famously polluted) extension of the bay.

One pier away, a huge freighter is being loaded with cement, while directly off my port side half the FDNY Marine Division's fleet of modern fireboats stands tied off along the seawall. I line up for my landing, determined this time to run in at idle speed, even though it still feels way too fast. My knees have already begun to quiver involuntarily, rippling the fabric of my work pants. Before I found myself at the helm of a tugboat, I never had a real-life context for that cartoon-character concept of nervous, knocking knees.

Everyone keeps telling me, if you can run *this* tug, you'll be able to run anything. The *Gowanus Bay*'s antiquated, single-propeller, direct-reversing configuration provides limited maneuverability. The boat has no neutral, so if the engine is running, the propeller is spinning and the boat is in motion. At idle speed, the propeller turns 111 rpm. Considering that this 10-knot boat tops out at 275 rpm, it's clear that even at her slowest, the boat moves pretty fast. She doesn't sashay out the starting gate, she leaps. When I pop the engine into action, I have to be sure I mean go.

And once I have her going, there's the problem of stopping. Boats don't have brakes, so to halt forward motion, I shift into reverse to apply counterforce. But unlike modern vessels, this tug can't shift immediately from forward to reverse. It's a direct-reversing diesel that has no transmission, no gears. Going backward requires shutting down the engine, waiting for the propeller to stop spinning, then starting the engine again, this time in reverse. To avoid hitting anything, I have to take things slowly, plotting my moves like a chess player, thinking several steps ahead, ever ready to adjust for the unexpected.

But I get only so many tries. Starting the engine requires compressed air, and because the compressors can make and store only so much air at one time, each maneuver must be carefully chosen. In tight quarters, I "fly" the tug using just little bursts in the direction I want to go. Though many helmsmen would turn up their noses at running an oldie-timey boat like this, I like the mindful intentionality she demands: Waste nothing.

I have to take into account the wind and current, using the immutable, natural forces to my advantage instead of barreling through them like I might if I steered a more modern vessel, with bow thrusters and joystick controls. Every fragmentary decision counts in shaping the form and the flow. It's like writing poetry.

My primary objective, this time, is to maintain control of the steering. Last time I made my approach, I had cut power to the engine too early, and no matter how much I cranked the wheel over harder and harder, trying to steer away from it, some magnetic force kept drawing me toward a barge at the end of the pier. That time, the sound of blood rushing in my head made it hard to think, but finally it occurred to me to push the start lever and throttle up the engine, so the boat began, once again, to follow my instructions. Though I'd made the correction in time, the incident taught me how unpleasant it was to slide around at the mercy of the swirling currents. Now I know I have to keep the propeller turning until the last possible second: A rudder can't steer without water flowing over it.

Pointing a boat toward land feels pretty counterintuitive. But that's precisely what docking requires. I aim the nose for the notch, favoring the right on the way in so that if I do hit something, it will be the fat tires hanging off the side of the barge instead of plowing through half the fireboats in New York City. Then I cut the engine, and hold my breath.

Fortunately, this time, the lineup is everything I hope for—a straight shot in. I let the boat drift closer to the rotten wood piles that hold it off the concrete wall. An easy touch of the rubber bow fender against the decaying timber gets us close enough so Tim can get a line to shore. The gentle crunch of the wood giving way doesn't worry me; those piles are just a mirage. Then I kick the engine ahead just a touch, springing off the line to swing in the stern. A murmur of activity begins on deck—a stern line made up, Karl wrapping a rope amidships—and we're done.

I have a moment to myself in the wheelhouse. My fingers click the running-light switches into the Off position. My thighs thrum with leftover electricity, soaked in their adrenaline bath. The ink I scratch into the logbook, "20:30, lines secure Brooklyn Navy Yard," gets lost in the dusk. But my heart gives a little yelp of glee as my head pauses in the sheer joy of a lesson learned, a goal accomplished, an intention satisfied.

✦ ✦ ✦

The first car I owned had a stick shift. My dad had scored me a good deal on a silver '85 Volkswagen Rabbit, and even though I hadn't driven a car with a manual transmission more than a handful of times, I figured I'd learn. I drove the Rabbit across the country from New England to California, but all those highway miles in fifth gear still hadn't given me much shifting experience. When I made it home to San Francisco, though, the steep hills offered more than enough practice. While stopped at a red light on a nearly vertical incline, it took a delicate touch to pull out the clutch while feeding the engine just enough gas to keep the car from stalling.

I had to master this skill as a point of family pride. After all, I was the daughter of a woman who drove a Subaru for six months without a working clutch, deciding by ear and feel when the gears were aligned so she could upshift. "I was so good you couldn't even tell," she crows. "The secret is you have to listen to the rpms of the engine. You rev the engine higher than you need to so that when you take your foot off the gas and the car starts to slow down, you can just slide it into gear."

Where I lived in San Francisco's Lower Haight, parking spots were scarce and often the only spaces I could find when I returned home from school late at night required parallel parking on a hill on the left-hand side of a main thoroughfare. The brief moment when the timed lights on this three-lane highway turned red gave me my window of opportunity. The pressure of jockeying into the spot before three lanes of traffic charged in my direction demanded that I learn quickly. Learning to steer the army tug poses similar challenges, but with one hundred gross tons of momentum behind every decision, the stakes are much higher.

✦ ✦ ✦

All summer long I practiced steering and pined for the chance to pilot the tugboat north of the George Washington Bridge—to cross that same landmark I had passed with the fireboat four years earlier. On a gorgeous, blue-skied day in September 2005, as we set out for the Tugboat Roundup in Waterford, about 130 nautical miles upriver from Pier 63, I finally have that chance.

Since John Callahan organized the first Roundup in 1999, the annual event has grown into a weekend-long party. It's one of the few events on the Hudson that integrates commerce and recreation— sharing Hudson River industry, in the form of working tugs, with the public, and riding the line between river work and river play. Though the Roundup's official mission is to "preserve and promote the maritime industrial heritage of the New York State Canal System," I'm convinced that what draws the tugboaters is the chance to drink beer and swap stories. Without John planning this event, we boat nerds would all stay isolated in our own little worlds, hunkered in our engine rooms and wheelhouses. Instead we come to Waterford to play.

"I just want people to appreciate what we have, and what we had," says John, a former administrator for the New York State Canal Corporation who now splits his time between steering commercial tugs and a newly launched consulting firm.

Waterford, a small, working-class village twelve miles north of Albany, is John's hometown. On a map, the regular grid of Waterford's streets fills a V-shaped plot of land bordered on the south, west, and east sides by a blue Y of water representing where the naturally navigable Hudson ends and the Erie and Champlain canals begin.

Despite its crucial role in U.S. history, the Erie Canal is not what has me twitchy with anticipation today. Truthfully, I'm excited to play reindeer games with this tugboat that the crew struggled so hard to bring up from down south. The weekend's festivities will begin with a tugboat parade, with townspeople lining riverbanks and standing on bridges to watch the procession of boats tooting their air horns for waving children.

The first Roundup I attended was in 2002, when Tim and I went to represent the fireboat, which was receiving an award for her service at Ground Zero. That year, and the next, I arrived by car. This time I'll be arriving by boat, and I can't wait to introduce little gray *Gowanus Bay* to the crowd.

At 8:45 on the morning of September 7, Huntley, Tim, Karl, Rob, and I head up the North River, the stretch of Hudson that extends from the southernmost tip of Manhattan Island to the Piermont Marshes of the Tappan Zee. As Tim and Karl cast off lines, I spin the wooden ship's wheel to set the rudder, then slide the brass control lever into the start position, popping the engine into action. The boat lurches forward, eager as I am for the voyage to begin. It will take us seven hours to get to Kingston, the halfway point where we'll tie up for the night, and I settle in for the long journey ahead.

An hour after setting out from Pier 63, we glide under the George Washington Bridge and into the Hudson's wide maw. Here again, on my left, are the Palisades, now in full view, tall columns of rock behind trees turning bronze, gold, and crimson. Geologists say this cliff face of thick diabase, a dark, igneous rock, "intruded" itself between layers of sandstone and shale between 186 and 192 million years ago. Rising in places to more than six hundred feet above the river, these cliffs, which the Lenape called "We-awk-en," meaning "rocks that look like rows of trees," line the western shore of the Hudson north from Jersey City past the Tappan Zee before sinking into marshland near Piermont.

In the mid-nineteenth century, the Palisades were quarried for high-quality, low-cost building materials, ship ballast, and concrete aggregate. Near where this bridge now stands, quarrymen blasted out a staggering 12,000 cubic yards each day. The river echoed "morning, noon and night . . . with heavy explosions of dynamite as one after another of the most picturesque of the columns in the stretch between Edgewater and Englewood Landing toppled into ruin in clouds of gray dust," as one report noted. This prompted progressive New Jersey women's groups to rally to the conservation cause, helping to bring about the establishment, in 1900, of the Palisades Interstate Park Commission, which purchased and preserved the land. Industrialists John D. Rockefeller Jr. and J. P. Morgan were among the key funders.

Ahead of us the Hudson shimmers a deep brown, as it often does after a rainstorm, when downpours stir up both sediment and what we on the fireboat have come to call "salad": the gobs of green grasses drifting along in the current that make swimming slightly less pleasant. Knowing that rain also releases bigger debris into the river, I keep my eyes peeled for "dead soldiers"—heavy logs that must be kept clear of the prop.

The river looks different when you're in it. After a morning in a boat with John Mylod, an old-time shad fisherman in Poughkeepsie, Lawrence Downes of the *New York Times* lamented the disappearance of the Hudson's "working character," remarking upon how different it is to experience the river "at the working level, on the factory floor." The view from a balcony, an office, or a train allows only passive appreciation. You can sit and watch and wait for the light to shift, or the vista to change as some vessel glides into view. But when you're *in* the river, the shifts become not just pretty changes in the viewshed but variables to consider, details that affect your movement through the water.

Tugboats are no Porsches. Designed for power, not speed, they move pretty slowly, even at Full Speed Ahead. At full throttle, with the push of a strong current, the *Gowanus* tops out at a mere 12.9 knots, or 14.8 miles per hour, affording plenty of time to take in the sights, including the traces of bygone industry that continue to fascinate me. But seeing the river as it is today feels kind of like meeting a relative decades after the only picture of them you've ever seen was taken. The Hudson I've come to know through antique photos—the crucial commercial corridor that was so essential to the growth of American industry—has gone missing.

✦ ✦ ✦

More than a century ago, these shorelines were lined with manufacturing enterprises that harnessed the Hudson's resources, fueling the push of industry that helped to carve out a new United States separate from Britain. The river strengthened our status as a sovereign nation, but now the vestiges of Hudson Valley manufacturing lie hidden under the grass and tucked between the trees. The scene out the wheelhouse windows looks nothing like I imagined.

Among the vanished industries is brickmaking. Today's bucolic, tree-lined banks belie the fact that material gouged out of the shore-line once supplied scores of brickyards along the river's edge. By 1910 the Hudson Valley was the largest brickmaking center in the world. It's likely that any brick you see in Manhattan that was laid before the 1960s was crafted out of Hudson River clay. Yet the traces of their manufacture are now remarkably difficult to discern.

Aerial photos of the shoreline around Haverstraw, in northern Rockland County, reveal an archipelago of small islands and ponds left over from the mining of vast beds of natural river clay. In 1883 forty-one different brickyards operated here along the bay's western shore, producing three hundred million bricks bound for New York City alone. But with the remaining lagoons and inlets now formed into marinas for pleasure craft, the clay pits are now almost invisible.

A largely manual trade, early brickmaking required little infra-structure. Raw materials were mixed by foot. Oxen hooves and people's feet blended clay and sand that molders would forcefully thwack by the handful into rectangular molds. Then they would stomp on the clay to squish it into the corners of the molds to give the finished product clean, straight edges. In yards that had been rolled flat and level, the molds were set out to dry. Then the men stacked the bricks in wood-burning kilns for fourteen days of firing.

Because brickmaking required so little equipment—and therefore minimal initial investment—many entrepreneurs entered the business, drawn by New York City's insatiable market. James Wood, an Englishman who emigrated with brickmaking knowledge on a ship aptly named *Industry*, launched a brick-manufacturing enterprise in 1815 that helped bring Haverstraw to international prominence. Fourteen years later, he revealed a discovery that kept local brick-makers at the cutting edge: By adding a new ingredient to his clay mixture, fine dust from anthracite coal called culm, production time could be slashed from fourteen to seven days.

Brickmaking was just one of the region's industries embracing the power latent in lumps of anthracite coal.

✦ ✦ ✦

On January 7, 1825, a crowd had gathered at the Tontine Coffee House, the turn-of-the-nineteenth-century home of the New York Stock Exchange where wealthy New York City men met to buy, sell, and trade. These men watched with rapt attention as Maurice and William Wurts set about igniting their shiny black stones.

Stones don't burn. That's what most people in New York believed at the time. Though soft, bituminous coal imported from Britain had long been used in small manufacturing, the jury was still out on whether stone, or anthracite coal, discovered locally in northeastern Pennsylvania, had any commercial value. The Wurtses thought it did, so they staged a demonstration that they hoped would inspire investors to sign onto their ambitious idea for a coal-shipping canal.

When the stones did burn, they produced an intense, low-smoke heat that warmed the drafty coffeehouse, enticing businessmen to invest in the Wurts brothers' plan to build a canal for transporting the coal from their Carbondale, Pennsylvania, mines to the New York market, launching the first million-dollar private enterprise in the United States.

In an age when an average farmer had to cut down an acre of trees to supply fuel for a year and spent a third of his time on fuel-related chores—chopping, splitting, hauling, and stacking—coal was a godsend. Recognition of anthracite's superior burning qualities came just as the deforestation of the Hudson Valley had reached startling levels. If not for the abundance of coal, a wood shortage might have stalled American industrialization.

To build the Delaware and Hudson Canal, the Wurts brothers hired the engineers who had designed the Erie Canal. Completed in 1825, the 363-mile-long Erie, which connected Lake Erie to the Hudson, opened up new markets for Midwest farm products in the eastern United States and overseas, and enabled westward migration. Despite the significant effect the D&H Canal has had on the Hudson Valley's economic development, its history is little remembered today.

Excavation of the D&H began in July 1825. Workers dug a ditch four feet deep and thirty-two feet across through 108 miles of untamed wilderness land using nothing but hand tools—picks, shovels, axes, and wheelbarrows. Blasting powder and saltpeter-soaked fuses helped break up rock formations that still today bear traces of the black powder. After a U-shaped trough had been carved out, men lined the trench with precision-cut stone blocks. Beyond these few details (recorded in the remembrances of a man named John Willard Johnston, who had witnessed canal building in his childhood home in Pond Eddy along the Delaware River) remarkably little history remains about the day-to-day operations of building the D&H Canal or the men who performed the backbreaking, dangerous work. In just sixteen months workers completed sixty miles of canal in the section between Rondout Creek and the Delaware River—more than half the total length. The canal was built in its entirety in just three years. One hundred and ten locks mitigated an elevation change of 1,073 feet—nearly twice the elevation conquered by the Erie. The D&H Canal Company managed to finish this extensive project so quickly because it outsourced, divvying up the work into discrete sections and hiring dozens of contractors, who, in turn, hired hundreds of workers to complete each portion.

In all the books I read about the D&H Canal, I found only one photograph of the men who dug the ditch. They stand in a row, shovels in hand, each with his own wheelbarrow and a wide-brimmed hat for sun protection. Their baggy trousers hang loose from suspenders slung over the shoulders of dirty, untailored shirts. They glower at the camera. One man, presumably the boss or foreman, stands in front with no shovel or wheelbarrow but wearing the same wide hat. Despite the uniformity of the portrait, their faces all look strikingly different, each registering unique hungers, schemes, lusts, and dreams.

When the first eleven boats traveled the canal's full length on December 5, 1828, they were laden with ten tons of coal each. Five days later, some of this Lackawanna anthracite reached New York City via the sloop *Toleration*. Over the coming decades, anthracite coal fueled virtually every industry, powering the swift rise of American manufacturing.

✦ ✦ ✦

"Is that a red?" I ask, meaning the buoy up ahead. Karl has the glasses, so the question is his to answer. He's been busy scoping out the cor-

Coal piles on Island Dock in Rondout Creek circa 1892, at the terminus of the Delaware and Hudson Canal, which opened in 1828. (*Collection of Friends of Historic Kingston. From Ford,* Images of America: Kingston)

morants—the sleek, black-plumed water birds sunning themselves on the rocks that poke through the river's surface near a little scab of an island off the eastern shore—but swings the binoculars back in the direction the tug is headed.

"Yup, that's a red."

"Yeah, okay, I see it now." I nudge the wheel slightly to port, one casual click of the electric steering motor at a time to keep the red on my right, then sneak a peek behind me. The tug's wake stretches downriver in an easy, straight line, indicating that I've come to trust the boat enough to let the rudder catch up with my intentions. That telltale, curvy snake wake that stretches behind any boat that's being oversteered doesn't come around much anymore.

This summer, while I ran the tug around New York harbor, Huntley taught me the basic rules of navigation and translated the radio lingo into English. Decades after radar and marine radios had become standard issue, captains still announce their intentions with phrases like "I'll see you on one" or "I'll see you on two." Harking back to an age when whistle toots offered the only boat-to-boat communication, their use of "one" or "two"—short for "one whistle" or "two whistles"—refers to the number of blasts once used by captains to indicate how they planned to pass another vessel. Maritime traditions die hard, and I love the salty stubbornness of pronouncing the syllables for "two whistles" over a VHF radio long after obsolescence has silenced the whistle blasts themselves.

Still, talking on the radio is not my favorite part of tugboating. My non-male voice stands out, drawing attention automatically to anything I say. Since I'm still getting a grip on naming local geography, I fear giving the wrong description of where the boat is and where we're going. As we head north, I plan out my words carefully before clicking the microphone button to make periodic security calls.

Rob, the tug's owner, has joined us for this first upriver trip. He stands in the wheelhouse, phoning friends to say, "Guess where I am? I'm on my new tugboat headed up the Hudson with Captain Jessica at the wheel." After a full round of calls he settles in for a long nap in the sun on the aft deck, looking thoroughly content.

At the north end of Haverstraw Bay (whose name comes from the Dutch word *haverstroo*, meaning "oat straw" or "wild oats") the river narrows again near the town of Verplanck. Parked at the end of a wood pier in a marina full of pleasure boats is a wooden, three-masted sailing ship, a replica of Henry Hudson's vessel *Halve Maen*. Owned by the New Netherland Museum, the replica ship was built in Albany in 1989 and now operates as a traveling museum "dedicated to public education about life in New Netherland during the seventeenth century."

En route to Waterford, we'll actually be passing Hudson's point of no return, where, upon taking depth soundings, he and his crew finally realized that the river was not a strait between seas. Though the waters were too shallow for the *Halve Maen*, modern advancements like dredging and canals will allow the *Gowanus* to pass through Albany, then Troy, and finally through the Federal Lock on the way to Waterford's seawall, the point of convergence between the Mohawk and Hudson rivers and the Erie and Champlain canals.

We're cruising just north of the first highway to span the Hudson south of Albany—the Bear Mountain Bridge, which opened in November 1924 to link Bear Mountain, on the west bank, with a peak nine hundred feet above the river known since at least 1697 as Anthony's Nose. No one is certain to which Anthony the name refers. Washington Irving said it was named for Anthony the trumpeter with a nose "of a very lusty size." Others say the nasal promontory was christened in honor of Saint Anthony, who also had a rock formation on Breakneck Ridge named after him called Saint Anthony's Face until it was quarried away.

I don't want to take my hands off the wheel, but I'm hungry. I duck out of the wheelhouse, leaving Huntley in my spot. While heading to the galley to slice some cheese for crackers, I see, at the end of a strip of land on the east bank of the river, a glum little edifice—a weather-beaten, unfinished, two-story house, stalled in the midst of construction, with a sign still hanging on the side: "We Build Dreams."

Returning to the wheelhouse, clutching the cheese plate, I step up the gentle uphill slope of the bow, listening to the water curling off the stern with an audible sigh as the boat slices through the river. When the water splashes back down, all white and agitated, it kicks up a distinctive salty smell.

We're not far from my favorite spot on the Hudson, a narrow passage that cuts two tight turns around sloping, rock-face hills, their tops carpeted with multicolored bushes and scrub. Here there's no need to block out power lines, marinas, or town houses in order to see the river the way Henry Hudson did: the foliage, the rock face, the eddies spiraling in the water that look just like the little curlicue cyclones drawn on today's charts.

About fifty miles north of New York City, as we pass Garrison on the right and the U.S. Military Academy at West Point on the left, Huntley advises me to make a security call. From this vantage point there's no way to see if another vessel might be headed south, and without fair warning, passing could be perilous. The river drops to more than 177 feet deep here, and the narrow channel amplifies the push of the current. When you're running with the tide, it spits you out, adding a knot or two to your speed, and when you're bucking tide, it can bog you down, cutting your speed by the same amount.

This is World's End, the deepest part of the Hudson. Here the river curls in a tight S-curve around a rugged, 160-acre landmass that's now called Constitution Island, but was referred to, early on, as Martelaer's Rock (a corruption of the Dutch *martelaar's reik*, or "martyr's reach") by sailors leery of the difficult tack and the river's powerful, swirling currents. A century later, these tricky turns offered an advantage to General George Washington and his army in their fight for American independence—especially once the fledgling country's earliest engineers and ironworkers crafted a giant chain to string across the river in an effort to thwart British warships.

✦ ✦ ✦

America was born on the Hudson. This is heresy for me, a New Englander whose Massachusetts ancestry dates at least as far back as 1630, to admit, but I've come to understand the Hudson River as a fulcrum in the history of the United States. For centuries after Henry Hudson's voyage, pivotal moments on the river determined the fate of the region and the direction of the new nation as a whole.

Though I was raised just a few dozen miles north of the site of the 1773 Boston Tea Party, I didn't grasp the full weight of what the Second Continental Congress had taken on when they committed to forming an independent nation until I learned how the Revolutionary War unfolded on the Hudson River.

The delegates had not stumbled blindly into war. Recognizing the Hudson as a key strategic asset, the Continental Congress began fortification efforts five weeks after the battle at Lexington, and more than a year before declaring independence from Great Britain. On May 25, 1775, the Continental Congress resolved to send "experienced persons" to examine the Hudson Highlands to "discover where it will be most adviseable and proper to obstruct the navigation" of enemy ships before they reached Albany. The river had long served as a crucial corridor for global commerce, but now it had a new political and territorial significance on the stage of world events.

To defend against superior British naval forces, the patriots used local knowledge of river currents and geography to build redoubts at critical spots. By fortifying the highlands at the S-curve of World's End, where the river narrowed to less than a quarter-mile wide, colonial leaders planned to force British warships to make the already difficult tack under a barrage of cannon fire.

Meanwhile, back in England, King George III had set his sights on the Hudson River too. As Richard Ketchum writes in his book *Saratoga: Turning Point of America's Revolutionary War*, the waterway was deemed "the continent's chief strategic military thoroughfare," which in 1776 "pointed like a long, vengeful sword at the heart of the renegade American colonies." Two months after the Continental Congress passed its resolution, the king posted orders to:

> command the Hudson . . . to cut off all communication by water between New York and the provinces. . . . By these means, divide the provincial forces . . . break the spirits of the Massachusetts people, depopulate their country, and compel absolute subjugation.

Clearly King George III understood the Hudson's central role in the colonists' ability to maintain cohesion. If the king controlled the river, he could cut off the movement of troops and supplies between the northern and southern colonies, concentrated as they were along the Eastern Seaboard.

The patriots first fortified a spot six miles downriver from World's End, at the mouth of Popolopen Creek, erecting forts Montgomery and Clinton just north of Bear Mountain. Then, in 1776, the army stretched a chain on wooden rafts across the river from Fort Montgomery to Anthony's Nose to thwart enemy warships—a staggeringly difficult undertaking for the time, especially given the empty coffers of the fledgling nation. Though this first chain failed to withstand the river's strong currents, it succeeded in laying the groundwork for the "Great Chain" constructed two years later.

By 1777, General George Washington was certain that possession of the Hudson River would make or break a Continental victory, and assigned engineer Tadeusz Kosciuszko the task of designing a new stronghold called West Point. The Great Chain became a crucial component of the fort's defenses. The links were made of iron bar stock about two inches square, shaped into loops about 12 inches wide and 18 inches long. The weight of the iron links was buoyed by logs about 16 feet long, which were pointed at the ends to offer less resistance to the currents, and anchored to give them stability against tidal forces.

Though the British never dared test the multiple batteries and the Great Chain guarding the river at World's End, the Continental Army came dangerously close to losing control of the Hudson, and with it the war, when after years of dedicated, courageous service, Benedict Arnold turned traitor right here on the Hudson.

In 1779, Arnold communicated to a British general his willingness to switch sides for a fee. The following year, he convinced Washington to grant him command of West Point, and soon after scheduled a midnight meeting with British major John André near Stony Point, on Haverstraw Bay, to sell maps and plans of the fort to the Crown. André was captured in Tarrytown on his way back to British lines, by three patriot militia volunteers who discovered the plans in his boot. The treason was revealed, André was hanged, Arnold escaped (and was given a pension by the British army), and the British gave up trying to capture the Hudson.

Decisive defeats and victories in battles for the Hudson ultimately determined the outcome of the war. West Point never fell into British hands, and still stands as the oldest continuously occupied military post in America. On Trophy Point, a hill overlooking an oft-painted view of World's End, pieces of the Great Chain remain on display—a swivel, a clevis, and thirteen links (one for each of the original United States)—commemorating the unlikely triumph of a nascent nation over a military superpower.

✦ ✦ ✦

Three miles north of World's End, the Hudson widens out into Newburgh Bay, home to one of the most distinctive ruins on the river: Bannerman's Castle, on Pollepel Island. The castle was built by Francis Bannerman VI in 1901 as an arsenal to house the wares of his prosperous military surplus business. Now a partial ruin, the castle lends a haunting enchantment to the eastern shore just before the disappointment of Newburgh coming up on the west. I say disappointment because of the scars remaining from action taken in 1970, when, during a few July days, urban renewal pushed its blades into a waterfront lined with shops and homes and storefront churches, reducing one of the city's oldest neighborhoods to rubble. That demolition cleared the way for the abandoned lots and the hillside that's now lined with cookie-cutter condos, testament to the aesthetic cost of neglecting the riverfront's architectural roots.

Just ahead is Crum Elbow, a spot I like just because of its cool name. The moniker, a pidginization of the Dutch *krom elleboge* ("crooked elbow"), suggests exactly what this reach of river looks like where the Hudson makes a sharp bend between two rocky bluffs.

As we continue north, the radio announces that a Buchanan tug is headed our way, pushing a loaded barge. *How narrow will the river be where we finally meet and have to pass?* In a car on the highway we're accustomed to traveling with just a few feet of space between cars on either side. Here on the water, just a foot of clearance would seem like a collision, since unlike cars, which are firmly rooted to the ground, boats move around more unpredictably. As it happens, we glide by the Buchanan tug at a wide spot in the "road," and I have plenty of space to skate by while checking the nameboard to see that the boat is the *Buchanan 12.* Tim and I had met a Buchanan engineer named Laddie while the fireboat was in the shipyard. Maybe this is his boat. I get on the radio: "*Buchanan 12*, this is tug *Gowanus.*"

"*Buchanan 12* here," a gravelly voice responds.

"Hi, Cap, can you tell me if Laddie's on board?"

"Yes, he is."

"Let him know that the crew of fireboat *John J. Harvey* says hi." Tim is standing in the wheelhouse, listening, and we both crack up when we realize what a weird, convoluted message it is, given the fact that we're on a completely different boat.

"I'll tell him," the guy responds, his voice conveying none of the befuddlement we expect. We're out here joyriding, but for him it's just another day at the wheel.

Seventy-five nautical miles upriver from Manhattan's southern tip, a curled finger of land juts out from the Hudson's west bank. A lighthouse standing at the end of the rocky jetty cautions mariners away from shallows at the mouth of Rondout Creek, in the city of Kingston. It's four o'clock and we've made good time.

✦ ✦ ✦

We set out again for Albany on Friday morning at eight thirty to make sure we don't miss the parade of tugs that starts at two. As we travel upriver from Kingston, the Hudson grows narrower, and I slow the engine as we pass by strings of pleasure-craft marinas to keep from bouncing them with my wake.

Long stretches of trees at the river's edge are punctuated by the occasional power plant, quarry, or cement dock, offering me the glimpse of Hudson River industry that I've been missing. I pencil notes in the chart so I can find out more later. In Ravena, a bright red barge labeled "Lafarge" waits at the dock as its holds get filled with cement that has traveled to the riverfront in a covered conveyor belt from the cement plant more than a mile inland. Reaching Ravena means Albany is just around the bend.

After a five-hour run we arrive to find a flotilla of tugs noodling around in the water, filled with people scoping out the other boats and snapping pictures while waiting for the parade to begin. I'm not the only one wearing a stupid grin as I wave to those I know, proudly presenting the tuglette (as the crew has taken to calling her), my newest little charge.

The more time I spend on the water, the more other boats develop personalities and become identifiable in some way. The Waterford Tugboat Roundup has helped add more names and faces to my list, and here they are assembled. There's the slender, seventy-three-foot *Urger*, the 1901 canal system showpiece, dressed in New York State blue and yellow; the U.S. Coast Guard cutter *Wire*, a sixty-five-foot ice-breaking tugboat; the *Herbert P. Brake*, a lumpy, squared-off tug hand-built from recycled steel by the late Bart Brake, whose salty legend outlives him; and another Roundup newcomer, a blue-and-gray tug called *Margot* that I worked on for a few days last fall, rebuilding injectors on a Fairbanks Morse engine even larger than the one we have on the *Harvey*.

Florida Joe, the engineer I worked with, stands on the aft deck of

Tug parade in Port Albany en route to the 2005 Waterford Tugboat Roundup. (*Photo by Jessica DuLong*)

the *Margot* wearing a straw cowboy hat and a blue-and-white-striped button-down shirt, open, as usual, halfway down his chest. When he sees me, the barrel of a man waves a happy-puppy hello.

The parade begins, and the *Gowanus* falls in line behind a brown, yellow, and red tug called *Frances Turecamo*, which belongs to Steve Trueman—the salvor who wants to build the old-boat shipyard/museum. Ahead of us the procession of tugs in all shapes, sizes, and colors moves so slowly it's all I can do to keep off Steve's stern. Looking out at the string of boats winding along the river, under a series of bridges, I stand at the helm, beaming. This is the most fun I've had in ages.

As we make our way into the lock, all the big tugboats snuggle up together, side by side, resting on each other's rubber fenders. Unlike other kinds of boating, tugboating is a contact sport—you're actually allowed to hit things. The fenders, often recycled from old tires or made new by extruding rubber into fat noodles, protect the steel hull. This means we can all pull into the lock, packed together like piglets.

The lock operates like a water-filled elevator, transporting vessels from one level of water to another. A boat pulls in, a gate closes behind it, then water is pumped into the lock chamber, raising the boat up to the level of the water on the other side. Then the front gate opens, and the boat continues on its way. (This process works the same way in reverse, too, so that when a boat travels from a higher to a lower water level, the lock tender pumps the water out.)

Meanwhile, on the other side of the lock, hordes of people stand waiting on the Waterford shore. I can't hear him, but John's father is announcing each tug as it pulls in, presenting her like a model sashaying down the catwalk. We have arrived.

✦ ✦ ✦

The Roundup culminates in a nose-to-nose competition in which two (or sometimes more) tugboats meet bow to bow (or nose to nose), then gun their engines to see which boat is stronger. The tugs battle to prove which has the most horsepower, until the captain of the tug that pushes the other boat backward announces victory with a blast of the air horn. The pointlessness of this exercise fits into a long tradition of horse pulls and lawn-tractor races where boys (and sometimes girls) enjoy showing off their toys.

I'm game, but still a little timid on the throttle. But the push-off ends up showing me how much power I have behind me on this boat. Maneuvering around other boats in open water—where making contact is sport and not catastrophe—teaches me a lot about how to convince the tug to do what I tell her to. Because many of the tugs attending the Roundup are small canalers, *Gowanus* reigns triumphant in many a competition.

The most challenging aggressor in our horsepower class is the *Chancellor*, another scrappy direct-reversing tug, built in 1938 for service on the New York State Canal System, once cared for by Steve Trueman, and currently in the stewardship of the Waterford Maritime Historical Society. At the *Chancellor's* helm today is a man named Bill Curry, well known for his penchant for explosives. He's coming for us, and we aren't backing down.

The trouble with single-propeller, direct-reversing tugs going head to head in a nose to nose, however, is the difficulty of lining up the bows. On one attempt we hit so hard that a cloud of antique dust from the *Chancellor*'s rope fender (called a beard) erupts into the sky upon impact. That hit breaks a few incidentals in both galleys, but when we finally line up and throttle down, the *Gowanus* shows her muscle. At the award ceremony later that day the mighty tuglette is awarded her first plaque.

Chapter Nine

TOWING WITH TOM

〜

"So, YOU LIKE this kind of work?" Tom asks, turning halfway around, hanging his torso over the ship's wheel. Three months after the Roundup—two days after Christmas 2005—I'm standing in the wheelhouse of the *Gowanus Bay*, on my first towing job, bound for New Jersey with Tom Teague, a seasoned tug captain. He asks this question of every new mate he trains, and I wonder if they appreciate how lucky they are to learn from someone who takes time out of the doing to explain the how and why.

Tom started working on tugboats the year after I was born and got his first captain's job nine years later, in 1983. He calls himself an old-timer, and though he's certainly logged enough years to merit the title, he doesn't look the part. Barely in his fifties, fit and wiry, sometimes clean-shaven, sometimes with a closely cropped gray beard, Tom doesn't have that leathery, sun-beaten look that lots of boat guys do after so much time in the business.

For the past fourteen years he's been steering a boat called *Janice Ann* for Reinauer, one of the big East Coast towing companies. These days his work mostly involves pushing ethanol barges back and forth between points in the Port of New York and New Jersey: Jamaica Bay, Sewaren, Newtown Creek. It sounds kind of like running a ferry, but Tom says he doesn't mind the repetition. He says he's "riding it out," though he doesn't ever plan on retiring. "It's not hard, it's not nerve-racking. It's just a job. They give me money, and it's a good boat. Being a deckhand—that's a brutal job. But the captain . . . You can sit up there and steer and tell people to bring you coffee. Really, it's not so hard when you get settled in."

Hearing how effortless this work is for Tom while I'm pining to develop piloting skills of my own makes me even more impatient to learn. After spending nearly five years getting my engineering bearings, I've finally filed the initial paperwork toward earning my Coast Guard engineering license. Now I am here on this trip with Tom, hoping to add two entirely different skill sets to my repertoire: steering and towing. How can I not? Tugboats are for towing. Now that I have a tugboat at my disposal, I want to learn how.

Tom and I met on the fireboat, where he drops in on occasion with the *Janice*, tying up alongside between jobs. In years past, when Manhattan's West Side had a working waterfront, there were plenty of places for a tugboat to tie up while waiting for the next assignment to come in. These days, Tom complains, there's nowhere to go, so he's happy to be able to make up a line to the *Harvey* every so often.

Today is Tom's day off, but I've asked him to run a towing job for us so I can watch and learn. The job is actually a favor for a friend, Carl Selvaggi, a monument maker from Bridgeport, Connecticut, who owns a fifty-six-foot 1941 tugboat called *Spooky Boat* (so named because he procured it in Amityville, New York, hometown of *The Amityville Horror*). Carl's been renting a slip in New Jersey, but the marina is closing and now he has to get the boat out. The plan is to tow *Spooky* with the *Gowanus* up to Kingston.

By the time Tom gets off work and we finish loading supplies, it's 9:00 p.m. So when Tom, Tim, monument Carl, deckhand Karl, and I set out from Manhattan for the Kill Van Kull, the waterway on the north side of Staten Island, the harbor is shrouded in darkness that's pierced by a dizzying array of lights. Navigating one of the busiest commercial channels in the port requires discerning the difference between the blur of city lights onshore, vessels' running lights, and the buoy lights on markers in the water. Running a boat at night poses challenges entirely different from operating in daylight, so even though it feels awkward not to have my own hands on the tug's wooden wheel, I'm glad Tom is at the helm.

Not steering, I have plenty of time to take in the view. Huge freighters and tugs with their barges linger out in the anchorage of the Upper Bay. At any moment a container ship might slip through the channel past Constable Hook and into the big water of the bay. The night skylines of New Jersey and Staten Island bleed together, lit up with a barrage of twinkling yellow, red, white, and green that forms a whole universe of shifting constellations. Who says you can't see stars in the city?

✦ ✦ ✦

Though today's freighters, tugs, and container ships run on diesel, they are nonetheless the modern-day descendants of the first commercially viable steamboat, which was launched by Robert Fulton off Manhattan's Hudson shore on August 17, 1807.

A crowd had gathered that day to ogle the odd-looking contraption—ungainly at 150 feet long, thirteen feet wide, drawing two feet of water, with paddles on the sides. Ladies with parasols raised against the summer sun, hanging off the arms of men in breeches and high-collared, frilled shirts, had interrupted their Monday to promenade the rural Greenwich Village riverbank and watch the experimental vessel depart for Albany. Though the boat had already steamed successfully around the tip of Manhattan, many had come hoping to see an explosion.

Here, at the dawn of the industrial revolution, only a handful of steam engines existed in the country and the devices remained alien to most people. Living in a great shipping port, New Yorkers were surrounded by boats—the harbor was filled with a forest of ship masts of square-rigged brigs, single-masted sloops, and schooners—but never before had they seen a contraption like "Fulton's Folly."

That disparaging term had followed Fulton through more than a decade of experiments in which he tried to utilize Europe's latest technology, the steam engine, in a boat of his own design. "Never did a single encouraging remark, a bright hope, or a warm wish cross my path," Fulton later wrote. "This is the way ignorant men compliment what they call philosophers and projectors."

One of his first attempts, on the Seine in Paris in 1803, failed when, during an overnight storm, the engine and boilers broke through the bottom of the vessel and sank. But by 1807, Fulton thought he had found a solution by taking a methodical, scientific approach to his design and utilizing models and experiments to troubleshoot potential problems. He brought to the table an artist's eye, a mind keenly attuned to spatial relations, and recognition that his work required employing old parts in new ways: "The mechanic should sit down among levers, screws, wedges, wheels, etc., like a poet among the letters of the alphabet, considering them as the exhibition of his thoughts, in which a new arrangement transmits a new idea to the world."

Perseverance and a strong mechanical aptitude had been essential. So had money. Fulton's patron, Chancellor Robert Livingston, was a member of a powerful Hudson River family, had served as a delegate to the Continental Congress, and had been a member of the committee that drafted the Declaration of Independence. He had lent his financial and political patronage to others racing to build steamboats, without success. But if Fulton's contraption could navigate between New York and Albany, the payoff would be tremendous. As part of an earlier venture, the New York State legislature had granted Livingston the exclusive right to operate a steamboat on the Hudson, provided it moved at least four miles per hour (about 3.5 knots) against the current.

Though a speedy sloop could travel roughly four to six miles per hour with fair tide and winds, it still had to wait at anchor under unfavorable conditions. Traveling great distances consumed weeks, or even months, and was governed by the seasons, since snow and ice could render dirt roads and rivers impassable. Women and children rarely ventured far from home, and certainly not alone. But after Fulton's steamboat, all that would change. This new mode of propulsion offered the promise of reliable transport that prevailed over nature, transforming even people's concept of time.

Confident his steamboat would make it to Albany intact, Fulton ordered his crew to cast off lines and the vessel slipped away from the pier into the river. All appeared to be going well until suddenly the boat lost power. Fulton begged his passengers for their patience, made some slight adjustments, and off they were, under way again toward the chancellor's Clermont estate. "All were still incredulous," Fulton later recalled. "None seemed willing to trust the evidence of their own senses."

Cheers from spectators on the shoreline greeted Fulton's contraption along the way. But others were afraid. "The crews of many sailing vessels shrunk beneath their decks at the terrific sight, while others prostrated themselves and besought Providence to protect them from the approach of the horrible monster which was marching on the tide and lighting its path by the fire that it vomited," recounted a writer of the day. One farmer who witnessed this chimera on the river rushed home to warn his wife and friends he "had seen the devil going up the river in a sawmill." After dark, the specter became even more terrifying. One onlooker called it "a monster moving on the waters defying the winds and tide, and breathing flames and smoke."

Even against the tide, the craft surpassed the government's four-mile-per-hour measure of success. Then, at a little past two, just as the steamboat reached Spuyten Duyvil, marking the northern tip of Manhattan, the speed picked up to five miles an hour.

After an overnight in Clermont, the party set out once again, this time with Chancellor Livingston aboard. When they reached Albany eight hours later, what Fulton dubbed his *North River Steamboat* (though it came to be known variously by others as *Clermont* and *North River*) had traveled from New York City to Albany, a distance of 126 nautical miles, in a combined total of about thirty-six hours. Though its average speed was no faster than that of a sloop under favorable conditions, the boat demonstrated consistency in the face of wind and current, which was unheard-of at the time. Incalculable though his joy may have been, Fulton could not have realized the full impact of his accomplishment. The steamboat, writes Kirkpatrick Sale in *The Fire of His Genius: Robert Fulton and the American Dream*, "would be the single most important instrument in the transformation of America in the first half of the nineteenth century." Indeed, Fulton's success facilitated the country's meteoric rise as manufacturer to the world.

By 1850 more than 150 vessels traveled up and down the Hudson, ferrying as many as two million passengers. In addition, steamboats revolutionized the movement of goods over water. Though schooners carried cargoes of grain and vegetables downriver to New York City through the end of the nineteenth century, the introduction of scows and barges that could carry weighty cargoes like cement, stone, bricks, and iron—on schedule—transformed the nature of river traffic. Today, many of these products continue to be transported via the Hudson, including petroleum and "clean oil" products, which are the bulk of what Tom Teague now tows.

✦ ✦ ✦

As we make our way past the containership terminals of Newark Bay and into the mouth of the Hackensack River, we have to wait for numerous bridges to open so we can pass beneath them. I have plenty of time to ask Tom how tugboating has changed since his first job, hauling acid waste offshore to dump it into the ocean. "The water is so beautiful out there," he says, with the slight Southern lilt he came by growing up in Elkton, Maryland. "It is so pretty and clean and we were puttin' brown stripes across the ocean. And the fish came to it, because it was warm. The fish were in it, you know, the whales and the porpoises and all that stuff out there. And I said, 'This is legal?'" But it was. Every time they went out, an Environmental Protection Agency helicopter followed them to make sure they went the hundred miles offshore. Despite this example of direct visual observation in his formative tugboating years, Tom says one of the biggest differences between today and when he started is that now vessels are under constant surveillance.

"It used to be you'd get on the boat and that was it. You were invisible," says Tom. "Now everybody watches us." He's referring to Vessel Traffic Services (VTS), a joint effort of the U.S. Coast Guard and the Department of Homeland Security responsible for coordinating vessel movements in the port, much the way air-traffic-control stations monitor plane traffic. VTS has cameras mounted throughout New York harbor sending a constant video feed of images with startlingly vivid detail. (In fact, a guy I know got busted for drinking while operating his—noncommercial—boat because the cameras captured pictures of him holding a beer at the helm.)

The surveillance bothered Tom, not because he was doing anything wrong but because he was unaccustomed to operating on such a tight leash. He missed the days when, given a job to do, he was trusted to decide how best to do it. "I used to move three or four barges at one time. They won't let us do it now because of insurance. It's just been regulated to death. It's ridiculous." Tom says this bureaucratic micromanagement began after the *Exxon Valdez*, a 986-foot freighter carrying more than fifty-three million gallons of oil, ran aground in Alaska's Bligh Reef on March 24, 1989. The resultant spill of eleven million gallons stretched 460 miles, oiling 1,300 miles of shoreline. "Then they came up with OPA, the Oil Pollution Act of 1990. That was the beginning of all of this." Tom recognizes the value of these regulations. What frustrates him is that incompetence sets the standard for the rules.

These days Tom feels like a major-league player stuck in a minor-league game. "They've dumbed the job down so much with all the electronics that do the thinking for the guy instead of the guy figuring it out for himself. I used to run up and down the coast with just radar and a compass—no GPS, nothing like that. You had to figure out your speed, distance, and time. You had to navigate. Well, now all the electronics do that for you. That's my take on it, being an old-timer. I like the job and I'm pretty good at what I do. I just don't like all the bullshit that's been piled on top of it."

While we wait for the bridge operator to raise the next lift bridge, I look out over the glittering lights on the electric towers and smokestacks of New Jersey. "Seems like the more technology we have, the more we lose our grip on common sense," I say. "It's almost like those muscles that used to get flexed all the time start to atrophy from lack of use. Everything's gotten so virtual that we're losing our ability to deal with the physical world around us. Now all of life seems to happen through a screen."

"Yep," agrees Tom, explaining that he sees this problem with the new mates he has to train. "When they first come on the boat, they don't ask about horsepower, they don't ask about the rotation or size of the propellers, they don't ask about the gears. They ask about the electronics. They go right to the wheelhouse: 'What d'ya got?' An electronic chart is required now by the Coast Guard and the guys come on the boat, they draw a line on the electronic chart, and then

they follow the line. It's like a video game. If they didn't have the electronics, I don't think they could drive the damn boat." Tom bemoans
the lost art of navigation, a skill endangered by reliance on computers. "The bottom line is this: If the battery goes dead, you lose your
electronics. And if you can't drive the damn boat without them, then
that's a problem."

While navigating on my own, I've been making a point to always
refer to the paper charts first, using the GPS as a backup. Learning on
an old boat like the *Gowanus* helps reinforce the lesson, since every
now and then the battery on the 12-volt system craps out, leaving me
screenless, the way it was back when this tug was built.

Tom's job used to be about towing from point A to point B, but
now he has to document it all too. "There's payroll, safety reports,
and the logbooks—one on board and one for the office." Because you
can't fill out paperwork while you're steering, the captain has to fill
out forms during his off-hours, which further cuts into his already
scant time for sleep.

Tom has essentially been sleep-deprived for the majority of his
adult life. Like most crews, the guys on Tom's boat work two weeks
on and two weeks off. The boat operates twenty-four hours a day on
six-hour shifts that rotate during that whole two-week period. "You
never get enough sleep," Tom explains. "I mean, the best you can get
is maybe five hours at a time. And they've done studies. Lack of sleep
is like bein' drunk. You can't concentrate. I've been doing this so long,
the guys knock on my door at three in the morning: 'The barge is
aground!' I get up. Okay, bang, bang, bang. I don't know if it's instinct
or what, but you never get enough sleep and you're always on when
you're on the boat. You never fully relax." No wonder every time I see
Tom on the *Janice*, he has a mug of coffee in his hand.

I'm already learning my first lessons about tugboating: Tides and
bridge openings are not timed around your sleep schedule. It takes
us until twelve thirty in the morning to finally reach our destination: a town called Little Ferry, where we'll wait for high tide to bring
enough water to enable us to drag *Spooky Boat* out of the mud. We
hit the bunks at around one o'clock, then at 5:30 a.m., Tim fires up the
generator and the main engine, and we're back at it again.

The people in the sleepy Jersey town slumber as Tom maneuvers the boat through the still, black Hackensack, which in this spot looks more like a creek than a river. Tim walks over on land, then climbs aboard *Spooky* to receive a line. Despite the dark, Karl manages to throw a rope close enough that Tim can snag it and wrap the line around *Spooky*'s bitt so we can yank the boat off the mudflats into deep enough water to tie the boat alongside. Tom gives calm, well-paced explanations about how to make up the tow, arranging *Spooky*'s bow well forward of the *Gowanus*'s nose and setting up the right configuration of lines. Soon we're headed southbound, and Tom shows me how to adjust the rudder to compensate for the drag of the tow. Off to our left, the New York City skyline stands silhouetted against an orange sky.

✦ ✦ ✦

After their first successful steamboat passage from New York City to Albany in 1807, Fulton and Livingston quickly added to their fleet. Their monopoly allowed them to set steep prices that ensured sizable profits until the Supreme Court overturned their hold in 1824. That year, Fulton and Livingston had been operating five passenger vessels on the river, charging $7 a head. But after the ruling opened Hudson waters to all, competition sent ticket prices plummeting. Sixteen new steamboats arrived on the scene, and by 1845 the fare had dropped to twelve and a half cents. Speed and luxury proved to be the most important selling points as the new boats vied for customers. Boats raced each other up- and downriver, cutting each other off as they darted their way into wharves to be the first to pick up waiting passengers. Profit-seeking outweighed safety, resulting in a number of ugly accidents, including collisions and explosions caused by pushing boilers and machinery past their limits for greater speed.

Steamboats increasingly replaced sailing ships for moving people and cargo. Throughout the 1830s and 1840s, steam ferries doubled as towboats. Even with a full load of passengers, the earliest ferries were known to abandon their routes for lucrative work towing ships in and out of port. Thus the birth of the towing business in New York harbor and along the Hudson was inextricably linked with passenger service. Moving goods was not so different from moving people, and combined revenues from both activities were often necessary for operators to stay in business.

Before long, as technology advanced and cargo needs changed, the towing industry separated from the business of carrying passengers. A Brooklyn ordinance forbade ferryboats from diverting from their scheduled routes to take towing gigs, and ferries deemed too slow for passenger service were converted into the first vessels used exclusively for towing. The first New York vessel to attempt to turn a profit solely by towing according to George Matteson, author of *Tugboats of New York*, a history/photo album of towing in the region, was *Hercules*, built in 1832.

The earliest towing procedures involved lashing barges on either side of a steamboat, but soon, operators embarking on much larger and more varied tows employed new strategies. In the late 1830s, a new technique called towing "on the hawser" permitted towboats to carry mixed flotillas behind, rather than alongside, the steamer. By 1846, fifteen hawser boats operating on the Hudson used this new technique, which became standard practice on the river for the next seventy-five years. Hawser towboats maintained regular schedules, setting out to the north and the south, picking up and dropping off at points along the way—a routine that lasted through the 1950s.

Images of some mid-nineteenth-century tows look, to my modern eye, like disasters waiting to happen. The precariously long strings of miscellaneous canalers, sloops, schooners, and barges trailing behind a lumpy side-wheel steamer look nothing like the tows you see on the river today. A photograph in *Tugboats of New York* shows the side-wheel towboat *General McDonald* pulling three two-masted schooners, a two-masted barge, a two-story market barge, and myriad canal boats and barges behind. The rope securing this massive flotilla to the stern of the towboat is hardly visible against the backdrop of the river. Instead of pulling the boats behind, it looks like the *McDonald* is being haunted by them. Beside her chugs a classically shaped, model-bow steam tug with a rounded house and tall stack. The job of this helper tug was to drop off and pick up tows at shore points along the route, while the *McDonald* steamed along at a steady pace. These tugs and towboats became part of a system of transport that was essential to the New York economy.

A late-nineteenth-century mixed tow in the Hudson River pulled by side-wheel towboat *General McDonald*, with a helper tug. (*Collection of the Steamship Historical Society of America. From Matteson,* Tugboats of New York)

By the turn of the twentieth century, larger companies with the capital and flexibility to adjust to the needs of their customers began squeezing out smaller operators, and improved towboat technology subdivided the industry into specialties. Following the boom years of the mid- to late-nineteenth century, when coal, ice, bricks, bluestone, and farm products all wound their way south to the great emporium of New York City, commercial traffic began to slow.

Today's river is nowhere near as busy, but specialization remains evident. Each tug wears the signature colors of its company, and if you watch the traffic on the river for long enough, the identities and work patterns of specific boats begin to emerge.

Buchanan tugs, identifiable by their red, white, and blue stripes, tend to run some of the largest Hudson River tows, pushing or towing strings of as many as fourteen stone barges at one time. Reinauer tugs, dressed in buff and red; K-Sea tugs, in white with cardinal trim; and Bouchard tugs, with their signature crimson houses and white rails, move petroleum and "clean oil" products in barges topped with mazes of piping and equipment sheds that, from afar, look like platforms supporting tiny cities. Among the few tugs on the river that still have that old-time tugboat look are *Crow* and *Cheyenne*, owned by Port Albany Ventures. They can often be seen hauling scrap steel. Today another classic tug, a little gray army ST with *Spooky Boat* alongside, is joining them on the river.

Many of the crews aboard these workboats would tell you it's just a job, but these men and women are carrying on the tradition of the Hudson as a working river. As I watch and learn from them, I become part of that tradition too.

✦ ✦ ✦

When we finally reach the Hudson, the river greets us with an ever-thickening fog bank that drops visibility down to less than half a mile. Now I'm really glad we have an expert at the helm. As Tom steers the boat through the fog and rain, I read the charts aloud, offering advance notice of the next buoys' positions and wiping the condensation from the windows, the white film melding with the low-lying clouds that block the land from view. Running a finger over the smooth paper charts to trace our progress, the crescent of grease under my nail hovering over the mark of a beacon, I check to see if the flashing white light we can make out on the horizon is the four-second green we need to find next.

The river has been whitewashed in rain and fog, and navigating blind demands heightened awareness. While Tom makes minute adjustments to the radar unit's gain and sea clutter settings, I focus all my attention on what he's doing, cataloging the details so that I might someday be this kind of captain.

As we travel north, the fog clears enough for us to see a field of icebergs ahead. Without a visual warning, the sound of that first impact would be terrifying. The groaning and rasping against the bow of the *Gowanus* makes me want to turn the boat around. I worry that sharp shards might gouge the hull, but Tom's calm steels me against my own impulse to retreat. Loud as it is in the wheelhouse, the echo of the scraping below the waterline in the crew's quarters is downright spine-chilling. But the "this is nothing" tone of Tom's stories reassures me. "When you're pushing, it piles a mountain of ice up in front of the bow until it just stops you."

"What do you do then?" I ask, mopping the condensate off the window with a paper towel for the gajillionth time. "Do you wait for the *Wire* to come and dig you out?" A sixty-five-foot U.S. Coast Guard cutter stationed in Saugerties—a town about nine miles north of Kingston—the *Wire* serves as an ice-breaking tugboat. Charged with keeping the shipping lanes clear, the vessel bellies up like a walrus onto the surface of the ice with its rounded hull, crushing the frozen sheets under its weight. This work is crucial to keep commercial traffic flowing. When fuel barges get stalled on the ice, shipping costs increase, which, in turn, raises oil prices in local markets.

I should have known Tom wasn't one to wait for rescue. Instead, he explains, he'd tell the deckhands to release the lines on the barge so the boat could pull away, then he'd run the tug up the river a bit to carve out a path. "You do your own ice-breaking?" I ask.

"Yep. The only time that you get a break is if there's a big tow coming down with a light barge. If you're stuck, and you see him coming down, you can ask him to pass close by, so after he's clear you can jump into his track and go." Fortunately, we don't need to try any of Tom's ice-thwarting tactics, but when an iceberg gets caught between the two boats, we stop and poke it free with a boat hook.

✦ ✦ ✦

On my trip to Waterford for the Tugboat Roundup, I had drawn pencil marks on the chart where mysterious masonry stacks poked up through the trees. A little research revealed that many of these are chimneys from power plants that ran machinery for the many icehouses that once lined the riverbanks. Though I can't see the stacks through the fog, crunching through the commodity they were built to help harvest gives me a sense of how icy the Hudson can get.

Today the river remains navigable year-round because icebreakers and workboats keep shipping channels clear. Unlike the days when the *Norwich*, a specially built icebreaker from 1836 dubbed the Ice King, plied the Hudson to and from Rondout, the river is never allowed to freeze over. The *Norwich* was usually the last boat down the Hudson in the winter and the first boat up in the spring. With the protection of a layer of copper sheathing on her hull, she could power up onto the ice, which broke under the force of her weight, then move ahead on the newly cleared path. This skill made her a favorite in the Rondout community, which remained essentially locked in once the "highway" of the Hudson froze over each winter. Townspeople eagerly awaited *Norwich*'s arrival because it heralded spring.

Today, ice is a nuisance, an impediment, but before the widespread use of mechanical refrigeration took hold in the 1920s, Hudson River ice was a product, harvested in the winter, then sold throughout the spring and summer. Some ice lasted even longer than a year, with previous winters' bumper crops filling in for thinner harvests in subsequent seasons. Ice harvesting was a major industry for the mid-Hudson Valley, with 135 icehouses between New York and Albany, from the mid-1800s to the early 1900s. The trade supported the families of as many as 20,000 off-season boatmen, farmers, bark peelers (who stripped hemlock trees for tannins used in leather tanning), and brickyard workers, who often spent ten-hour days in subzero temperatures, snowstorms, and gale-force winds, marking, planning, scraping, sawing, and hauling. New York City alone demanded 1,500,000 tons of ice each year.

Ice-harvesting and brickmaking industries worked hand in hand, with workers shifting occupations by the season. Counterintuitively, given the natures of their products, while few brickyard relics remain, the ice industry left spectral reminders up and down the river: powerhouses topped with tall brick stacks.

These buildings—constructed of brick to prevent fires, and separated from the wooden icehouses where the ice was stored to prevent melting—contained steam plants that ran conveyor belts called endless-chain elevators, upon which millions of two- to three-hundred-pound blocks of ice, hand-sawed out of the river, were moved into the huge ice houses, packed with straw and sawdust, and stored through the year. The wooden structures were massive—several stories high and up to three hundred feet long, with double walls from twenty to thirty-six inches thick, the space between them packed with sawdust for insulation—a remarkable feat of engineering, using the simplest of materials.

✦ ✦ ✦

By the time the *Gowanus* passes the Esopus Lighthouse, the whiteness of fog has been replaced by a winter evening's early darkness. Here is where generations of tug operators have sounded off a "Port Ewen salute" to pay homage to a statue of the Madonna cradling a tug in her arms, erected at the town's Presentation of the Blessed Virgin Mary church as a monument to local boatmen. A string of blinking red and green buoys traces the path to the entrance to Rondout Creek and the end of our voyage.

I wipe the drips from the windows again, joking that we'll have to stop breathing if we ever want to see, and position the spotlight along the north side of the creek at the stern of a tugboat named *Susan Elizabeth*, a member of Steve Trueman's fleet. As we approach, Tom squats down to check his lineup through the railing and describes to me all the choices he's making and why. Then he lands *Spooky*'s bow at the stern of the *Susan*, in a single, graceful maneuver, utilizing the ebb current and the wind.

From here in the creek, I can see the ice move on the Hudson. I know if I stood here long enough I could watch it switch directions with the tide. All winter the ice will shift back and forth—three steps forward, two steps back. That's how I see my time on the river, too, as I continue my hunt for yesterday's river by working on the Hudson of today.

Part III

∿

PRIDE AND PRESERVATION

Lightship No. 115, Frying Pan Shoals, 1929-1930.

Mark Peckham

Chapter Ten

"ARE YOU LICENSED?"

WORKING WITH PEOPLE like Tom inspires me to learn. So when I walk into my first day of engineering school two weeks after my first tow, I'm excited about the chance to study, in a classroom setting, all the theory I have been picking up aboard the boats.

Anticipating a change in the fireboat's Coast Guard status that might end up requiring its operation by licensed engineers, Huntley has asked Tim and me to get our "tickets." Since paperwork isn't Tim's strong suit, I have gathered all the forms, researched the prerequisites, and hunted down a two-week test-prep program that's about to begin.

The continental breakfast in the hotel lobby is too free and convenient to pass up. The coffee is lousy, but I bring the cup with me on the complimentary shuttle that drives us to our first day of class because wrapping my fingers around the warm Styrofoam offers some measure of comfort. I don't realize that this cup will draw the first round of unwanted attention in my direction.

I'm walking up the ramp toward the door of the building amid a group of about ten or twelve other students when the instructor walks by and informs me that coffee isn't allowed in the classroom. "We just got all new carpets," he says. "We want to keep them that way."

"Oh, okay," I answer. "I'll just finish it out here, then." I pound the last bit of liquid, then toss the cup.

"We've had fistfights in here—one guy spilled coffee on another guy's books."

"Oh, you don't want that," I say, all first-day-of-school agreeable, my make-nice knob cranked to ten. If this man is going to be my instructor for the next two weeks, I want to repair my starting-gate infraction and end up on his good side.

I pick a spot in the second row, but the padded seat of the chair is set so low the desktop comes up almost to my collarbone. I don't want to spend the day like a kid in need of a booster seat, so I reach for an adjustment lever. Finding none, I climb out of the seat and squat down for a better look. No lever.

As my new classmates, all guys, file in and take positions at the long, narrow tables, I clear my throat absentmindedly, and a mustached man in the front row turns around to look at me. I flash back to something a female firefighter once told me while I was reporting a story about women working at Ground Zero. "All the women and men were working together, helping each other. But the minute you start to talk, somebody will turn around to look," she said. "They don't expect to hear a woman's voice."

The instructor—let's call him Hal—introduces himself and offers the class a preamble, telling us that the key to passing the Coast Guard's difficult engineering tests is to walk in with confidence. "That's what this course is for—to give you the confidence that you can pass." Hal looks to be in his seventies, stands about five-five, and when he walks to the front of the class, he lists a bit to starboard. Arthritis? I wonder. A stroke? He explains the structure of the course, then adds, "If you have any problems, ask the girls in the office." Most of the "girls" in the office are in their fifties, at least, and though I sometimes use "girl" in reference to myself (in that boys versus girls, schoolyard way), Hal's use of the word in this setting makes me slightly nervous. I chalk it up to a generational difference.

But his next comment offers little reassurance. "We don't often get ladies in this class, but we should have more," he says pointing in my direction. "We had one girl, she sat back there and she was smart as a whip." What does she have to do with me? I think, though I realize that with scarcity comes comparison. I am being pitted against, or paired with, some woman I've never met before, but I brush it off, figuring that testing new students to see where they stand is pretty typical first-day teacher behavior.

I keep my head down, flipping through the spiral-bound books that the "girls" in the office handed us when we checked in. One book, thick with text, includes pages photocopied from a navy manual, with sections about compression ratios, the viscosity of lubricating oils, and valve-spring vibration. There is a lot of new material here. The other is a book of illustrations that we might encounter on the Coast Guard exams. These worry me even more. Mechanical drawings use their own language of symbols to render three-dimensional objects on a two-dimensional page. For me, these illustrations are barely comprehensible.

Hal thrusts a stack of papers at me. "Here. Will you pass these out?" he asks me, specifically, even though to do so requires that he lean over between the guys in the front row. I take one sheet for myself, then, without getting up, pass a few sheets forward, and hand the rest of the stack to Tim, sitting to my left, who takes one and passes it on.

Hal turns on the overhead projector to display a page of long questions, each with a row of multiple-choice answers. He starts with number one: "The amount of fuel delivered by a helical plunger fuel injection pump is controlled by (a) varying the pump discharge pressure; (b) varying the pump return pressure; (c) rotation of the pump plunger; or (d) rotation of the pump barrel. Anyone think they have the answer?" No one raises his hand. "You," he says, pointing at me. "What's your name?"

"Jessica."

"Think you have the answer, Jessica?"

My face floods with heat. "Rotation of the pump plunger," I say, hesitantly. "C."

"Well, let's look and see. C. That's right."

Whew. Lucky break. Now I'm off the hook.

The next question comes to me too. "When comparing globe valves to gate valves, globe valves . . ." And the next one. Over and over. I get some right, some wrong. It doesn't matter. Either way the next one comes my way. Hal doesn't call on any other students. "Crank web deflection readings will give a positive indication of . . ."

Before long this absurd interrogation starts to seem like a bad comedy skit. The air conditioner hums, and every few minutes Hal reaches over to slide the thermostat up or down. I notice little balloons of flesh beneath his untucked, sky-blue polo that poke out above his waistband. The questions keep coming, and I feel all eyes on me.

"Next question. Jessica. Low horsepower, polyphase, induction motors can be started with full voltage by means of . . ."

✦ ✦ ✦

In my five years as a marine engineer, I've acquired a few strategies for managing the unwanted attention I endure because I'm female. When entering a new situation, I fortify myself against that look: *A girl engineer?* My chin locks. My cheek muscles tighten. My eyes steel. I find a neutral place to set my impassive gaze until people have appeased their curiosity so I can get on with doing my job. My blank expression opens no doors, offers no invitations, and that impenetrability allows me to get back to work faster. It's a way of letting the awkwardness roll off.

A carpenter I once interviewed for a story about women in nontraditional occupations described it best: "It's like you're constantly on a catwalk," she said. I knew instantly what she meant. She was describing that same weird watched feeling I'd had at the *Slater* during the first Hudson River trip. By this point I've grown accustomed to feeling like a caricature of myself whenever I step into a new environment. *Jessica: Fireboat Action Figure . . . Now with Posable Limbs!* But until now, the ways I'd been singled out for different treatment were relatively minor.

One of my first major lessons in how weird some men get about women doing "men's" work came at a shipyard in Norfolk, Virginia, in January 2003. Pamela (the tug captain from the first Hudson River trip) had hired Tim and me to come down to work on a 1933 steam-powered buoy tender named *Lilac*, which had recently been purchased by a preservationist group. Enlisted to help prep the boat for the tow to her new home in New York harbor, Tim and I were working to reposition an anchor. I had lifted a twenty-pound chain hoist above my head and was trying to clip the hook into a loop in the ceiling when two gloves reached over my head, grabbed the hoist, and yanked it out of my hands.

The gloves belonged to a yard employee known as Joe the Rigger.

"Here, I got it," he said, and I just stood there dumbfounded, frozen, my head racing: *Well, it's the yard's chain hoist, maybe there's some restriction about non-yard crews using yard tools. Well, he is a rigger— maybe he's required to do all the rigging. Well, maybe he just needs something to keep him busy away from the foreman.* I suspect, however, that Joe the Rigger would never, ever have taken a chain hoist out of a man's hands. Period. Tim watched me turn red, but I kept my mouth shut, not allowing myself to fume until after yard hours.

"If it happens again, just take it back," Tim counseled. "Say, 'It's okay, I got it.'"

The next time I worked in a shipyard, in Bridgeport in 2005, I was much less likely to have a tool pulled from my hands. Still, I braced myself. By then I understood what has been explained to me by multiple male friends when I asked for their help understanding the thought process: The first thing most (straight) men do when encountering a woman is categorize her as fuckable or not fuckable. And when I'm the only woman around, that objectifying attention is magnified. Thankfully, the men doing the categorizing don't usually share their verdict with me outright, but it's often not hard to pick up on their assessment.

Next, they often assume that I must be somebody's girlfriend who's come along for the ride. Rarely does someone jump to the conclusion, without some context, that I run the engines that brought us here. A girlfriend is peripheral, so I'm often presumed irrelevant until proven otherwise.

How you carry yourself says a lot. I've learned that to earn some guys' respect you have to play the game by their rules. Often a lot of the groundwork is laid in the little spontaneous circles of bullshit conversation. When the stories start bouncing back and forth, sometimes chiming in with a comment or story of my own is the best way to convey my experience and establish myself as just another worker on the job. I try to blend in.

I've dealt with a few issues aboard the fireboat and during my work on the tug, but only with outsiders, never crew. There was the guy who wiped his greasy hands on my pants, apparently confused about where his body ended and mine began. The balloon-animal artist who passed me a note asking me out while I was standing at the control pedestal, engines running. The female bank executive who slipped me her card after a trip. The numerous guys who have tried to kiss my hand instead of shaking it, or call me sweetie or honey instead of using my name.

All of these experiences have taught me a few things about how to divert unwanted attention. So when I find myself singled out in the engineering classroom, I try to use what I've learned.

✦ ✦ ✦

I start with the most basic tactic: reason. "Why don't you let these guys have a chance to show all they know," I propose congenially, after Hal asks me yet another question.

"Jessica," he continues, ignoring my suggestion, slinging yet another one my way. "Precision engine bearing inserts are manufactured with a small portion of the bearing ends . . ." The room is thick with tension.

I try humor: "You know, if I keep answering questions, they're all going to get mad at me, thinking you're playing favorites."

"I just want these guys to see how smart you are 'cause it will make them study harder," he replies. The students shift in their seats. From where I'm sitting, I can't see their reactions to the instructor's baffling behavior.

The chemical fumes from the new carpet hurt my head. I try keeping my eyes low, scribbling in my notebook—writing just to keep my hand moving. Little pills of pink eraser—tiny remnants of my mistakes—bounce across the fake-wood laminate surface of the desk. *Don't respond and maybe he'll get bored and go away.* My heart pounds.

Hal's tone and body language have kicked my head into a slide show of incidents from my past: My dad screaming at me after I messed up bolting the tire on my mom's car, the boys in high school who called out nasty things to me from the bench in front of their dorm, all the slights and lewd attention I've shrugged off in my years as an engineer—it all starts spiraling. I keep my eyes on the page, trying to focus on the words in the navy manual to reset my head.

"The purpose of a slew rate controller in a circuit . . ." Over the space of an hour and a half, the entire class period, the instructor directs every single question to me.

Finally, the lunch hour offers a reprieve. When I walk out of the classroom, I do my best to hide that I'm shaking. Tim follows behind.

Conversation between us is terse, covering little beyond the fact that a deli up the street might have sandwiches. I'm not hungry. I wait for Tim to say something, anything to acknowledge what the teacher has just put me through. This had gone way beyond some kind of let's-rib-the-new-guy ritual. I'm hoping for something as simple as, "Wow. That sucked." Or "I can't believe that guy is being such a dick." Or "Are you all right?" We're crewmates. We've been through some situations together, and I expect him to have my back.

Not that I expected him to say or do anything in the classroom. But now that we're outside, I look for some acknowledgment, some support. He's dumbstruck. My mentor, usually so ready to brainstorm a solution, doesn't know how to help, and I feel completely alone.

When I can no longer take the silence, I blurt out my fears—the swimming of my own head: "What am I going to do? The class is already paid for. I can't just walk away. But I don't know if I can stand two weeks of this."

I have to walk into the afternoon session with a plan. That morning I was caught off guard, but dealing with a known enemy calls for preparation. Choosing the wrong response could make this kind of targeting a thousand times worse, but I have to try my luck. But hey, maybe Hal's lunch break has given him a moment of clarity. Maybe he'll finally get over himself.

I keep my head down on the way to my seat, careful to avoid eye contact with any of the other students. As far as I know, every single one of them feels the same way Hal seems to—that I have no business being here. Right now, I don't even trust Tim. Hell, I don't even trust myself. Maybe I *don't* belong here.

The instructor enters the room and tells us to open the book of illustrations to number MO-0082. "Which of the operating characteristics listed is correct concerning the blower shown in illustration MO-0082?" reads the question. I study the curved black lines on the smooth white page. *This is a blower. Okay, now what are the choices?*

I read through the answers, sifting through phrases like "inversely proportional," "rotor housing," and "compression of air," hoping some clarity might appear.

Fight-or-flight instincts suppress any logical mental processing, making it hard to see through the hormone bath to the correct answer. I can feel Hal's eyes on my face. Red heat rises to my cheeks, and my heart clunks ragged in my chest. *Shut up*, I scold it. *You'll give me away.*

"You," I hear him say. "What do you think it is?" I don't look up. "What's your name?" I don't flinch. So Hal looks at Tim. "What's her name?"

"Jessica," says Tim. After all, what else can he do?

"Okay, I'll remember that," Hal replies. "So what's the answer, Jessica?"

"You don't have to remember my name. Maybe if you don't remember it, you'll stop calling on me," I say.

"Oh, I want to know your name. I want to know it so well it's the name I call out to my wife."

The gloves have come off. "Look," I say, trying to breathe, trying to lower the register of my voice so my words won't come out so pinched and tight. "*I* know I'm the only girl in the class. Everybody here knows it. But I'm not sure what your issue is. I'm just trying to learn the same material as everyone else. So can't we just get on with it?"

"Well, I just need to make sure you're getting it, since you don't have as much experience as the rest of these guys."

"How do you know how much experience I have? How do you know how much they have?" I later learn I have more sea time, and am gunning for a higher license, than at least half the students in the class.

For the first time, Hal shifts his gaze and calls on someone else: a guy from Aruba, who, although he will ultimately take the exam at home in another language, has come a long way to take this course. Presumably, he's hoping to learn something, not sit here watching some pissing match. "C," he says.

"That's right. Next question," Hal continues, adding, "Jessica," like it's a new idea.

"Aren't you bored?" I say. "I know the rest of these guys must be. I'm sure they came here to learn something."

"I'm not bored. I won't be bored for two weeks."

"I'm not answering any more of your questions."

"Fine. I won't call on you again. We'll see how you do on your test." He winks. I pray he keeps his word.

"You can see I have a way with the ladies," he says to the class, looking for a response. No one says anything.

He addresses me just once more that day: "And how's my favorite student doing? Are you with us?"

"Yes," I say. But the rest of the afternoon is a blur. The lines on the drawings, the letters on the white board, all run together. I can't focus.

When I was studying psychology at Stanford, I learned that sex-based stereotypes can interfere with intellectual functioning and performance. Studies show that women who are told a math test might reveal differences in their aptitude compared with men's perform worse than women who take the test without that predisposition. It's called stereotype vulnerability, which, as researcher Claude Steele explains, is "the unsettling expectation that one's membership in a stigmatized group will limit individual ability." This vulnerability might explain why highly skilled university women drop out of programs in math, engineering, and the physical sciences.

Poor performance, Steele argues, might result from distracting thoughts and the interference of anxiety ensuing from women's fear that their performance will reinforce negative stereotypes about their group. Rather than simply focusing on the task at hand, stereotyped groups seemed to suffer from divided attention that alternates between concentrating on the task and worrying about what their performance might mean. I've found myself living the research.

Once Hal singles me out, I'm no longer allowed to just be a student, like the guys around me. I'm thrust into the position of, somehow, representing all women. All that weight does not help my head stay focused on the work. Yet I am determined to succeed. To make a point.

That evening, after I find out the teacher is also the owner of the school, my hurt turns to venom. The good money that was spent on this class—which gives me every right to be here, every right to learn—is lining this man's pockets. Over dinner, I do my best to explain to Tim why I'm so upset by what happened. "If you had just been pissed off, I could have understood that," he tells me. But he doesn't relate to the isolation I feel in being targeted for my femaleness. He can't appreciate the impact of the cumulative damage from all the inappropriate comments I've brushed off over the years.

Most men have been singled out for attack at some time in their lives. But harassment that carries with it the force of centuries of subjugation of entire segments of the population has a different flavor. Such discrimination carries the institutional power of an entire culture behind it. Tim's life experience has provided no context for understanding it, and when I suggest that as the reason why he doesn't get it, he agrees.

But after he has a little more time to process, Tim offers his support in the best way he can—with a strategy. "The best thing you can do is prove him wrong by doing well," he says. And he promises to do everything in his power to help me.

I study like mad for the first in-class quiz—a practice test of sample questions pulled from the Coast Guard exams. My eyes burn from trying to focus on the tiny lines of schematic drawings, from staring, unblinking, as question after question scrolls across my laptop screen.

The disk I study from includes more than six thousand possible questions, and a staggering number of them have absolutely no bearing on my job (though in some cases the antique equipment Tim and I work with helps us answer the outdated questions that leave the rest of the class shaking their heads in puzzlement). There are questions about steam boilers, repairing refrigerated containers, and even whole series on MODUs (mobile offshore drilling units), commonly known as oil rigs. This collection of questions suggests one blanket test for many different engineering jobs. And I have no way of knowing which of these questions will end up on my exams.

Even though the scope of material is impossibly vast, at least this studying thing is familiar territory. How many all-nighters did I pull in high school?

Down in the hotel lobby I sit with Tim and another student from class and we talk through questions, hunting through old textbooks we've assembled on our own to try to locate background material and explanations, since the teacher not only doesn't provide them but forbids the class from bringing in outside material. Tim understands a lot of these concepts already, and makes sketches and devises analogies to help us understand.

The next morning, all that studying pays off. I not only pass, I earn one of the highest marks in the class, which I discover when Hal broadcasts our scores to the whole room. If I work hard, maybe I'll manage to grasp enough of this material to pass the actual exams.

A week or so into the course, a classmate confides, "It sucked what the teacher did to you." I thank him for saying something, explaining that I couldn't tell if everyone in the class agreed with him. Hearing him say "We didn't understand what the guy's problem was" is a relief.

✦ ✦ ✦

A week after I fly back to New York, I head to Boston for my Coast Guard exams. Contrary to Hal's stated objective—and my performance on his exams—I do not walk into the room confident I can pass. In fact, it takes all my concentration to keep from throwing up. For three weeks I've been churning through the material trying to wrap my head around the principles of refrigeration, electricity, and diesel. Every time I close my eyes, I see row upon row of potential test questions scrolling across my lids, as if on a screen.

I walk into the testing room. I sit down. I read the questions. I bolt to the bathroom. Fortunately, there's no limit to the restroom visits permitted during the test. I get up three or four times an hour over the course of the six-hour test. It's all I can do not to just keep walking, straight past the bathroom and out the front door. I stare myself down in the mirror. *Don't quit. Not now. Just get through this.*

In the end, I pass. But any sense of relief or accomplishment I might feel is tarnished when the test supervisor shows me the questions I got wrong. I can't believe some of the mistakes I've made. The clutter in my head had created an obstacle course for my thinking. But I passed, and now I just have to make it through five days of fire school.

✦ ✦ ✦

A month later, I'm standing poised and ready, my leather-gloved hands cupped around the charged hose that's so fat with water pressure it's difficult to hold. Black smoke rolls out through the metal shutters of the cement block building in front of me. The soles of my rubber boots sink deep into the soot-covered mud under the weight of the sixty pounds of gear I'm wearing: thick, three-layered pants with suspenders, a red turnout coat with yellow reflective tape, a knit hood under my hard-shelled helmet, and a self-contained breathing apparatus—the steel canister strapped across my back with hoses leading to my full-face mask. I'm encased head to toe, listening, in the pause of waiting, to the Darth Vader sound of my own breath through the regulator.

I stand second in line behind the nozzle man with two more men behind me—all of us holding on to the hose. My placement puts me in charge of the radio that's strapped into the slot in my coat. I listen for the instruction to move in. Word crackles over the Handie-Talkie and we blast through the doorway to hunt down the blaze and search out victims.

A quick sweep of the first floor reveals neither. "Hit the stairs!" comes the shout from one of the guys behind me, and the nozzle man spins around, tracing the hose back out the way we came in. Pulled from the front and pushed from the rear, I struggle to stay vertical as we tromp up the stairs, my feet threatening to slide out of my heavy boots. We round the corner to the second flight into a hallway choked with white smoke. My mechanized breaths come quickly. The harder my muscles work, the more oxygen they demand and the less time I'll get out of the air canister on my back before the telltale clicking signals that it's time for me to leave the smoke-filled building. I try to slow my breathing.

A voice on the radio garbles something I can't make out. The second team must, by now, have entered the building from the rear. My grip on the hose offers my only hope of not getting trampled, and I hesitate to let go with even one hand to operate the radio as we continue down the corridor, moving toward the heat. I can hardly feel the buttons through my gloves, so I paw blindly at the thing, calling out for a repeat transmission. "Go! Go! Go!" hollers the guy at the rear, slamming the front three of us into each other Stooges-like. As we approach an open doorway on the right, I hear a rushing sound, like wind, and a low crackle that grows louder with each step. We've found the fire.

The nozzle man shuffles into the room on his knees and I follow close behind, sliding my shins along the cement floor. A corner of the room is filled with flame. Hose in position, the two guys behind me break off to search the floor for victims. The nozzle man cocks the hose up toward the ceiling, preparing to quench the superheated gasses gathered there. "Ventilating!" I shout through my mask. I let go of the hose and crawl to a nearby window, swinging open the metal shutters. He slides the lever at the end of the hose, and the water hits the ceiling, condensing instantly into steam, then sending a cloud down to help smother the fire, starving it of air. The radio squawks again. "We're evacuating a victim from the second floor."

I fumble with the button. "Copy that," I say. Even with the window open, the heat from the steam banks down. Through the smoke, I can make out the other two members of my team hoisting the victim, carrying him down the hallway, struggling to maintain their grip. They rush by with seriousness of purpose as I crouch down to slide back into the room with the fire.

The "victim" is, in reality, a bundle of fire hose tied together, shaped into mock arms and legs. The fire we're fighting has been lit by our instructors, nothing more than a couple of bales of hay in a concrete "burn building" designed not to ignite. Still, this advanced firefighting class grants me new respect for the work real firefighters do every day.

✦ ✦ ✦

Two days before fire school, my back seized up, and I had no doubt that stress about the course had triggered the spasm. I feared being singled out again by the teacher or the students. It was one thing to be targeted in a classroom setting; here I'd be dealing with fire.

Over the next five days, according to the academy's Web site, I would learn search and rescue, ventilation, large-hose-line handling, confined-space rescue, multiple-story firefighting, and advanced firefighting tactics and strategy. "Students will spend large amounts of time in live firefighting," the page read.

Worry loves to fixate, and mine obsessed about gloves. If I just had the right equipment I might feel prepared, confident, like I had the right to be there—the very feelings that had been shaken by my encounter with Hal. I knew from experience that (a) finding gloves in my size was next to impossible, and (b) fingers flopping around in oversized gloves are next to useless for getting a job done. So I called the school and ended up speaking with the owner. I explained my small-hands problem and asked if it would be best if I searched out my own pair of fire-retardant gloves.

"Not to worry," he reassured me. "We have everything you'll need." His respectful manner offered some reassurance. But who knew what my teacher or my classmates would be like? My whole body had clenched up.

Pulling into the parking lot of the academy in March 2006, I could see the group of students gathered by the front door of the firehouse, some clutching paper coffee cups and a few smoking cigarettes. I wasn't ready to face them, so I just sat there in the driver's seat, wanting to forestall the moment when I put myself up for judgment. "Come on, Jess," Tim encouraged. "It's gonna be fine."

When the instructor summoned the group inside, I filed in behind them, entering a fire-truck bay that reeked of old exhaust. The parked truck sent me back almost a decade, to a time when I taught pre-school in San Francisco and the day a local fire company came to visit. We had shepherded the little ones outside for a glimpse of their gleaming cherry truck with its shiny chrome rims, nozzles, and other apparatus. Fire companies visit schoolchildren for all sorts of reasons, including familiarizing them with the trucks and the look of firefighters in their turnout gear so in the event of a future, smoky encounter the kids won't be so frightened. They probably also do it to plant seeds among the children so they might someday grow up to be firefighters. I'm pretty sure that the goal isn't to woo teachers to the trade, but that's exactly what happened to me, albeit briefly.

Naturally, it was the apparatus that lured me—the truck with all its pumps, gauges, and equipment. That and having seen firefighters—men and women—in my neighborhood, jogging in packs as they set out for nearby Golden Gate Park. I thought I might like to belong to a group that worked together in a physically demanding job that served the community. During a lull in the kids' questions, I asked one of the guys how one goes about becoming a firefighter. He kind of cocked his head, unsure of the impetus for my question, but told me where to get information about taking the civil service exam. I doubt he (or I) expected I would follow through, but I signed up to take the test. A few weeks after my appointment confirmation arrived, an acceptance letter from Stanford came, offering me the opportunity to finally finish my degree. I cast aside any future I might have had in firefighting. Now, more than a decade later, here I was in fire school, curious to see what I had missed out on . . . if I could just let go of the stress.

To my immense relief, the teacher, Sean, turned out to be a good guy and a great instructor. He treated us all as equals—exactly the approach that brings out the eager student in me. We learned that fire is defined as "rapid oxidation, with energy released as light and heat." He taught us the four classes of fire, its five stages of development—from ignition to decay, and how to prioritize the order of fire attack. We learned about ventilation, search and rescue, and lots more. Then it was time to get suited up with gear.

On the application the school had cautioned that students had to be in good physical condition, capable of intense physical activity while wearing sixty pounds of equipment. I ran semiregularly, lifted weights, and boxed off and on, so I figured I was up to the challenge. But until I tried to move in all that gear, I couldn't be sure.

On the way to the trailer where the school housed a whole warehouse of turnout coats, pants, and boots, the instructor joked with Tim and me, saying something about how the two of us defined both ends of the size spectrum for this class. Tim was no doubt the biggest, and I was the smallest, though there was one guy who was not much bigger than I. The teacher's good-natured humor allowed the knot in my back to soften. With coat, pants, and boots in place, it was time to get our gloves. Sean tossed me a pair, and they fit.

✦ ✦ ✦

I'm standing with my hose team, waiting outside the burn building for our last round of fire exercises. The instructors have disappeared inside the multistory building to hide dummy victims and ignite hay bales in various locations throughout the building. They complain that now they're allowed to burn only hay. "Before, we burned pallets. We burned tires. We got some ragers going then."

After a few quick, get-in, get-out exercises, Sean lights a big fire in a small room and has us kneel on the floor, letting it build. He wants us to experience the physicality of flames, which shoot in a column up to the ceiling from the corner in front of us where the fire began. When it reaches the ceiling, it spreads out, licking across in a parade of colors: blues and blacks, yellows and reds. The heat itself seems to take on different hues, as if manifesting in physical form. As the flames roll farther, spreading out above us, they move animal-like, consuming the superheated gases, then continuing on in a constant quest for more fuel. I can see why firefighters call it the Red Devil.

When the fire reaches the edge of the ceiling, it begins to climb down the wall behind us. I'm now surrounded on three sides, but I'm not afraid. The roar and crackle, the pops and sizzles all compete with the mechanical noise of my breathing through the regulator. I kneel there, awed by the colors and the raw power. The heat banks down and I start to sweat, but can't taste the smoke through my mask. My gear protects every inch of flesh, shielding me, allowing me to sit inside fire without being burned.

Then my regulator starts rattling to warn me I'm low on air. Time to go. "That you?" hollers Sean, and I nod. "Get out," he says. "I'll cover your spot." I hand Sean the Halligan, a multipurpose tool like a crowbar used to find and expose any smoldering or hidden pockets of fire, and head for the stairs. On my way down, a weariness hits me. The weight of the air cylinder, the boots, the heavy helmet compressing my neck—they offer a window into the exhaustion real firefighters work through during their real, life-or-death battles.

✦ ✦ ✦

A few weeks after I submit papers demonstrating my completion of Advanced Firefighting, I receive a certificate in the mail from the Coast Guard confirming I'm now a licensed engineer.

Come springtime, two FDNY Marine Division guys in dark blue polo shirts and shorts come by the fireboat for a friendly visit, asking to take a look at the engine room. They don't ask me questions—a lot of guys don't—but they seem interested, so I volunteer some details. I explain that the diesels are hooked to generators that power the prop motors, then rattle off a few more things about how the pumps are direct-drive and how I engage the air flex clutch to start the flow of water.

One guy concedes, "I'm just a firefighter on the boats." And I can see he clearly isn't grasping the details. But the second guy seems to be following along as I talk about the flexibility of the boat's design, praising the redundancy of the system that allows us to swap pumping and power to different engines as needed.

In a pause, he blinks at me. "Are you licensed?" he asks.

For the first time I say, "Yes."

Chapter Eleven

LOVE OF LABOR

∽

"WE'VE BEEN EVICTED," says John Krevey, proprietor of Pier 63 Maritime, the public pier and events space that's home to the *John J. Harvey*. It's May 2006, and I'm on the deck of the fireboat, at the top of the engine-room stairs, relishing the last few minutes of fresh air before being banished down below, when he comes to the edge of the pier to make his announcement. Engines are already running and a boatload of senior citizens sit waiting for their boat ride while Harry, the caterer, pokes at the barbecue, readying the coals for links of still-pink sausage that sit squished together in their vacuum-sealed plastic.

"All tenants need to be out by June seventh. So we're all out." By "we" Krevey means not only Pier 63 itself (which is actually a barge that can move) but all the boats that tie to the barge/pier, including this one. When he says it, Krevey's face conveys no discernible emotion. And then he duckwalks away, retucking the shirttails of his beige button-down into his blue jeans and tugging his belt unnaturally high above his waist. This day has been a long time coming, but that doesn't mean any of us imagined it would ever actually happen. What will happen to our Shangri-la? Where will *John J. Harvey* live?

✦ ✦ ✦

John Krevey's brain doesn't work like most people's. His tenacity has enabled his survival through two decades of turbulence along the Hudson's Manhattan shores. He has made a New York name for himself as the man who runs Pier 63 Maritime, which plays host to a hodgepodge of diverse events. On any given day, visitors can find a crawfish boil or a troupe of acrobats in full swing, hear paddlers chanting in Polynesian as they propel an oceangoing outrigger canoe, attend a tap-dance festival or Bahamian cultural celebration, view a photo exhibit hung on the walls of a caboose, or dance to hip-hop or house music in the cleared engine space of a once-sunken lightship. Whatever draws them initially, visitors also get a taste of the river and learn a bit about New York City's maritime heritage from signs that explain the background of the historic vessels moored here, including the fireboat. It was Krevey, in fact, who first encouraged Chase, Huntley, David, and friends to bid on the boat. On the *Harvey*, we call Pier 63 "Kreveyland." Krevey is the ringmaster, and Kreveyland his circus.

Some years back, Krevey bought a caboose from a guy near Steamtown, Pennsylvania, a mecca for railroad enthusiasts. His goal had been to set it up as an office for the pier, but the plan stalled briefly when a homeless woman took it over, barricaded herself in, and claimed the caboose as her own. "I know my rights," she said, launching into a creative, but faulty, legal argument. "I've taken up residence. You have to get a court order." Krevey managed to repossess the caboose, of course, and nonchalantly adds the incident to his long list of the bizarre hassles that come with running a public-access pier.

Krevey says that Pier 63 "just evolved." It was "never intended or conceived or created," but emerged as a series of tiny steps in a single direction. Krevey wanted to be on the water, and he thought people living on an island should have access to their shores. His struggle to maintain his pier put him at the center of a decades-long skirmish in the centuries-long battle that has been playing out along the Hudson since the earliest days of waterfront development.

"A lot of people do a lot of talking and planning that goes nowhere," says Krevey, who, over the years, has spent way too much time at community board meetings. "You could practically build a whole new waterfront if you added up all the time all these different groups have spent in meetings. You sit and talk to people who don't want to listen anyway. They've already got their agenda. Give me a shovel."

Krevey came to New York from Seattle in 1978. "In Seattle, waterfront real estate was the most expensive. But here real estate on the waterfront was the cheapest. I was an electrical contractor and needed a place to run my business, R2 Electric, so I rented a building at the foot of Pier 63. That was around 1981. Back then the waterfront was a dirty, rat-infested place. The building had garage doors with those old-style parquet windows. They were so dirty you couldn't see out. There was no interest in looking at the river. What could you see? Rats and dirt and pollution. Everybody knew back then that you couldn't possibly touch the river; you'd get all kinds of diseases. 'Who lives down there? Nobody. Who would go down there? No one.' That was the atmosphere I walked into in New York City twenty-five years ago." Since then, all that has changed. But the transformation began long before Krevey arrived.

✦ ✦ ✦

Change has been the single constant along Manhattan's Hudson River shore. Rocky bluffs and lush wetlands greeted Henry Hudson upon his 1609 arrival into what is now New York harbor's Upper Bay. While the New Jersey side of the Hudson River featured shallow tidal embayments, the New York side had rocky escarpments with deep water right up to the shore. Back then the Battery was separated from Manhattan Island's southern tip whenever the marshland between them flooded during high spring tides (determined not by the season but the positions of the sun and moon). These same high tides are reputed to have divided Manhattan farther north as well, flooding a swath of marshland near Corlears Hook (between the Manhattan and Williamsburg bridges) on the East River all the way through to where Fourteenth Street meets the Hudson.

When European colonists arrived, commercial pressures led them to fill in the marshlands and the irregular banks on both the Hudson and East rivers to create bulkheads and wharves. They dumped household refuse, and rocks and soil collected from land-leveling projects and basement excavations, and built docks that stretched out into the harbor. While the earliest waterfront development began on the East River because it was naturally better protected from winter ice floes, West Side development followed thereafter, and by 1800 most of Manhattan's southern tip was ringed, on both sides, with wharfs and piers.

Before 1856, the year New York City first established clear policies about how far piers could extend into the river, the waterfront's development had evolved based solely on the needs of individual businesses. Slaughterhouses and leather tanneries took advantage of the river as a convenient dumping ground for their noxious wastes, creating cesspools of filth and breeding grounds for diseases like typhus, cholera, and yellow fever. Given the foul ambience created by these industries, nearby residential areas devolved into teeming slums.

Any attempts to improve conditions were thwarted by power struggles within the labyrinth of independent agencies that each claimed jurisdiction over some part of the waterfront. Development stalled and the piers suffered. Initial conflicts that divided proponents of commercial and industrial uses and those advocating public access echoed throughout the course of Hudson shoreline development for the next century and beyond.

During the heyday of shipping, commercial interests always trumped any others in debates over waterfront use, since the obvious economic benefits that piers brought to the city overshadowed all other considerations. But when shipping began to decline, the power dynamics shifted. By the depths of the Great Depression in 1933, the tonnage of goods moving through New York harbor had been slashed in half, and New York City started turning waterfront property over to real estate interests and recreational uses. The maritime character of the Hudson's Manhattan shore began to fade.

New technologies pushed different priorities to the forefront of city planning. Car travel over the George Washington Bridge (completed in 1931) and the Holland and Lincoln tunnels (1927 and 1937, respectively) began to reduce ferry traffic. And bustling piers and streets lined with waiting cargo soon devolved into what Mary Beth Betts calls "a fragmented terrain of highways, bridges, esplanades, and parks under the disparate control of several city agencies."

In an endearing 1937 travelogue documentary called *Manhattan Waterfront*, the harbor's significance was proclaimed in florid detail in classic newsreel voice-over style:

The industries of Manhattan's magic waterfront are many-sided and never-ending. . . . The falling shadows of evening bring no silencing to its towering skeletons of steel and fast-dropping and -rising clam-shell buckets unloading barges of coal, sand, and gravel, or its great dry docks capable of lifting great ships so that men may work under their monstrous keels. . . . No age, no century in history, no place on any continent has known such a monstrous melting pot of human and industrial accomplishment as is clustered about the Manhattan waterfront.

Despite this aggrandized portrayal, Manhattan's industrial water-front had already begun to fade as the impact of the Depression rippled out to waterborne businesses. New, higher tariffs curtailed international trade, and financial pressures reduced transatlantic travel by more than half, from one million voyagers in 1929 to fewer than 500,000 by 1935.

A narrow island with clogged roadways and limited rail access was no place to move goods. Manhattan cargo handling had long defied the obvious practical obstacles. The crowded island lacked the space necessary to keep shipping on its shores and had no citywide infrastructure, like rail facilities linking shipping terminals to ware-houses. For this, some historians have blamed railroad executives too blinded by their own profit seeking to act collectively. They misman-aged freight facilities, and refused to establish the infrastructure that might have kept Manhattan shipping on the map longer.

New York harbor's infamous corruption also played a part in this commercial decline. In 1948 and 1949, Malcolm Johnson exposed the harbor as an "outlaw frontier" run by an organized crime syndicate that held the port in a stranglehold. His series, published in the *New York Sun*, was the basis for the Academy Award–winning film *On the Waterfront* (1954), in which Marlon Brando plays an ex-prizefighter turned longshoreman who struggles to stand up to his corrupt union bosses. Unchecked by law enforcement, the waterfront racket system of theft, extortions, and kickbacks tacked hundreds of millions of dollars onto annual freight costs, and those dollars helped drive busi-ness from Manhattan. Shipping on the island ended not only because of geographic reality and technological advancement, but as a casu-alty in the battle between public good and private greed.

As the decades progressed, ships and their cargoes grew larger and larger, which pushed more and more loading work to the less-crowded Brooklyn and New Jersey shores. Shipping was bound to move off the island once break-bulk (storing diverse cargoes side by side in open ship holds) was replaced by packing like goods into standardized boxes called containers. Manhattan real estate was deemed far too valuable to accommodate the acreage necessary for handling thousands of these 40 x 8 x 8½-foot boxes.

The shift away from break-bulk cargo and toward containerization was cemented in 1956 when trucking entrepreneur Malcom McLean inaugurated the U.S. container shipping industry by putting fifty-eight containers aboard a retrofitted tanker ship, the *Ideal-X*, and sailing them from Newark to Houston. Because they were equally suited to transport by truck, ship, and railroad, McLean's containers never had to be opened en route. This new system, developed here in the Port of New York/New Jersey, caught on worldwide, and the growth of containerization sealed Manhattan's fate. By the 1960s the island had ceased to function as a major port as shipping operations moved to nearby areas.

Commercial shipping had defined the Hudson's Manhattan waterfront for centuries. What would take its place? For decades that question provoked power struggles for leadership among different city, state, and community ·groups and agencies. Today one group, the Hudson River Park Trust, is determining the look and feel of Manhattan's western edge, and its vision has had huge repercussions for Krevey and his pier.

✦ ✦ ✦

Ten years after he'd moved in, Krevey was still living and working in a building with nothing more than a thirty-day permit. This was during the era of Westway, a massive federal project that proposed running an underground highway along Manhattan's West Side by dumping landfill between existing finger piers and tunneling through it. First planned in 1974, Westway became one of the most disputed public works projects in the nation before it was finally canceled in 1985. Had the Westway plan succeeded, Krevey's building would have been demolished. Instead, his lease limbo continued, so Krevey, being Krevey, bought a small, decrepit barge and filed an application with the state to open a marina.

"Here was this city on an island and there was virtually no boating," Krevey explains. "The few things around were in disrepair. The Seventy-ninth Street Boat Basin was full of dilapidated boats that didn't run. They were embroiled in lawsuits for having live-aboards. And there were no other marinas. Chelsea Piers was abandoned. There was no World Yacht. Commercial shipping was gone. The piers were falling into the river. And here I had a warehouse on a pier. Of course it was cheap; nobody wanted it because the river had a stigma. So I thought we should start a marina."

He wrote to the state office charged with permitting such things, explaining that he intended to build his own docks and put some boats in. The state, remarkably, agreed. "The marina was never very successful financially, but I did this for years," Krevey says.

If Krevey was going to run a marina, he figured he should have a boat. Fortunately, fate provided him with one, in the form of a 1920s wooden cabin cruiser that had sunk at his dock. "It wasn't much to look at when it came in, but it had two diesel engines that ran." The owner gave up on it after it sank, but Krevey decided to raise it. "I got some pumps and raised it up and got the engines going." He put a little money toward fixing it up, and named it the *Useless*. "But I did use that boat," he says. "We went to Fire Island in that old junky cabin cruiser, and I became a boater. This boat became a big focus for friends, a whole social, community thing. And I had a nice place to keep it where no one seemed to care." The boating bug that bit Krevey has afflicted many, but rarely have the symptoms of illness reached the glorious level of derangement that Krevey soon exhibited.

The *Useless* would not see the sun for long. Eventually it settled at the bottom of the Hudson, where it stayed, for good this time, to become a home for marine life—its wood planks feeding crustaceans called marine borers that burrow into ships, piers, and other wooden structures in salt water. "A friend of mine who had been in the Coast Guard told me one day, 'You know, John, wood is food.' That stuck with me. I figured I'd better switch to metal." So he did.

The sunken vessel he fell for next was a 1929 United States lightship that had served as a floating lighthouse before it shoaled over in Whitehaven, Maryland, on the Chesapeake Bay's Eastern Shore. In the 1980s, Krevey's electric company was doing better than ever. "I was financially successful and of course no one is content with that," he says, laughing. "But it wasn't like I had enough money to go to the boat show and buy a forty-foot sports fisherman for a quarter of a million dollars—you know, buy a normal boat." And besides, that wouldn't have been very Krevey-esque. "I started to get interested in lightships. These were historic boats. They weren't making them anymore, and there weren't many left. Lightships were a part of American history, and I have a very strong sense that historic things are the most beautiful things," he explains. "All I needed was to find a good hull." The reality—that he had no permanent claim to the waterfront space he was occupying—didn't seem to faze him. Nor did the fact that he wouldn't be able to park his new boat along the seawall like he had the *Useless*, since the water there was only three or four feet deep, and a lightship would need twelve.

A diver who knew the Whitehaven lightship assured Krevey the vessel's hull was like new. Named *Frying Pan* after the Frying Pan Shoals, thirty miles off Cape Fear, North Carolina, where it served from 1930 to 1965, the ship had worked warning mariners of shallow water. Fifteen men had lived aboard to keep the light atop the sixty-five-foot mast burning and the foghorn at the ready. When Krevey first saw the *Frying Pan*, it was sitting on the bottom, but not fully submerged. After years of neglect, the ship had rolled to a forty-five-degree angle. "At low tide the skylights were above water, but at high tide the only thing sticking out was the mast," he recalls. Even Krevey knew pursuing this boat was nuts: "This was one of those things that you just have to be crazy to do. *I* even thought I was crazy," he concedes. "How can I buy a 133-foot, six-hundred-ton boat when I have no place to take it? But a fixer-upper is my kind of deal. So I bought the *Frying Pan* for eight thousand dollars."

This was a stupid idea. Krevey likens it to dating someone you know you shouldn't "when everything's bad about this person, but they have a nice smile or something that attracts you and it's just what you want to do and there's no stopping you even though there's no logic to it. That's what this was." What helped him justify the purchase was an article he read about a lightship-bell collector who had paid $10,000 for a ship's bell. Krevey knew *Frying Pan* had a thousand-pound brass bell engraved with "1929 United States Lighthouse Service." That had to be worth at least ten grand, he thought. "My devil side and angel side were arguing. I just decided I was buying this bell with a boat attached."

His other justification was that the boat would be his summer home. Instead of real estate, he'd invested in "aquastate" for which he'd pay no property taxes. "I used to tell people, 'My summer house moves faster than your summer house!' That pretty much summed up what I felt about having this boat. I could move to any state and anchor offshore, which I proceeded to do for the next three years. There was no plan and no purpose. It simply existed and there was no rent to pay as long as I was offshore." But *Frying Pan* was no yacht. Even after he raised it and mucked out tons of silt and shells from the inside, the ship was far from turnkey. When Krevey got the boat, the motors and generators had already been stripped out. So, until he hooked up a replacement engine, *Frying Pan* was dead in the water. Boarding the ship while it was at anchor was no picnic either, given the ship's high sides, which had been designed to withstand the storms and hurricanes that sent other ships to safer harbors.

Friends would join him in the summertime. "It had twenty-six rooms. Plenty of space for guests," he explains. *Frying Pan* spent a year in Baltimore, a year in Philadelphia, and a summer in Annapolis, Maryland. "We were out there sitting in the harbor on this old rusty boat with all these beautiful yachts going around us. It was great!"

Come wintertime, though, Krevey made the three- or four-hour drive to look after the boat alone. "It was pretty rugged. It would be twenty degrees out and I'd be in a sleeping bag with no heat. It was just what I did. I was young and tough and it was my boat and I loved it. Well, you know what it's like," he says, gesturing in my direction. "You're in the engine room and it's hot and messy. If you were to describe it to anyone else, there'd be nothing appealing. That's the lost art of getting your hands dirty. This wasn't a labor of love, it was the love of labor—being on the water and building something, which is maybe something certain Americans have lost touch with. I was industrious and wanted nothing better than to work in these miserable conditions. And what I learned about survival on that boat I now take to running a successful business in ways I could never describe." Today, Krevey attributes all his subsequent success to this one decision, to buy the *Frying Pan.*

✦ ✦ ✦

In his stubborn self-sufficiency, I can't help but see Krevey's pioneering efforts on the waterfront as a throwback to the efforts made by Manhattan's first settlers (and other early Americans), people who charted their own destinies in a no-man's-land along the shore. The earliest New Yorkers grew and cooked their own food, made their own clothes and shoes, forged their own tools, built their own houses, and shod their own horses. In the eighteenth century, the typical family consumed at least 75 percent of the goods the household produced. Whatever they couldn't provide on their own, they bartered for with neighbors. But as our fledgling nation developed infrastructure and industry, this subsistence-based existence gave way to a market economy—first-world, but dependent.

In today's postindustrial economy, when the U.S. is losing the facilities and the know-how to produce many of the goods we use every day, our dependence on exports from foreign nations to maintain our way of life suggests a new kind of vulnerability.

At the height of the Great Depression in 1933, one in four Americans who wanted to work was unable to find a job. Images of the day show men clustered outside shuttered factories and city employment offices—the sheer numbers of them a grim indication of just how unlikely it is that they'll ever be put to task. In the 1930s, before modern safety nets like food stamps and welfare, and when basics like food and clothing were significantly more expensive, faith in personal responsibility prevailed.

The American dream was predicated on the notion that one's individual merits determined one's station in life. But the Depression's bankrupting of rich and poor alike rattled the core of American values. Suddenly being a hard worker wasn't enough to succeed. When the stock market crashed, laborers were thrust into a new economic landscape where it wasn't so much about what you could make but what you could sell. During these dark days, survival demanded creativity and resourcefulness—the same qualities required of the Hudson River Valley's earliest settlers and later waterfront pioneers like Krevey.

✦ ✦ ✦

After three years of gallivanting around, anchoring in different cities, Krevey decided it was time to take advantage of *Frying Pan*'s potential as an events space. So in 1990 or 1991, he and three friends, Eddie, Simon, and Bebop ("That's the only name we ever knew him by. He was a nightclub bouncer"), decided to bring the ship up the Chesapeake Bay and through the Chesapeake and Delaware Canal to New York City. A wild winter voyage ensued (involving *Frying Pan* getting lodged in what Krevey calls "a one-billion-pound ice cube" so that the crew had to walk a mile across the frozen Chesapeake to reach land to buy more food—in this case, doughnuts—) before the lightship finally arrived in New York harbor. And, of course, Krevey still had no place to park the thing, since the water at the bulkhead behind his electrical shop was too shallow. Nor did he have a lease.

"We got bounced around from spot to spot," Krevey recalls. "We anchored behind the Statue of Liberty for about a year, and we anchored six months to a year off the Seventy-ninth Street Boat Basin." *Frying Pan* needed a real home. Krevey decided to buy a barge to use as a makeshift pier. Installed at the bulkhead behind his shop, the barge would become Pier 63, located just north of the once-famous Chelsea Piers, lauded in the early twentieth century as among the greatest achievements in Hudson River waterfront development history.

The push to build along the shore began after authority over the waterfront was granted to the Department of Docks. From Gansevoort Street north to West Twenty-second Street, the department constructed a row of magnificent buildings with long-span steel trusses and grand, sculpted exteriors embellished with pink granite facades. These large, modern piers, designed by the architectural firm of Warren and Wetmore (which was simultaneously designing Grand Central Terminal), reflected the working harbor's crucial importance to New York City. Officially opened in 1910, thirty years after the initial proposal, the Chelsea Piers were seen as Mayor George B. McClellan Jr.'s dream come true for "waterfront with an architectural appearance worthy of the city."

On these piers, after disembarking from White Star and Cunard luxury liners, the glitterati posed for the paparazzi, who obliged them with popping flashbulbs and pictures in the paper. Other arrivals—immigrants who boarded ferries bound for Ellis Island to be processed before establishing new American lives—received considerably less attention.

For decades Chelsea Piers thrived, but history often better remembers tragedy. Some of the Piers' landmark occasions were characterized by misfortune, such as the arrival at Pier 54 of the *Carpathia* in April 1912 with 675 survivors of the *Titanic* aboard. The *Titanic*, the largest passenger steamship in the world at the time, had been bound for Pier 59 at West Twentieth Street when she struck an iceberg on her maiden voyage and sank.

Three years later, in May 1915, the luxury liner *Lusitania* departed from Chelsea Piers. A few days later it was torpedoed by a German U-boat off the coast of Ireland, killing 1,198 people, including 124 Americans—deaths that mobilized public opinion in support of the United States' entry into World War I.

These events, though tragic, bore no direct impact on the Chelsea Piers themselves, but the stock market crash of October 29, 1929, was a harbinger of port decline. A few days after the crash, when the Cunard Line's ship *Barengaria* docked at Chelsea Piers, throngs of reporters pounced on arriving passengers to ask what it felt like to have departed on their voyage wealthy and returned bankrupt.

Decades later, the Chelsea Piers declined, eventually becoming another neglected maritime ruin on Manhattan's waterfront. This was the decrepit Hudson shoreline that Krevey originally found, but within a few years of his arrival with *Frying Pan*, the four surviving piers were redeveloped for recreational, instead of industrial, use in accordance with New York City's shifting priorities.

For fifty years the Chelsea Piers had served New York City's working waterfront needs, but now they are a thirty-acre playland, opened by private developers in 1995 and operated under the

Chelsea Piers name. Today's visitors enjoy batting cages and driving ranges, massages and ice hockey, catered events and children's parties—activities that could happen anywhere in the city, since few are water-dependent. The trend away from using waterfront property for water-specific uses poses an ever-growing threat to New York City's maritime heritage.

✦ ✦ ✦

To park *Frying Pan*, Krevey needed a barge. So he went knocking on doors in Staten Island. Any barge in good condition was way out of his price range, so he chose one that was full of holes. "It's not that there wasn't a vision; it just wasn't a very practical one," Krevey concedes. "The barge had fifteen compartments. The same as the *Titanic*, and it was headed in the same direction as the *Titanic* too," he says, laughing. "When I first got it, you couldn't walk across the deck without worrying about falling in. It had soft patches everywhere, but we fixed all the leaks." Krevey's new purchase was actually a particular kind of barge, called a car float.

Car floats were once a key component of Manhattan shipping. Since the island lacked sufficient, integrated rail freight lines, goods that arrived by rail came to New Jersey, then crossed the Hudson to Manhattan via car float—essentially a long, flat-decked, steel barge with two or three sets of train tracks on it. Just as railroad passengers crossed the river on ferries, so, too, did boxcars. They were rolled onto barges mounted with rail tracks, then a tug would tow the loaded barge across the river.

Typically the tug nestled between two car floats with their bows lashed together, "like a gentleman with a lady on each arm," reports Tom Flagg in his book, *New York Harbor Railroads in Color*. This configuration required tricky maneuvering, but New York tug crews got lots of practice, as more railroad freight cars traveled by car float in New York harbor than in all other places combined. In 1937, 5,300 cars per day were moved this way. And even during the decline of the early 1960s, 1,600 cars still made the trip across the Hudson each day.

Once his car float barge was delivered by tugboat, Krevey secured it so the short end met the land behind his building and the long end reached out into the river, creating a makeshift finger pier. With this he succeeded in extending his domain out onto the river. He moored *Frying Pan* in deep water, and opened his barge-cum-pier for public access. And the public came. Where else could you sit on a "pier" that rose and fell with the tide, sipping a beer while watching the boats go by? Pier 63 wasn't just *by* the river, it was *on* the river. Boats came too. Not long after Krevey got the barge in place, a diverse fleet clung from all sides—from sailboats to tugs to lightships to fireboat *John J. Harvey*.

When I first visited the fireboat in 2001, Krevey's public-access Pier 63 Maritime had already been operating for about five years, and year by year his facilities continued to grow. The bar expanded to offer snacks and, later, a full restaurant menu. Krevey and a crew of welders built enclosures over the end of the barge, and a roof overhead so the space could be used in any weather. He rented out the barge and *Frying Pan* for everything from international heritage festivals to hip-hop dance parties. Part of the magic of Kreveyland was how it brought together disparate people, all drawn by the offbeat ambience and access to the Hudson.

Once the eviction order came down in May 2006, all this was in jeopardy. Krevey knew it was only a matter of time, but he hoped there would be space for his public-access pier in the newly developing Hudson River Park.

In 1998, the New York State legislature established a new agency, the Hudson River Park Trust, and granted it authority over the riverfront land on Manhattan's West Side. Charged with creating a five-mile waterfront park from Battery Place to Fifty-ninth Street, the agency began to transform Manhattan's Hudson shoreline.

Krevey's troubles stemmed from the fact that the jumbled, rusty, theater-set aesthetic of Pier 63 Maritime didn't fit with the Park Trust's dreams of a park with grass, trees, and stainless steel, which included little evidence of New York's maritime heritage. The group had inherited Krevey and his project, and by many accounts, they were none too pleased. While some members offered support, others seemed to go out of their way to squeeze him out, a task that proved to be more difficult than some might have imagined.

✦ ✦ ✦

Moving day, June 7, arrives but Krevey isn't leaving. He's secured an eleventh-hour stay of execution until the end of the summer so he can at least keep the pier open through the rest of the season. In exchange, he agrees to clear the whole north side of the barge to make way for demolition crews assigned to tear down Pier 64, one of the few remaining historic covered piers along Manhattan's Hudson River shore. Clearing the north side is no small feat, but an important compromise that Krevey hopes will ease tensions with some members of the Park Trust.

Krevey's barge is massive, about the length of a football field. Hanging off every inch is a vessel of one sort or another. Krevey's longstanding generosity has led to an accumulation of boats over the past several years. In addition to *Frying Pan* and *John J. Harvey*, there is a vintage ex-NYPD police launch called *Big G.*; a ketch called the *Laissez Faire* (which someone who works on the pier has redubbed the Lazy Ferret). Then there's the schooner *Anne*, whose captain and shipwright Reid Stowe began planning in 1986 to embark on the longest voyage in history: A Thousand Days Non-Stop at Sea, "living on the sea instead of the land" for the duration of the 2.74-year voyage, without refueling, resupplying, or pulling into any harbor.

Each boat on the north side comes with an assemblage of clutter—accoutrements such as concrete floats, sanitary lines, and fixed gangways. All these vessels strung together with a mass of lines look like an exploded bottle of Silly String. And yet Krevey has a plan. He'll move *Frying Pan* from the north side of the pier around the end to the south side, where *John J. Harvey*'s berth had been. The other boats on the north side will need to find new accommodations, but *Harvey* will tie up alongside the lightship.

This move has been planned for high water because who knows if *Frying Pan*'s bow can cut through the mud and silt that have accumulated over the years. There was talk of sending a diver down to scope out the subaquatic terrain, but that hasn't happened. Instead, Krevey fires up *Frying Pan* and hopes for the best.

When I arrive at the pier, Krevey has already made it around the end of the barge and is cruising along the south side. "And you said we needed a tugboat," he yells in my direction, when he sees me watching. "Hah!"

In honor of today's move, Krevey wears a white pocket T-shirt that spells out "FRYING PAN" in big blue block letters across the back, and a skipper's cap, white with a black braid above the shiny black brim. Operating under her own power is an uncommon occurrence for a boat that, depending on the whim of city inspectors on any given day, has variously been certified as a permanently moored vessel and a building. Today *Frying Pan* is acting distinctly boatlike: coughing black smoke out the stack, kicking up water behind the propeller, and curling back layers of mud on the river bottom with its pointed bow.

All the while, Krevey whirls around. "Slack out that line. Quick! Before we lose it!" He doesn't exactly bark—his voice peels out too high and tight to qualify as barking—but he spins on the heels of his brown leather shoes, heading aft, then forward, then aft again, reconsidering each move faster than his feet can heed his contradictory wishes.

His "deckhands" are even less responsive than his feet—not out of insubordination but inexperience. Krevey always has a gang of workers available on the pier to run his restaurant and bar, and handle the construction of barge improvements he's always dreaming up. A few of his employees, mostly short, strong, immigrant men, come highly skilled, like the fine-featured welder, Shafiek Mohamed, who learned his trade on a Guyana beach where captains ran their steel-hulled vessels into the sand for repairs. The welders would wait for the tide to go out, then rush in to patch holes that had to be sewn up before the tide came in and floated the boats again. On Pier 63 Shafiek is famous for patching a gusher in the corroded skin of the barge by stuffing T-shirts in the hole while he welded, seemingly unfazed by the water rushing up past his knees. Krevey's other workers change from week to week—hardworking men in perpetual motion. Their challenge today is playing deck crew.

"Bring that line forward," Krevey yells at the guy on the stern deck, who is fruitlessly, and dangerously, attempting to hold the 632-gross-ton ship steady by tugging on a sun-faded yellow polypropylene line with just one turn around the bitt.

Meanwhile, the nose of the boat creeps forward toward the back of Krevey's office, where a wooden deck, littered with planters, juts out over the water. Fifteen feet, twelve feet . . . The boat inches closer toward its own reflection, which shows in the deck's glass doors. Krevey is looking the other way. "It's not coming. Let's winch the stern in." He hails the bow man to a spot amidships where an extension cord dangles. The stem inches nearer: ten feet, nine feet . . . The bow man curls a single turn of the stern line around the winch, but the winch won't move. It has no juice. Krevey dives into the engine room to rejigger the electricity.

The lightship looks even more mammoth as the sharp bow cuts through the mud in the spot the fireboat has occupied for so many years. *John J. Harvey*, red and white like the lightship, looks Lilliputian in comparison, though the boats are about the same length. Not only does *Frying Pan* plunge four feet deeper below the waterline, but the air space she fills is enormous. The difference in scale registers even more clearly from where I stand, as the hull blots out some of the sky and most of the silhouette of two tugs tied up one pier away.

Finally the bow comes to a stop three feet away from the wood deck. Krevey and his crew make fast lines, and the north side of the barge is clear. Now that he has acceded to the wishes of the Park Trust, maybe, just maybe, they'll work out a space for his rusty Shangri-la in the midst of their stainless steel.

Chapter Twelve

SINKING

Repairs and Reparations

∿

In May 2005 I woke from a dead sleep, sobbing, my face, hair, and pillow soaked with tears. I had dreamed *John J. Harvey* was sinking. Once I composed myself enough to reboot my cognitive processes, I realized the boat was, at that moment, about as far from sinking as it had ever been since the day I'd first been aboard. For some weeks the boat had been sitting on blocks in the shipyard, out of the water and up on dry land. I figured the nightmare was a result of my newfound intimacy with the physical substance of the boat and my growing awareness of her vulnerability. By then I had a sense of the materials with which she had been constructed, patched, and protected over the years. I understood their properties, their potentials for failure.

✦ ✦ ✦

For the past three weeks, I've been working with Tim and a crew of volunteers in Kingston, reconstructing the aft tower—the fifteen-foot-high structure on the back deck upon which three deck guns sit. It's August 2006 and we are exhausted. The tower, made of steel, has been rapidly melting away, approaching becoming what Tim calls "just a mirage."

The problem with joyride water displays in the lower Hudson is that salt water eats steel. Every time we spray salt water, we bathe the boat in a corrosive solution that burns its skin, creeping into every opening in the paint, digging into the metal, altering it at the molecular level. Every pinprick of rust grows, bubbling up the surrounding paint, which exposes additional steel to the elements. Like cancer, rust spreads.

As engineers on a preservation project, our job is to retain as much of the original fabric of the boat as possible. That means we can't simply rebuild the tower outright. Instead we cut away the rotten parts, like salvaging bad fruit. Using an acetylene torch, we burn out small, rectangular sections and weld in pieces of new steel. The immensity of the job means I get lots of practice with the torch and learn how to weld. Days spent climbing up and down the tower ladder in the sun, hefting hammers, pry bars, welding leads, and cutting torches, along with my helmet and gloves, are nothing like working in the shade of my engine-room hole. I roast in my brown suede welding sleeves and bib. My face breaks out from the sunscreen I apply twice a day, and from wiping the sweat from below my cutting glasses with a dirty-gloved hand, or a bandanna dunked in old, melted cooler ice, which jams more crud into my pores. The skin around my mouth dries out from the welding gasses, chapped like it's winter, and in moments of concentration I catch myself chewing the peeling skin on my lower lip.

At the deck level, we shovel sand from the sandblasting and haul ice-filled coolers, and the cases of spring water that keep us hydrated. We sweep wet sand off the deck with that stiff-bristled push broom with the handle that keeps spinning off again and again. Over the past three weeks, I have vanished into the space of the work and begun to feel like a machine with no space for emotion. I process only thoughts that get the work done—cutting and welding pieces onto the tower and managing our resources: allocating time, supplies, and bodies to the tasks at hand. When it comes time for the seven-hour trip south back to Pier 63, my inner reserve tank is running on empty.

Once we finally pull off the dock and I have no choice but to stay in one spot, I'm relieved to be back in my hole, out of the sun, eyeing my gauges, just waiting for Bob to ring down the next command. I'm glad to be down here with the throttles, levers, and gauges. I no longer have to manage or cajole anyone, or hunt down replacement equipment for volunteers when their tools break. All I have to do is drive.

But then Tim comes forward from the back of the engine room, a dark expression on his face. He leans in to my ear so I can hear him above the engines: "We're taking on water."

My first thoughts are, Oh, God. From where? And how much? But Tim doesn't stick around to give me answers. I jump up, charged and ready to act, but can do exactly nothing. I have to stay here at the control pedestal to respond to Bob's commands while Tim darts around collecting rags, then dashes to the back of the engine room. I follow his trajectory to try to get a sense of where the water's coming from, but I can't make out anything from here.

I try to stay put, but can't stand not knowing what's happening. After a quick glance back at the gauges, I sprint down the walkway between engines, back to where the propulsion motors live, yanking my silver Maglite out of its holster and spinning the lens to focus the light. I point the skinny beam into the bilge, lighting up the shiny waterline on the frame beneath the prop motor to gauge how fast the river is coming in. It's hard to tell. Then I shine the light all the way aft to where Tim is crouched over, stuffing rags into holes in the perforated bulkhead.

He moves methodically, not frenzied or panicked, and it eases my mind a bit to see his focus despite the cloud of fatigue through which we've both been stumbling. I can see he's making progress stopping the flow. Reassured that he hasn't gotten himself stuck in any machinery, I bolt back to my spot.

A bulkhead is a dividing wall or barrier between different compartments in a boat, and the one into which Tim is currently stuffing rags is supposed to be watertight. But it, like so many of this poor boat's structures, has wasted over time. Because the bulkhead forms the forwardmost wall of a ballast tank we never use, the repair hasn't been a top priority. After all, it's not like the holes opened up to the river, just to an empty tank. The question now is, Why is that empty tank suddenly filling with water?

Tim doesn't stop to update me on his way up the engine-room stairs. I stand poised, doing my job, but still feel useless as I wait for whatever signal will come down from the wheelhouse. In the pause, my mind replays stories from newspaper clippings I've read over the years in which the engineers die.

Nine of Her Crew Killed
Machinists and others were in the engine room . . . of the American Line Steamship *St. Paul* . . . when the explosion happened. [December 19, 1895]

Wrecks of Great Fire-Scathed Ships
Fifteen members of the engineers department of the steamship *Main* after they had lain for nearly eight hours in an empty coal bunker in the bowels of the blazing ship, the vessel being for all that time in the very vortex of the conflagration. Brass and copper within a few feet of their prison melted, and ran like water. [July 2, 1900]

Old Ferryboat Sunk by a Sea-Going Barge
Adolphus Barker, an oiler . . . got caught in the engine room by the inrush of water . . . went down with the ferryboat. [December 30, 1906]

And then there was the electrician on the *Muenchen*. Twenty-three-year-old Gustav Franke, third electrician, was last seen at his post, attempting to effect repairs on a damaged generator after the lights went out following the first explosion. In the papers the next day his name appeared, alongside John Harvey's, in a two-person list of the dead.

✦ ✦ ✦

While I busy myself with my doomsday ruminations, Tim has gone up to the wheelhouse to consult with Bob. It's time to make a decision. Up ahead is the Mid-Hudson Bridge in Poughkeepsie, where a handful of people who rode the train to meet the boat are waiting to take the ride back to Manhattan. Meanwhile, the wheelhouse is crowded with tourists. Tim doesn't want to alarm them, but he has to communicate what is happening to Bob. "Bob, we're sinking," he whispers.

"What?" says Bob.

"We're sinking," Tim says, a little louder.

"What?!?"

Then Tim blurts the words out, and all the heads snap around. The two of them debate: Should we go to straight to the shipyard now, or turn around and go to Kingston? Tim calls Huntley to get his vote.

Down below, I monitor the rising water, dashing every few minutes to the rear of the engine room with my flashlight, then running back to the stand. The level seems to have risen more than an inch since my first look, which can't have been more than ten or fifteen minutes earlier. There isn't much I can do about it, but the checking makes me feel better. At the very least, I want to know well in advance if the water plans to make contact with the propulsion-motor commutators.

Only a few feet of air space now remains between the rising water's surface and those huge, rotating drums lined with copper bars, each of which seethes with 625 volts of DC. Fortunately, since we're far enough north that the river is still fresh instead of salt, the conductivity of the water, and therefore the risk of electrocution, is greatly reduced. But, if the water hits them, the whole electrical system could short out, leaving us dead in the water.

Considering the vulnerability of the commutators makes me think about a top-secret basement in New York City during World War II. Known as M42, it contained the AC to DC converters used to supply electricity to Grand Central Terminal. Guards were instructed to shoot on sight any unauthorized personnel in the area, since sabotage to the equipment would stop all train service, and with it halt all troop movements across the Eastern Seaboard. The military understood that because the copper-covered commutators spun out in the open air, a weapon as simple as a bucket of sand thrown on the equipment would be enough to cripple the whole system.

The telegraph bell startles me. Both propellers have been blazing Full Ahead. So when Bob rings down for Half Astern on the port side and Full Ahead on the starboard, the whole boat shakes as she jerks around, making a full about-face in the water and confronting her own wake. With this maneuver I know the decision has been made. It looks like the passengers at Poughkeepsie will be taking the train back home again too. We are heading back to Kingston.

From our spot in the river, Kingston is eleven nautical miles away, while the nearest shipyard, in Staten Island, is more than sixty. Huntley calls ahead to Feeney's, a workboat-repair facility two and a half miles up Rondout Creek in Kingston, owned by brothers Tim and Sean Feeney. Tim Feeney tells Huntley they'll be standing by with pumps.

Meanwhile, the onboard bilge pump is working its heart out to keep up with the incoming water, but falling behind. Still, the rate of inflow stays pretty even. Whatever hole has let the river in doesn't seem to be getting any bigger. Good thing. We still have more than ten miles to go.

On deck there's a general buzz of confusion about why we've turned around, but no panic. Tim makes it clear that the situation is under control. Somehow the steady flow rate, combined with the fact that the Feeney's crew is waiting for us at the other end, throws an odd sense of calm over the whole affair. Sinking—at least this slow-motion version of it—is nothing like I expected. Here we are, actively taking on water, and all we can do is run the boat toward safety.

Before long I notice the whole engine room (which means, of course, the whole boat) has sloped down at the stern. The back of the boat is sitting so low in the water that everything—gauges, levers, and portholes—is cocked back at an unfamiliar angle. It's like I've been driving a car, looking at the dashboard from the same vantage point, for years, and then somebody suddenly tips the seat a few notches forward, skewing my perspective by a few degrees. The next time Tim steps within hearing range, I summon him over to make a suggestion. "Think we should shift the fuel to the forward tanks?" I ask.

"Good idea," he says, and goes back to open and close some valves in the manifold to let the fuel gravity feed from the stern tanks into the belly tank. Slowly the angle pitches back closer to normal. This maneuver grants a welcome six inches of additional clearance between the prop motors and the water level in the bilge.

As promised, the Feeney's crew is ready with pumps when we arrive.

But it takes time to pull out enough water to identify the source of the leak: a hole in the pipe that encases one of the propeller shafts on its way through a tank in the stern. A fist-sized chunk of the pipe (called a stern tube) has rusted away and fallen out, giving the river a straight path into the boat through the cutless bearing—the bronze sleeve that supports the shaft where it penetrates the hull.

This is no small, manageable hole in the hull that we can address with a temporary, in-water patch. This repair will require a huge undertaking: pulling off the propellers, separating the couplings that join the propeller shafts to the propulsion motors, and sliding the shafts out of the boat. This work, without question, necessitates a trip back to the shipyard a year earlier than planned. And since Feeney's small yard is fully booked, we'll be heading back to Bridgeport. Our season has come to an abrupt end.

✦ ✦ ✦

On December 5, 2006, when we pull into the shipyard that treated us so well last time, it feels like a homecoming of sorts. We know some of the workers. There's Obie, running the toggles of the travel-lift controller, and Norman, the tall Jamaican guy who's always cracking jokes. It all seems promising. Then one of the shipyard engineers approaches me as I stand alongside the travel-lift pit watching the boat rise out of the water. He asks me a couple of technical questions and seems surprised when I answer them. Then he asks me when the boat was built.

"In 1931," I tell him. "She turned seventy-five two months ago."

"I have a machine that will take care of this boat," he says, with a thick accent that I can't place.

"Oh, yeah?" I say, not quite sure where he's going with this.

"It's over there," he says, pointing, then scissors his fingers in my direction. "Snip, snip, snip." Hardly an encouraging start to our stay.

Once the boat is out of the water, the new service manager refuses to do the work the way we need it done. Because of OSHA regulations, he tells us, any space to be occupied by yard workers needs to have two egresses. Since the work entails being inside a tank, that isn't possible without cutting out the bottom of the boat—a major undertaking is neither in our budget nor in the best interest of the boat. This means we have to do the work ourselves, and due to shipyard restrictions, we are only allowed to use certain tools and equipment. The situation deteriorates quickly after the manager in charge of our project just disappears one day, and then the service manager vanishes too—apparently fired. The yard is in turmoil, and with the boat on land—their land—we're at the shipyard's mercy.

✦ ✦ ✦

Bob, Tim, Karl, and I all have commitments that preclude us from moving to Bridgeport for the duration of the yard work, as this project will require a much longer stay than last time. So we work from Thursdays through Saturdays, staying in an empty house right up the street from the yard that's owned by our friend Carl Selvaggi, owner of *Spooky Boat*. When volunteers come up from New York they, too, stay in the place that we dub the Harvey Dream House.

On Thursday mornings I take the subway from Brooklyn to Grand Central Terminal and board a Metro-North train bound for Tarrytown. On his way from New Jersey, Tim takes a quick dip off the highway to pick me up. The drive from Tarrytown to Bridgeport gives us uninterrupted time to plan the next phase of work, based on how many volunteers we expect and what parts and supplies have arrived since last week. Strategy sessions aside, for me the real benefit of this train-carpool routine is the view of the Hudson. I always miss the river in winter after boating season ends.

As the train thrums down the tracks on the east side of the river, I press my face against the dirty glass, cupping my hands around my forehead as a visor against the glare. Bare, ragged tree limbs stand stiff with cold along the banks. Rocks jut through the snow at the shoreline where garbage sits trapped in ice caked in the shallows. Ice on the river this far south, where seawater brine conquers fresh mountain runoff, means the water is at least a couple of degrees colder than zero Celsius. Salt water freezes at a lower temperature than fresh. Tim and I have, on occasion, depended on the buffer granted by those few degrees when the furnace crapped out on the fireboat—a spread that spells the difference between broken and unbroken pipes. Small bits of frozen river hug the shore, cordoning off mounds of sea grass—turning them into their own little islands. Framed by the yawning branches of bare trees, the cracked ice—like panes of shattered glass along the water's edge—makes my river look cold and private. A couple of seats ahead of mine a guy talks on his cell phone: "I'm training up the Hudson. It's gorgeous. It's beautiful."

These tracks follow the same riverside rail beds laid in the late 1840s under the direction of John Jervis. Following his work on the Erie Canal and his service as chief engineer on the D&H Canal from 1826 to 1828, Jervis had earned international attention for overseeing, from 1836 to 1842, the design and construction of the Croton Aqueduct, which delivered the first clean water supply to New York City. Three years later he turned his attention to railroading and spearheaded the first successful project to connect New York City to Albany by train.

At first, constructing a rail line on the banks of the Hudson was viewed as an impractical, unprofitable pipe dream. Investors hesitated to back Jervis's plan because they knew that New Yorkers were attached to the luxurious accommodations that steamboats provided—which railroads wouldn't be able to supply for decades to come. The investors also grasped the construction obstacles posed by the mountains of the Hudson Highlands, which rise steeply at the water's edge. The project was considered by many to be a "wild, visionary, and unpromising enterprise."

But New York was already behind the rest of the nation in building infrastructure, and Jervis warned that any further delay might jeopardize New York's shipping preeminence. Among the more than 15,000 miles of track that had been laid by the mid-1800s were railways linking Lake Erie to Albany and Albany to Boston. Without a link between Albany and New York City, midwestern goods might bypass New York and head straight to Boston's port instead. This threat ultimately inspired action, and Jervis's enterprise was incorporated in June 1846. The board of directors included Hudson River manufacturers who determined that their investment in the future Hudson River Railroad would pay off once they could ship their products year-round, even after the river had frozen. They raised $3 million, and construction began on the stretch from Manhattan's

Thirty-second Street to Breakneck Ridge in Cold Spring, the leg that contained the most challenging obstacles of the 143-mile route.

Trains need rails that are straight and flat—conditions that do not occur naturally. Because they couldn't follow the irregular curve of the shoreline, rail workers had to create straightaways to span creeks and streams and cut across the Hudson's coves and inlets. They piled jetties of rock fill until the man-made peninsulas were high and solid enough to build upon. Then they erected narrow platforms on top for the rails. Still today, where the river swings wide, the train seems to be skimming over the water.

Jervis designed the track bed to hug the riverbank, sitting five feet above the water level of the highest tides. At other places where the river's winding turns proved inconvenient, the engineer ordered workers to cut through the projecting points of land. The river's low grade proved advantageous, easing construction immensely. At only one point did the tracks stray even a mile from the water's edge.

The biggest challenge came in the Hudson Highlands, a fifteen-mile stretch between Peekskill and Newburgh bays, where the Hudson cuts through the Appalachian Mountain chain and mountains of more than a thousand feet slope directly into the river, precluding any flat overland runs. Workers burrowed through the stone to create tunnels, cutting or blasting two million cubic yards of rock out of the sides of mountains, including Saint Anthony's Face and Breakneck Ridge. Workers constructed eight tunnels, each twenty-four feet wide and eighteen feet high, between New York and Poughkeepsie.

The first engine steamed from the railroad's principal station on Chambers Street in Manhattan into the station at Poughkeepsie in 1849, and two years later, the tracks reached East Albany. Passenger traffic quickly exceeded 500,000 per year, as New Yorkers took advantage of transportation that cut the travel time from New York City to Albany to four and a half hours, from more than eight via steamboat.

But not everyone along the Hudson was pleased with the railroad's arrival. Among those dismayed were estate dwellers whose views of the river across their sprawling properties were now interrupted by train tracks. Indeed, the construction of the Hudson River Railroad prompted "the first known public outcry over the loss of scenery and the intrusion of industry on the Hudson," according to Frances Dunwell in *The Hudson: America's River.* James Fenimore Cooper, Thomas Cole, and others had also expressed concerns, but the public did not oppose the construction of the railroad through scenic places until the plans were set.

When workers raised and flattened the thirty-foot-wide strip of track bed along the shore at Tarrytown, Washington Irving was among those pained. "If the Garden of Eden were now on Earth," he grumbled from his nearby estate, Sunnyside, "they would not hesitate to run a railroad through it." Yet even he came around after experiencing a trip on the train, traveling distances that he could never otherwise have accomplished within a single day.

The jostle of the railcar is soothing as it paints its path to the north, galumphing along the narrow track bed etched out of the riverbank. My only problem with the train ride to Tarrytown is that it has to end, dropping me back into the mundane reality of the six-lane highway that leads to the red-and-white-striped tower at the power plant across from the shipyard that signifies the termination of the pause before work.

✦ ✦ ✦

Ten months after we arrived in Bridgeport with the boat, she still isn't fixed. We, and a handful of incredibly dedicated volunteers, have logged thousands of hours toward her repair. Despite having to work with the equivalent of one hand tied behind our backs due to shipyard regulations, we have made significant progress. We painted the restored aft tower, protecting all the new steel. We needle-scaled and painted areas of the hull in the engine room and in the stern tank where the stern tubes live—halting the cancer before it can spread. We repaired the perforated bulkhead where the river had poured into the engine room. We poured a new concrete floor in the wheelhouse. Over and over we climbed down the steel ladder into the aft compartment, then shimmied past a fuel tank—backs flat against the wall— then squeezed through a manhole into the stern-tube compartment. This is where we enacted the most important repairs—replacing the wasted stern tubes with solid new pieces, custom-built to fit.

We also installed a set of new cutless bearings to support the shafts, which were a completely different style from the old ones. The original bearings—bronze sleeves lined with galvanized rubber that fit around the shafts—were an odd size. Making customized sleeves would have cost $20,000, which the boat didn't have, and would have taken six months—time that the yard wouldn't give us. So we ordered stave-style bearings, and when they arrived, within days, Tim installed the sections—essentially long and skinny, but thick, sections of rubber shaped like barrel staves. As is the case with so many hand-to-mouth operations, time and money drove the decision to buy the cheaper bearings. That decision would ultimately cost the boat plenty.

When we were finally closing in on the finish line, Charlie, our surveyor, came to inspect our progress. His report called our work first class. "The repairs were done conscientiously and with great care." This gave us all confidence, fleeting though it would be.

"It felt really good for a minute there," says Bob, sitting at the kitchen table in the Harvey Dream House, drinking a Corona. He's talking about the few minutes that afternoon when we finally moved the boat under her own power. She was back in the water and we were testing the bearings while shifting her position at the dock. "Even if it didn't last too long. We could remember why we do this."

"Yeah, it did feel really good," I say, taking a sip of rum—the ice tinkling against the jelly-jar glass as I raise it to my lips. Even Tim, who's not much of a drinker, is working on his second beer. We are nursing our wounds.

In those few brief, fleeting moments, Bob and I clicked back into how things used to be, tethered to one another by telegraph chain, sharing the charge of anticipation as we moved in sync, each doing our different jobs, one notch off but together, like an echo or, maybe, singing in a round. Bob swung the pointer to Stand By and I stood by, Slow Astern on the port, and I shifted the lever. For a moment everything was as it should be.

And then a dying-animal screech, like a creature howling in pain, scraped ear-piercingly high over the low grumble of the engines. Suddenly the gauge showed zero rpm, indicating that the propeller had stopped turning. But the needle on the amp gauge shot past 1,000. In the space of a millisecond it shot up further, past 1,350—the critical-failure mark I'd been taught to watch out for on my first day at the stand. It shot all the way up to 2,000 amps before I managed to yank the lever back into neutral. And with that, the animal went silent. But Bob kept ringing down, first for Slow, then Half, then Full. He kept escalating the commands as he realized he wasn't getting what he needed to keep the boat under control.

Earlier that day, we had been laughing—something we hadn't been doing much over these last few months. The work and relations with the yard management had beaten us down. After getting a taste of all four seasons during our work here in Bridgeport, we were happy to be getting ready, finally, to take the boat home.

But in that instant, everything changed. When I responded to Bob's initial command, putting the prop motor into gear, the shaft had begun to spin for the first time inside its new bearing. At first, it slid around just fine. But then, the irregular surfaces inside the strut that supported the staves caused the rubber to catch and then twist itself around the shaft. The animal cry that pierced the engine room was the squeal of the rubber staves twisting around the shaft, squeezing it so tightly that it finally just stopped.

On deck, Tim told me later, the wind had tried to suck the boat out toward Long Island Sound. Bob needed power to control the boat, but I had nothing to give him. To try would burn out the prop motor. I rang back Stop to his every command. "There is no worse feeling," I told the crew later, "than being down there not able to give Bob what he asks for."

Tim finally managed to throw a line onto the pier, but weeks of work and thousands of dollars in parts had just been destroyed. Worse still, replacing the mangled bearings would require pulling out the shafts again. The boat was out of money and the crew was out of steam.

After shutting down the engines, I climbed the stairs at the back of the wheelhouse, the way I do at the end of every trip. It had been raining so hard all day that the part of the yard that the service department called the apron had flooded in low spots up to a foot deep. At least on this boat, unlike the tug, it was possible to get from the engine room to the wheelhouse without going outside.

At the top of the stairs I could see the whole gang gathered, occupying their respective places. Karl sat on Bob's bunk, looking down at his boots. Tim slumped in the brown pleather swivel chair, chin on his chest, eyes closed, and Bob stood with his back to the wheel, in his blue, quilt-lined flannel shirt. We had arrived at the shipyard last winter, and now it was fall. Bob and I just looked at each other. And that's when I noticed the rain—inside the boat. The drips were coming down through a hole in the roof of the pilothouse and landing on the floor beside the wheel. The four of us hung there in the thick, damp silence.

✦ ✦ ✦

Next, the shipyard kicks us out. Because they declined to do the work we needed done, they aren't making enough money to justify our presence. It doesn't matter that we can't leave under our own power. We are not allowed to stay.

A friend with a tugboat comes to tow us home. Matt Perricone, the new owner of tug *Cornell* (previously owned by Tom Teague of the *Spooky Boat* tow), lashes the fireboat alongside his boat to take us, under tow, back to New York City. I have been dreaming of leaving Bridgeport for months. I just never imagined it would happen like this.

The engine room is silent as we move through Long Island Sound. I spend the trip in the wheelhouse with Bob, who stands at the helm, monitoring the radio and the GPS. At critical points in the Sound, Matt, a bearded twenty-six-year-old who has been working on commercial tugs as an engineer for four years, makes the requisite security call on the radio. We hear it crackle through our radio in the wheelhouse: "Security. Security. Tug *Cornell* westbound at the Throgs Neck Bridge. Fireboat *John J. Harvey* alongside. Headed for the Battery and the West Side of Manhattan."

Bob gives me a look, and I know what he means. I step out the back door of the house and gesture up at Matt in his wheelhouse. He hangs his head out the window. "Hey," I yell so he can hear me above the sound of the water getting kicked up in the space between the two boats. "Do you have to rub it in?"

"What?" he hollers back.

"Do you have to announce to everyone on the radio that we're coming in under tow?"

"Yeah," Bob pipes in from behind me. "Maybe they'll think it's one of the city's boats," he says, the rivalrous spirit from his FDNY days still alive and well.

Matt laughs, but he gets it. The next security call he gives, he says, "Fireboat alongside," and as we travel closer and closer to New York harbor, he says simply, "Light one alongside."

It's dusk by the time we reach Manhattan. The lights on the Manhattan and Brooklyn bridges glint before us as we move down the East River, approaching Corlears Hook. In the dark wheelhouse, Bob stands at the window on the port side, looking off toward the Brooklyn Navy Yard, where the Marine Division fleet rests against the seawall. In the glow of the GPS, I think I see him bristle a bit when one of the little go-fast FDNY boats speeds out, heading straight toward us before hooking a hard right and zooming up the East River. Over the radio an anonymous voice calls out, "Good to see you back, *Harvey*." It sounds sincere.

Bob reaches up for the microphone. "Thank you."

Chapter Thirteen

SHAKING HANDS WITH
DEAD GUYS

Preservation and the Long Good-bye

❧

WHEN I GATHERED with my mother and her siblings to dismantle my grandmother's apartment, shortly after her death in January 2001, I fantasized about taking her things home with me and reassembling her world in my apartment, as if keeping her belongings together could somehow help me hold on to her life. Though I didn't go that far, I did preserve a few important items.

One was the double-leafed pine table where she and I had shared dinners of split-pea soup and grilled cheese, the finished surface scarred with tiny dents made by the tracing wheel she used to mark fabric. After she moved from the small Cape house where she raised her four children to a one-bedroom apartment in a retirement community, she lost her sewing studio. Now she had to do her projects on the same table where she ate, and where her nebulizer (which she called her Nebbie) delivered a cool, medicated mist to her lungs, slowly succumbing to emphysema.

Running my fingers over the marks in the table, while cupping in my palm another saved item—a sewing kit, the leather of the box so brittle it flakes off in my hand—reminds me of the power that objects possess to connect us with our history. There's no denying their stored energy. Harvard professor of clinical psychiatry John

Ratey explains that because our brains are able to link ideas together in memory, they are primed to suffuse objects with emotional value. I find it comforting to know that there's some hardwired aspect to my attachment to old things.

✦ ✦ ✦

One of Steve Trueman's tugboats is on the bottom. Again. Just like the day he first met her back in 1990. This time the seventy-seven-year-old *K. Whittelsey* has sunk off the dock of the Panco Petroleum Company in Stony Point, on the western shore of Haverstraw Bay. And the owner of the property is none too pleased. The first time it sank it had belonged to someone else, and the sinking spelled income for Steve, the salvage diver hired to raise her. Now the boat belongs to Steve, and money is flowing out instead of in. This sinking marks the beginning of the end of Steve's museum dreams.

A group of us have gathered to help Steve—the tugboat preservationist who had a fleet of six vessels when I first met him in Kingston—refloat his boat. Today's date, November 24, 2007, has been carefully chosen to take advantage of the spring tide, when the positions of the sun and moon create the strongest pull. Today's particularly low low-water will offer Steve only six hours in which to get ahead of the river that is trying to lay claim to his vessel.

Saving the past for future generations was the mission behind all of Steve Trueman's tugboat rescues. His goal was to preserve examples of lost technology through his fledgling North River Tugboat Museum, but besides collecting and restoring old boats, he was struggling to make any headway. "I'm a garage mechanic. I can't pull this off. I can't make this Mystic Seaport," he explains. Setting up the infrastructure that would bring his goal to fruition—rallying a board of directors and applying for grant money, for example—simply isn't his forte.

Though he says he met with Kingston city officials to try to convince them that a tugboat museum/historic boat repair facility would be a boon to the city, becoming a tourist destination by creating an ever-changing exhibit that would draw visitors and generate revenue, he "couldn't sell it to the politicians." Eventually he had to vacate Kingston, taking his boats with him. Afterward, Steve divided his fleet, stashing boats wherever he could at spots up and down the river. Spread out as they were, it was too difficult for him to keep an eye on all of them. The *K. Whittelsey*'s bilge pump had come unplugged, and before long the tug was on the bottom.

I first saw the tug underwater a week earlier when I passed by Haverstraw with the *Gowanus Bay* on a run south to Tarrytown. I was delivering a string of floating docks for the tug's owner, Rob, to property he recently purchased along Kingston's Rondout Creek. Since the *Spooky Boat* tow with Tom, I've done a number of towing jobs, following in the long tradition of tugboat apprentices who worked for free while they learned boat-handling skills. Lately Rob has been adding to his ex-military fleet (which he bills as "Fleet Obsolete") by collecting PT boats. I jumped at the chance to tow the latest addition to his menagerie—one of the small, fast "patrol torpedo" vessels employed by the U.S. Navy to attack surface ships during World War II—up from Little Egg Harbor, New Jersey, about fifteen miles north of Atlantic City by water. But it was on the Tarrytown dock tow that I first saw the sunken *K. Whittelsey*.

I had heard about Steve's misfortune through the old-boat grapevine, so as we passed by Haverstraw, I knew what to look for and where. I lined up my bow to slip between the three pairs of red and green buoys of the shipping channel that cuts a diagonal across the wide bay, and lifted the binoculars.

Driving by in a working tug felt a bit like licking clean a spoon of chocolate cake batter in front of a newly diagnosed diabetic. Here we were under way, going strong, while the *K.*'s bow pointed skyward and the stern had simply vanished underwater. The sight of it made me a little queasy, and I lowered the glasses. Steve had become a friend over the years, and my heart went out to him for that reason alone. But it was more than that. Once an old boat has your heart on a string, seeing another one in jeopardy hits home. I had to help him. When I heard about his plan for the coming Saturday, I decided to join in and lend a hand.

When I arrive at one in the afternoon, Steve is not around. Two hours earlier, the four two-inch portable gasoline pumps he'd rented were set up and running, and clearly not enough pumping power. They weren't able to keep up with the river water pouring in, let alone get ahead of it. So he drove off to max out yet another credit card to rent two more, larger pumps.

✦ ✦ ✦

Although many people know him as Tugboat Steve, he describes himself and his job this way: "I'm a commercial diver. I'm a captain, but it's not fair to call myself a tugboat captain, because those people do it every day. I can run a tug and that's what I do because we've always had tugboats in our dive companies. And being a poor little company, we get tugs that aren't in such good shape and make them run. It's the way you learn. By working on junk all the time, we pretty much know where to put the duct tape. We can always get home. It may not be pretty, but we'll get home."

When Steve first came across the K. in 1990, she needed lots of duct tape. A couple of years after Steve raised her, when the owner started talking about selling or scrapping the boat, Steve spouted off about how somebody ought to save her, since she was a unique boat. "I moaned and groaned for months, calling all the museums on the East Coast trying to get someone to save her. It was an important boat, an important piece of technology." When no one else expressed an interest, Steve bought the K. in 1992.

Steve lights up while describing the boat's unique design. The K. has what he describes as a "hybrid" engine, built when diesel was still new technology, with features straight from the steam era, like huge, poured-babbitt (white metal, an alloy of tin, antimony, and lead) bearings like you would find in a locomotive. And when she was launched in 1930, Steve says, the K. Whittelsey's was among the largest diesels in a boat.

The boat was built—overbuilt, really—by a man named Daniel Whittelsey, who was both an engineer and the owner of a tug company called Oil Transfer Corporation. "There's no manual for the boat. She was one of only two like her, both designed by the same man. And she was the largest boat I know of that ran through the canals."

The engine itself is two and a half deck levels high. The pistons are "so big a guy my size can stand inside the cylinders wielding a jackhammer," says Steve, speaking from experience. And he is not a small man. Round in the middle, with glasses and a crown of silver-streaked long hair gathered into a ponytail, Steve looks the part of the wayward salvor, and the marks on his thick hands tell stories from a lifetime of labor.

One particular engine conundrum confounded him for a while: "I was puzzling over this part. I'd taken it apart, cleaned it, then put it back together, but I still wasn't sure exactly what it did. Then at two in the morning I woke up with a flashbulb realization. I said, 'Wait a minute. That has an oil line in it.' I got up in my slippers and went down in the engine room. I shone a flashlight and got under there. 'Holy crow,' I said. 'Look what they did. This part does five things. Some guy sat down and thought of all that.' Today we'd have fifteen computers that design and make a bunch of things that nobody in the world can fix. But here was this part that was beautifully made. All the edges had been filed off by hand. It was built in an era when people did stuff by hand. I felt like the guy who built that was sitting next to me, had showed me the part. It was such a neat thing to sit there with the guy and see what he did. And I thanked him for it. Every time I worked on that engine, that's what happened. When you're working with equipment like that, trying to figure it out, it's like shaking hands with dead guys."

I understand what he means. As I step across the worn deck plates in fireboat *Harvey*'s engine room, I think about the decades of engineers who came before me. I think about them each time I pass a clipboard that hangs from the back of the Number Two engine, its particleboard back crumbling at the corners, and the pages torn and faded. The sheets list the dates when oil was added. The last entry, scribbled in blue ink, is dated "9/18/93." Though today we use a log-book for engine-room notes, we let the clipboard stay. It's an artifact that reminds me of my place in time, and the hands of all the engineers who have tended these machines.

✦ ✦ ✦

Despite all the pumps spitting the river out of Steve's tug, the boat, with its rare "hybrid" engine, stays sunk. The four pumps scream, sucking up muck from the engine compartment through long corrugated hoses and spewing it over the top of the caprail. Attached to the railing on the upper deck is a hand-carved wooden sign: "Hudson River Towing and Salvage." The irony is painful.

As I stand watching from the pier, a pump sputters and dies. The only access to the boat requires walking a six-inch-wide plank that's suspended over the frigid water. I have less than stellar balance, but I have come to work, not watch. So I take slow, careful steps across, make it over, and see that Tim is aboard, slip-sliding around on the gratings slick with oil that floated to the surface when the river filled the engine. I head for the pump, shimmying sideways up the caprail, which runs the length of the boat from the bow to where it disappears underwater at the stern.

Fussing with the gas can to refill the pumps, I quickly lose sight of the simple fact that I am climbing around a half-sunken boat. Not long ago I had the idea that when a boat sank, it had met its end. Now I realize something usually happens next.

✦ ✦ ✦

Why do we save old things? Since I began working to restore a three-quarter-century-old piece of maritime history, that question has taken on new weight and importance. I wanted to talk with someone who has given preservation a good deal of thought, in part because I hoped to understand why I had allowed this obsession with old workboats to consume my life.

Mark Peckham has been the National Register unit coordinator for the New York State Historic Preservation Office for more than twenty-five years. A good friend to the fireboat, he helped nominate *John J. Harvey* to be listed on the National Register of Historic Places and Things—a designation that had made the boat eligible for the restoration matching grant from New York State. I visited Mark at his house in New Baltimore, New York, built right along the Hudson River, thirteen miles south of Albany.

The house, which Mark designed himself, sits back one hundred feet off the west bank of the Hudson, just south of Coeymans Landing—one of the oldest landings on the river. Mark relishes his weekends at home, listening for passing vessels to record in his logbook. Over the past two years he has filled countless pages with lovely sketches of tugboats, barges, tankers, and cargo ships, brought to life with dabs of watercolor. Below each illustration he pens a description: date and time, vessel's name and origin, cargo and destination—whatever he can glean before it passes out of view. "It's my way of keeping in touch with the river and getting to know the boats," he explains.

Mark speaks in a calm, low, measured voice that reflects his thoughtfulness. But every now and then a mischievous grin pops out, his eyes gleam, and it's easy to picture him as the nine-year-old who, after a day of Hudson River swimming, hid a little fish in his trunks because he wanted to take it home with him. "It started to smell in the car." He laughed. "Then it stank up my bedroom." Finally his parents, who disapproved of Hudson River swimming in the first place, confronted Mark and confiscated his souvenir. "Back then you could smell the river from about half a mile on either side," Mark says, but still, he loved it, stink and all.

Today Mark is an expert diver with a mind-boggling ability to explore shipwrecks and map out the contours of an underwater vessel by feel, then reproduce it visually in two and three dimensions. His house is decorated with small reproductions of tugs, ships, and sailboats, including some whose hulls he cut out of logs with a chain saw. He also builds life-size wood boats. Next on his agenda: constructing a twenty-six-foot, flat-bottomed sailing scow that he can hoist into his backyard at the end of the season. At his day job, Mark champions historic places and things that would otherwise get destroyed in the constant crush of development.

Preservation is predicated on the notion that physical objects are steeped in the breathable essence of time's passing. The physicality of spaces, edifices, and artifacts evokes a bygone age, offering a visceral sense of the past—the chance to step through yesteryear and wonder and imagine who and how we might have been had we lived then. "History is an inspiration for the present and for the future," Mark says. "We ought to retain a physical, living record of how people overcame challenges, because that gives us confidence to overcome challenges in our time. That's what preservation means to me. If you take the artifacts away, the setting away, and all the places away, how can you communicate with that past?"

In 2006, a partnership of heritage organizations in the United Kingdom organized a three-month program to collect answers to the question "Does history matter?" More than a million people of all ages and stations participated, and their responses illustrate how our individual lives fit into the larger whole.

C. Walsh submitted that history "puts our little lives into perspective. It helps us to see ourselves as part of our world's journey."

"Without history," offered Paul Irving, "we are just creatures. History gives us a place and a soul."

In his 1961 lectures, collected in the book *What Is History?*, Edward Hallett Carr called history "an unending dialogue between the present and the past." Like looking at satellite images of the street where you live, or the house you grew up in, communication with the past grounds us in where we are and helps us see our lives in a larger context, through a wider lens. Grasping history's messages is more intuitive than literal, but the information connects us to our place in time.

No single philosophy brings people like Mark to the business of preservation. Some of his colleagues say preservation is about honoring our ancestors who built these resources and aren't here to speak for themselves. Others say preservation is about representing the interests of our grandchildren and their offspring, who can't be here to save these resources, though they'll need them someday. Still others focus on what a sense of the past offers people today. This is what Mark calls the paradox of preservation—that preserving historic places and things simultaneously serves people in the past, present, and future. "We have the responsibility to save now what people will want later, whether they realize it now or not."

✦ ✦ ✦

A handful of people have rallied for Steve's tug raising—one of whom is walking around in a wet suit pulled halfway up, the empty arms loose and dangling. There isn't much conversation. Those of us who don't know each other don't even stop for introductions beyond head-nod acknowledgment. With guys, there's often no need for small talk. Tim and I work together to keep the pumps fueled up and running until Steve returns, but it's clear that the pumps he's bringing are the only hope we have of raising this boat.

When Steve does return, I can't believe how beaten down and frantic he looks, like a hunted dog. He's underdressed in a sweatshirt under an unbuttoned flannel shirt, with no hat. He looks right through me without even saying hello. "I don't think we're going to make it," he mutters, shaking his head.

Steve has just driven all over the county to rent these two extra pumps, and as the sun begins to drop out of the sky, we're racing against the clock. Still, he just stands there dazed, taking no steps to get the pumps onto the boat so they can do their job. Steve is absolutely cooked.

Seeing this, Tim and I kick into gear, sliding the hundred-pound units across the plank, trying to manhandle the machines without landing them, or us, in the drink. The rest of the gang pitches in, refilling the smaller gas can from the larger, and testing the hoses Steve has brought to be sure they will fit.

We fire up these new pumps, and the boat begins to quiver. This movement seems promising, but it still isn't enough. Deciphering how much pump power you need to raise a boat is all math, really. Subtract the water coming in from the water going out. The formula factors in the diameter of the hole and the pressure of the water pouring through it to determine how much pump volume you'll need to first catch up with, then overtake, a leak.

The whole back deck, where Steve had cut away wasted steel with every intention of replacing it, is now just a big, rectangular, eight-by-ten-foot opening. Like too many of Steve's projects, this replacement stalled midstream. He simply has too many boats to keep up with all their needs. Instead of new steel, which would have kept the river out, he covered the hole with nothing more than a tarp over a row of two-by-fours—hardly watertight. And since a six- or eight-inch opening also passes from this back compartment directly into the engine room, there is no way we are going to raise this boat without first blocking the flow through that hole—not even with the two extra pumps.

While the tide was going out, I watched a row of old pilings rise up above the water. Now it's approaching five o'clock, and those pilings are beginning to disappear again. The river is filling back up because the tide has swung the other way. We're losing our daylight. And our fight.

The diver has to plug the hole to the engine room. He lumbers to his car to get the rest of his gear. It takes him forever, and he insists that Steve carry the heaviest part, the tanks, across the plank to the boat. This lack of initiative and independence strikes me as strange, until I realize the diver is spooked. There is plenty to be afraid of. By the time he gets himself suited up, the sun has dropped out of view. Now the only light he has to dive by spills over from the lamps on the pier. He has to splash through the black river into the opening in the stern deck to locate the hole.

While all this is going on, I keep up with my business of refueling and adjusting the position of the pump hoses. Inside the boat, the water level is, indeed, dropping. Our progress is visible. *Maybe this will work, if the diver can just block that hole.*

Over the screaming pumps, I hear Steve call my name. I hunt him down by the sound of his voice to where he sits perched on an H-bitt on the deck below me, feet up so they won't hit the water. In front of him I see the diver, stuffed like a sausage into his suit, floundering at the water's surface. "I'm *his* spotter," Steve yells to me. "I want you to be *my* spotter."

"Okay," I holler back. "What should I do?"

"Just be there in case I need something." So I stand above Steve, who sits above the diver, who still won't dive. "I'm right here for you, buddy," I hear Steve saying. "Anything happens, I'm right here." He tries to offer some direction about where the hole must be. With my view from above I can understand the diver's hesitation to plunge into the black abyss. Steve's attempts to help him navigate sound like nonsense. Diesel fuel that floated up from the engine swirls in little rainbows around the diver, still at the surface, and the loose hose with his mouthpiece floats in the swill. There's a boom around the perimeter of the boat soaking up oil, but the diver is inside the boom. I think about how I wouldn't want my mouth making contact with anything that touched this water.

"I can't get through," he says. "There's something in my way." One of the boards that once held down the tarp has floated up at an angle and wedged itself so the diver can't find his way into the opening. "It's not moving. It's stuck." But he manages to swing the board free. He passes one end to Steve, who calls out to Tim to move it out of the way.

Rather than shimmy down the caprail like we've been doing all day, Tim walks down the deck of the boat until he's knee-deep in the diesel-y water. He does this, he explains to me later, to encourage the diver, to reassure him that there is someone out here who isn't afraid of getting wet, should he get into a bind. Tim removes the board, and finally the diver dives. He plugs the hole, jamming it full of rags, then scrambles off the boat as quickly as he can.

I turn back to refueling and discover the gas can is empty. I call out to Tim, but he says not to worry about it, the remaining pumps will either float this boat now or not at all. Relieved of duty, I cross the plank to the pier. An anxious pause looms over the group. Now I, too, stand among the spectators. All we can do is wait and watch.

I pick a spot on the caprail to try to gauge the waterline. At first the tug seems content to sit perfectly still. Then I realize the belly of the boat is rolling over to the side. She's squaring herself up. Slowly, slowly, the back rail rises out of the water like a whale breaking the surface for a gulp of air. Finally the stern of the boat begins to poke through.

Just then, in a shift of light almost too poetic to be real, the full moon that created the low low tide that made this tug raising possible rises high enough in the sky to cast moonbeams over the water. The beams shimmer a long trail in the rippled surface of the river like little arrows of light pointing right toward us, and the boat. In an instant, the whole stern crests, and the tug hops a little hop like a puppy bouncing a cheerful hello. I never expected her to rise so gently, so elegantly.

✦ ✦ ✦

Machines have souls. Never say anything bad about a car within earshot, or it might get back at you by breaking down. That's how I was raised. You talk nice to your car if you want it to behave. If it's trying to die, give it some encouragement, and maybe it will get you home.

Since we raised the *K.*, I've been thinking about how, for better or for worse, these boats have become Steve's identity, much in the same way my own sense of self has gotten all wrapped up in the fireboat. When I first stumbled onto the *Harvey*, I never expected it to take over. I couldn't have anticipated that I would come to need it so much. I can see how Steve has gotten caught up, and how hard it must be to let his boats go as he gives up on his museum.

Grim news travels fast. Steve has sold the *K. Whittelsey*—the boat that he has limped through the past sixteen years with, raising it from the bottom, twice—to a man named Mike Giordano, who makes his living snipping steel for scrap. The old-boat community is buzzing.

I call Mike to ask where and when he plans to cut up the boat, telling him I want to be there. The shipyard he names is in Tottenville at the southwestern tip of Staten Island. Though I'm not looking forward to it, I appreciate that Mike is willing to let me come and bear witness. On April Fools' Day 2008, I cross the Verrazano-Narrows Bridge, named after (a misspelling of) Giovanni da Verrazzano, who in 1524 became the first recorded European to enter New York harbor. When this bridge was constructed in 1964, workers drove three million rivets and fastened one million bolts to secure each 693-foot-high, 27,000-ton tower. The 4,260-foot distance between the bases of the two towers—one in Brooklyn, one in Staten Island—required bridge engineers to compensate for the curve of the earth, building the towers an inch and five-eighths farther apart at their tops than at their bottoms.

As I cross over it, I sneak quick peeks through the bridge railing at the ships and tugs with barges out at anchor in the Upper Bay. The Narrows, the tidal strait through which the Hudson River empties into the Atlantic Ocean, is the maritime gateway into New York harbor—the main thoroughfare for container and cargo ships as well as oceangoing tugs. But once I pass through the toll plaza on the Staten Island side, the happy distractions of the bridge and the ships fade into an anonymous stretch of highway and I remember where I am headed and why. This isn't like paying a shiva call or attending a wake, with the food and formality and loved ones all around—it's more like a deathbed visit.

I pull into the yard, and there is the *K.*, toppled over on her side.

The tug sits on land—not upright and supported by bracing chains and blocks like she would be were she here for repairs, but slumped over in the dirt. I wanted to be here sooner. Mike Giordano started snipping early.

A short guy in his late forties, Mike, in his company-logoed, collared, gray T-shirt, is sitting in the operator's seat of the excavator plucking at the *K.* with the snipper as if the boat were a chicken carcass bound for a soup pot. The screech of the tearing metal hurts. Though I have a pair of earplugs in the front pocket of my Carhartts, I don't fish them out. Putting them in would feel somehow disrespectful to the boat.

The whole stern has already been ripped apart. I can see through the back of the boat into the engine room. The aft deck, where, in Haverstraw Bay, the hole had let the river in, has been shredded, and the steel that formed the tug's structure, her skin, lies in a mangled mound.

"We whack these boats up like they're beer cans," Mike told me earlier, with a casual, nonchalant tone that stems from his decades in the business. "You put on the air conditioning, sip your coffee, and cut the boat up. The machine is like a giant pair of bolt cutters. You never even get your hands dirty. . . . I know some people love this old junk," he said. "I'm a scrap guy. I don't love anything."

Mike's machine is a yellow John Deere excavator, called a crawler because it rides on tracks instead of wheels. A single arm extends from the rectangular house, which can pivot side to side above the tracks. When used as an earthmover, this type of excavator is usually outfitted with a bucket at the end of the arm. But Mike has a custom model with a jawlike attachment that serves as a giant pair of scissors. Just as he described, the machine tears through Steve's boat as if it were an aluminum can, although from where I stand, the steel looks remarkably thick and solid for a vessel built in 1930.

The snipper attachment looks alive, like the head of a *Tyrannosaurus rex* topping a longer, more *brontosaurus*-like neck. The nut securing the upper jaw to the lower looks like a tiny eye, and although reason tells me that Mike's hands control its movements, I hold the tearing up of Steve's boat against the creature doing the damage. Seeing the machine as the monster helps me reconcile the fact that Mike seems like a nice enough guy.

When the beast sets its jaws around the propeller shaft, a long column of solid steel six inches around, the boat puts up a little bit of a fight. It takes a few pulls before the clenched jaw manages to rip the shaft from the rear of the engine, but soon it, too, lands on the pile.

The John Deere, Mike told me, had cost him $650,000, but with the skyrocketing value of scrap steel, had paid for itself within two years. "Twenty years ago, steel went for sixty to sixty-five dollars a ton. Right now, steel brings between two hundred and three hundred dollars per ton, depending on the type. The price varies from grade to grade." The scrap, he said, is headed for Turkey. "They're rebuilding the country over there." He plans to chop Steve's boat into four- or five-square-foot sections, load the pile onto the back of a truck, and drive it to Port Newark, where the final sale will go through a broker who will tell him which ships are coming into the Northeast looking for iron. "I'll just whack it up as quick as possible, then move on to the next boat," he said. "I'll break it up and never break a sweat."

Mike makes no apology for the fact that the pile he's accumulating means nothing more than money to him. And really, why should he? This is his business—recycling usable steel. He has been selling scrap metal for twenty-five years, and got his start "picking scrap out of other people's garbage, and scrapping junk cars," he explains. "There's a lot of superwealthy people picking up soda cans . . . I'm in it for the money."

Soon the machine has chomped deep enough through the stern to reach the deckhouse. The jaw bites into the side of the house, tearing apart the wall of the aftermost compartment, and as the machine yanks at the piece, I hear the staccato snap of rivets releasing like buttons popping off a shirt. I think about the men who drove these rivets, pretzeling their bodies into impossible positions to get at the hard-to-reach spots. After that snipping comment made by the engineer at the Bridgeport shipyard, I can't help but see the *Harvey* in the *K. Whittelsey*'s place.

As Mike continues picking, the sinking sun shifts the light, intensifying the contrast between the red boat, the blue sky, and the yellow head of the monster. Jagged edges of steel poke into the blue, and the pipes and wires in their braided steel sheathing splay out like entrails. Next, he reaches the engine.

The jaws devour the unique, "hybrid" engine one cylinder at a time. The head of the machine cocks sideways to get a grip, then clamps down on the first cylinder liner, plucking it from its fitted bed in the block. As the liner leaves the boat and hovers over the pile, the coppery glint of the head gasket dangling off a head bolt catches my eye. The ring sparkles there for an instant before the jaws close, crushing the cast iron, which crumbles into dust.

Mike told me his exact plans for breaking up the engine: "I'll cut all the bolts off with a torch. I'll lift the cylinders out. Then I'll bust the engine up into little chips with the weight of the flywheel." I do not want to watch this. The halt of the machine grants me a reprieve.

"I cracked a line," Mike says, referring to a hydraulic line on the John Deere, after climbing out of the cab to inspect his work. "I broke a line for some reason. I don't know if something flew off while I was cutting it. Now I gotta fix that in the morning," he says, adding, "See, these engines come right apart."

"Well, it's cast iron, right? It's got to be a lot easier," I reply.

"Oh, so it's easy, then?" he asks, smiling coyly.

"Well, it's easier than some would be, right? I mean cast iron's just dying to turn back into sand." I concentrate on sounding blasé. "But I was surprised at how brittle the pieces were."

"Well, that's a lot of power there too," he says, with obvious admiration for *his* machine.

"Clearly," I say.

He chuckles, adding, "That thing's punching through the metal like it's nothing."

"I'm amazed at how intact the hull is," I submit. "The steel is good."

"Yeah," he says. "It will take me just one full day. I've been on this, what, about three hours? One long day and it would be done."

"It takes a hell of a lot longer to put them together."

At that moment I remember a passage from a book called *Old Steamboat Days on the Hudson River,* published in 1907. The author, David Lear Buckman, mentions that Fulton's original steamboat was one of few early steamboats that didn't end up sunk or smashed in a collision. Instead, it remained in service long enough to "receive an honorable discharge by being 'broken up.' " Could what is happening to Steve's boat somehow be construed as an honorable discharge? I make the mistake of voicing my question aloud.

"I'm more interested in when they write me a big, fat check," Mike responds matter-of-factly. "That's all I care about. Like I said, it's all about the money."

Before I leave, Mike hands me a stack of business cards and says, "If you know anybody who wants to get rid of one of these wrecks, you let me know."

When I tell my brother Josh the story, he puts my thoughts into words: "That would be like handing your address book over to the Grim Reaper," he says.

Some time later, I ask Tim if he wants to see the pictures and video I took of the *K.*'s dismantling. He isn't sure at first, but then he says yes, so I click through the images on my laptop screen. "It's chasing all the ghosts away," he says, referring to Mike's machine. "They're going to need to find some other place to hide."

✦ ✦ ✦

The *K.* was the first of Steve's tugs to get cut up, but soon two more would follow. Out of his original fleet of six vessels, Steve has managed to save three: the *Chancellor*, which found a new home, some years back, in Waterford; the 1957 tug *Frances Turecamo*; and the railroad barge.

Steve wasn't there when the *K.* was towed out of Kingston to Staten Island. "I'm glad I didn't have to watch it go away. I have a real weak heart," he tells me. "I tried everything I could try. I tried to find anybody that wanted it," he says, his voice cracking. "It just breaks me up. I have an emotional attachment to the boats, but it's also just . . . I'm so tired. It shouldn't be this hard."

Chapter Fourteen

CITIZEN CRAFTSMEN

The Art in Craft

∾

ELIZABETH NORRIS UNDERSTANDS the power that objects hold to transcend the linear boundaries of time. In one smooth motion, the doctoral candidate in anthropology lowers her lean frame and reclines on her side to get a better look at the artifacts arrayed atop a sheet of pink newsprint on the gallery floor of the Putnam County Historical Society & Foundry School Museum. She has devoted the last seven years of her life to researching the West Point Foundry, a nineteenth-century ironmaking complex in Cold Spring, New York.

On a Thursday in March 2008, at the tail end of a long week, she is piecing together displays at the museum. This is the first exhibit she has ever helped curate, and the pressure is palpable. What can the average viewer understand about mining, forging, and shaping iron? What aspects of the foundry's complex history will hold viewer interest? What objects will best reveal the foundry's unique and pivotal story?

"Maybe we should get rid of one of these bricks," she wonders aloud. "Or maybe the sand, if the different types will just look the same to laypeople." From across the gallery, the objects she ponders look like nameless rusty lumps, some packaged in ziplocks, others tied with manila paper tags. Upon closer inspection, I see them take shape, identifiable features revealing clues about the purposes they served a century ago, before the earth consumed them, and before

Elizabeth and her student crews dug them back up. A cast-iron handle, a set of calipers, various files, a wrench. "I'm not sure these are all going to fit," she says.

Engaging an audience in a museum setting poses new challenges for a woman accustomed to leading on-site tours where visitors can gain a tangible sense of what industrial archaeology entails by watching students finger through the soil and seeing their dirty hands, clothes, and faces.

✦ ✦ ✦

The first time I visited the West Point Foundry site was in August 2003, the day after a massive blackout left fifty million people in the northeastern and midwestern United States, and Ontario, Canada, with no power in the middle of a nasty heat wave, reminding us all of how dependent we've become on electricity.

In New York City, people stranded by public transportation shutdowns slept in parks and on the steps of public buildings. They lined up ten or more deep at pay phones because circuit overloads had left many cell phones out of service. Some hosted huge barbecues in the streets to use up food before it spoiled, while others gathered on balconies, in backyards, and at bars to relish a night of being involuntarily unplugged. It was the most widespread electrical blackout in history, but on the fireboat we almost didn't notice it, because we make our own power.

That night the boat was docked fifty miles up the Hudson, in Cold Spring, and as the sun went down behind Crow's Nest and Storm King mountains, the whiny 2-71 Detroit diesel generator wailed away in the engine room, powering spotlights on the back deck. The crew was gathered, eating another fine meal prepared by our cooks, John Doswell and Jean Preece, when someone realized there wasn't a single light shining in the whole village of Cold Spring. Our floodlights blazed through the darkness—the only lights in town. Bob turned on the radio, which updated us on the poor Manhattanites melting in the ninety-degree temperatures and brutal humidity that had followed a record rainfall. Meanwhile, we lounged in the river breeze.

The next day we clambered off the boat, crossed the railroad tracks at the Cold Spring Metro-North train station, and walked down a mowed path that curled away from the river. We tromped through tall grasses that lined the marshlands of what is now called Foundry Cove—its liquid surface covered in patches of green algae.

Down a path toward a grove of trees and the promise of shade, we came upon a two-story brick building with arched windows, a central tower, and two chimneys. Our tour guide, an industrial archaeology student from Michigan Technological University's industrial archaeology field school, was nowhere to be found, so we poked around on our own.

Deeper into the site stood remnants of brick pillars, stone walls, and curious leaf-strewn dips and rises throughout the wide ravine. Here and there we came across clumps of red-black, lava-looking rock— slag, a by-product of the ironmaking process. This shady glen—once clear-cut of its hardwood to fire the furnace and now overgrown with young trees—was the birthplace of one of this country's earliest large factories. At the dawn of the American industrial revolution, its development exemplified the shift away from cottage-industry craftsmanship toward a new form of business that divided the labor and managerial classes.

✦ ✦ ✦

The West Point Foundry's history begins with a student from the first graduating class at the U.S. Military Academy at West Point, and the academy itself begins with General George Washington. After his inauguration as the first president, Washington urged the establishment of a military school to ensure that the country never again had to rely on ragtag, untrained ranks.

Devoted to the arts and sciences of warfare, West Point was finally established in 1802, with a first class of ten cadets, to eliminate America's wartime reliance on foreign engineers and artillerists. Among the earliest graduates was future general Joseph G. Swift, who became one of the foundry's initial proprietors. While the academy and the foundry were independent entities, a long, symbiotic relationship developed, forged through shared purposes and close personal ties.

✦ ✦ ✦

Located diagonally across the river from West Point at the northernmost point of World's End's notorious S-curve, the West Point Foundry made landmark contributions to U.S. history as it became one of the nation's largest, most successful ironworks of the nineteenth century. Its importance stemmed not only from its products and technology, but also from the company's embodiment of the social and technological changes at the dawn of America's industrial Iron Age. The foundry exemplified the transition between craft-based production and modern industrialism. Now that the United States was formally training its soldiers, the country needed to make its own arms and reduce military dependence on foreign-made weaponry.

In the early nineteenth century, the nation's leaders understood that domestic manufacturing was crucial for political freedom. For their role in freeing the country from dependence on foreign goods, artisans deemed themselves patriots. In New York, a group of craftsmen created the Mechanics Institute, which sought to support the crafts system and artisan pride. Among other programs, the institute sponsored a competition in which apprentices submitted examples of their best work for exhibition. Medals presented on July Fourth recognized how the "practice of useful experiment" dovetailed so seamlessly with the celebration of American independence.

Even as more and more U.S. industry shifted away from cottage-based production toward more modern, large-scale manufacturing enterprises, the notion of American innovation and ingenuity as patriotic contributions remained. After graduating from West Point, General Swift had returned to the school, working as superintendent from 1812 to 1818. Prior to that, he had served as commander of the U.S. Corps of Engineers and also as superintending engineer for fortifications in New York harbor. Then, in 1817, he teamed up with a man named Gouverneur Kemble, a member of a powerful landholding family whose brother-in-law, James K. Paulding, was secretary to the Board of Naval Commissioners and later secretary of the navy. Kemble had studied iron technology in Europe, and he and Swift planned to use their knowledge and significant military connections to establish a New York–based ironworks capable of producing heavy ordnance castings.

In April 1817, they secured two hundred acres on Margaret Brook (now called Foundry Brook) that offered everything ironmaking required: ample wood for charcoal, water power captured by damming the brook, local iron ore, plenty of loamy sand topsoil used for making molds, and convenient product shipping via the Hudson River. Within months the proprietors broke ground and set about erecting several shops and mills, as well as a dam to power a thirty-six-foot waterwheel, said to be the largest existing in the United States at the time. In April 1818, Kemble, Swift, and others were made a corporate body, and the government provided an advance of $25,000 to assist in the erection of the works. This simple transaction cemented new ties between the military and private industry. That same year the company produced its first shipment of cannons.

Kemble is credited with designing the company's structure, for which few, if any, American models then existed—a huge complex that handled every aspect of ironmaking from mine to market. One of the challenges of being at the forefront of a new industry, however, was the paucity of experienced foundrymen. Between 1820 and 1840, the sum total of skilled mechanics in the English-speaking world numbered only three or four hundred, and few of them lived in the United States. So Kemble set his sights on Great Britain, his representatives rallying a number of skilled metalworkers who were willing to move overseas for the promise of lucrative work. The British government, determined to protect its monopoly on ironmaking and other crafts know-how, had enacted laws prohibiting skilled mechanics from leaving the country to practice or teach their trade. But the law couldn't prevent them from absconding.

One account in a Cold Spring newspaper reveals the lengths to which foundry recruiters went to enlist skilled craftsmen: "Laborers were put on board a ship in Belfast, and then just as the ship was about to leave, mechanics substituted for the laborers, and the ruse was discovered too late by the British government."

In the early nineteenth century, ironmaking was an art, not a science, according to Patrick Martin, the MTU professor heading up the field school project. Furnace operators possessed a set of skills that were largely undocumented. "There wasn't a manual. You couldn't get a degree," he explained. "The know-how was passed down as craft, as an oral tradition." At the time, ironmaking possessed for the foundrymen some almost magical, animate qualities, which he describes this way: "Foundry workers didn't have instrumentation capable of assessing the chemistry or the physics. They couldn't measure furnace temperature because there was no thermometer capable of reading 1,200 to 1,600 degrees centigrade. Workers depended on clues from light, smells, and color. These installations were virtually alive. They changed as the charge got hotter, things expanded and contracted. Even the big masonry stone structure of the furnace moved. The furnace breathed. It drew air, demanding fuel in ways that seemed organic. When a blast furnace blows out—and that's the term they use for it—it's almost like blowing out a flame, but more explosive. The mass of stuff that's left in the bottom was called a salamander. In life, a salamander is a weird creature. It's not a frog and not a lizard, but something sort of in between. The term, like the creature, bespeaks a kind of a mystical reality. This is not the way we, today, tend to think of something strictly technical or industrial. Workers then discussed ironmaking in more biological terms."

✦ ✦ ✦

Having finally secured a cadre of skilled workers familiar with the magic of metallurgy, Kemble and his crews got down to business. Every step of iron manufacture was laborious: mining ore; chopping down trees and burning them into charcoal for fuel; smelting the ore in blast furnaces; casting the molten iron into molds; converting the cast iron to wrought iron in forges; rolling, cutting, and slitting the wrought iron into useful dimensions; machining and assembling finished pieces; and, finally, transporting them to market.

Naturally, given the government advance, the ironworks' first products were ordnance. But before long, the foundry supplemented this work with commercial products, especially in the 1820s and 1830s, when it produced machinery and engines for the cotton and sugar industries, sending equipment to the American South and to places as far as Austria, Nova Scotia, and the Caribbean.

In 1830 and 1831, the foundry built, for the South Carolina Railroad, the first American locomotives put into U.S. service, the *Best Friend* and the *West Point*. The company also constructed engines for many Hudson River steamboats, including the *Victory*, the *DeWitt Clinton*, and the *Swallow*. By midcentury, the foundry had expanded its product line to include stationary steam engines and boilers; a variety of mill equipment and machinery; pipes and hydraulic cylinders; elbows for the Croton Aqueduct and the Brooklyn dry dock; components for the original water mains in New York City, Chicago, and Boston; and parts for an underwater railroad tunnel between New York and New Jersey. These goods were crucial building blocks for some of America's earliest infrastructure investments.

In addition to its contributions to infrastructure, the West Point Foundry made landmark changes to the business practices employed in early America.

The soup-to-nuts approach Kemble took to ironwork, with different shops handling different stages of production, and products moving hand to hand between workers on their way to completion, foreshadowed Ford's first assembly-line factories and Andrew Carnegie's use of vertical integration. Kemble's approach was a far cry from the smaller, home-based production typical of seventeenth- and eighteenth-century America.

As manufacturing businesses grew, so did class differences between workers and owners and managers. In traditional craft-based enterprises, typically small and run by a few individuals who both managed the business and produced the goods, proprietors were themselves master craftspeople. But the needs of running a small shop differed entirely from those of orchestrating the works of a large-scale facility like the West Point Foundry. The complexity of operations demanded a new managerial class of employees who oversaw, rather than directly participated in, production activities. By hiring the right superintendents, Kemble left actual production up to the craftsmen and established himself as the head of a new managerial class. This division of labor was new in nineteenth-century America.

Despite the diversity of its products, the foundry's lifeblood was ordnance, as evidenced by the company's Civil War boom and postwar decline. From 1861 to 1865, the company reached its peak, employing nearly one thousand men and boys. In 1861, *Harper's Weekly* estimated that the foundry produced twenty-five guns and seven thousand projectiles each week. Over the course of the war, it supplied the Union army with more than a thousand cannons and a million projectiles. The most critical weapon produced was the Parrott gun (named after Robert Parrott, foundry superintendent from 1836 to 1866), which proved to be the foundry's most lasting legacy. The cast-iron cannon, fitted with Parrott's signature wrought-iron reinforcement strap that enabled it to fire more accurately at greater distances, helped secure the Northern victory.

Following the war, drastically reduced government contracts for armaments, along with the emergence of steel—deemed superior to iron for most uses—sent the company into an irreversible tailspin toward bankruptcy. By 1889 the number of employees had dropped to 150, and the company went into receivership. Although other industrial concerns occupied parts of the site after the West Point Foundry closed, many remnants of the decades of ironmaking remained remarkably undisturbed, offering MTU's archaeology students pay dirt in which to dig. The archaeology project—funded by Scenic Hudson, a Hudson River Valley environmental group that now owns the site—began in 2001.

✦ ✦ ✦

The next time I visit the foundry, years later, in June 2008, the MTU Field School is hosting its annual open house, where the public can take tours, listen to presentations, and get a close-up look at the excavation work. "We invite the public to come because when they smell the dirt and see the stains on people's clothing, they can better understand that what we do is physical and tangible," Elizabeth explains. "Archaeology involves the senses."

Offering the public this kind of somatic experience is exactly what we do on the fireboat. When adults and children board the boat and we take them off the dock, out into the currents of the river, they can't help but feel the engines grumbling below their feet, see the water peel away from the bow, smell the exhaust as it pours out the stack, and hear the force of air escaping from the deck guns just before the water shoots out. This kind of full-body, sensory experience takes on heightened meaning in the context of our increasingly more sedentary, screen-focused lives.

As I walk around the foundry site, I do smell the dirt. Here and there, among the new-growth saplings in the glen, students work alone or in pairs, fussing about in their holes, using trowels, dustpans, and whisk brooms like you'd see beside a fireplace. Most of this year's heavy digging has already been completed. Tape measures stretched along a short side of each hole help students track the positions of features they are examining—the remains of brick walls, iron pipes, or other structures and artifacts they have found. Already today a student has discovered a clay smoking-pipe etched with the words "Home Rule." The slogan, a battle cry for self-government, offers evidence of the Irish who worked here when the foundry's twenty-four-hour operations made this peaceful patch of woods a noisy, smoky, busy factory. Standing in the sun-dappled gorge, I try to imagine the place that nineteenth-century author Benson Lossing encountered during his visit in the 1860s:

> We could hear the deep breathing of furnaces, and the sullen, monotonous pulsations of trip-hammers, busily at work at the West Point Foundry, the most extensive and complete of the iron-works of the United States. Following a steep, stony ravine that forms the bed of a water-course during rain-storms, we descended to these works, which lie at the head of a marshy cove, and at the mouth of a deep gorge, through which flows a clear mountain stream called Foundry Creek.

Today the ravine is quiet, save for the chatter of visitors and the students answering their questions. One student, in beige cargo shorts and a backward cap, digging in a unit that had once been part of the foundry's massive machine shop, is busy color-matching soil samples by comparing spoonfuls of dirt with color chips in a bound book. "It's called the Munsell soil color chart," he explains. "Coroners use it for identifying skin and hair color too," he adds. Ashes to ashes, I think.

✦ ✦ ✦

Another way the MTU Field School helps people make a tangible connection with history and the foundry is by inviting foundryman Dean Anderson to demonstrate the art of casting. Under a white tent in the clearing in front of the office building, he moves step by step through the process: packing a wooden pattern in sand, carving channels for the molten metal to flow through, removing the pattern, pouring the metal in, letting it cool and harden, then removing the solid metal form, to the oohs and ahs of the crowd. Side by side with Dean is journeyman Amy Lahey, who has been apprenticing with him since 2004.

Now sixty-three years old, Dean has been working with metal since 1967 and is the proprietor of Super Square, a 4,000-square-foot metal fabrication shop in Newburgh, New York, where he uses traditional nineteenth-century practices to make ornamental metal structures and fixtures for homes. Some months after the open house, I visit the shop where Dean and Amy form, fabricate, cast, and forge custom metals. When I arrive, just after dark on a rainy December night, downtown Newburgh has the look of a small city that has fallen on hard times.

Super Square is located in a basement space behind and below B's Auto Parts. The first thing I notice when I open my car door is the rushing sound—like a highway of cars shooshing across wet pavement—of Quassaick Creek, swollen and surging along the back edge of the parking lot. In another age, Dean's foundry and metal shop might have been run by harnessing the water in this creek. Instead, Dean buys his juice, like the rest of the businesses along this strip, from Central Hudson Gas and Electric, which only within the last hour has restored power to the block after a storm-related blackout.

I have come to ask Dean why it's so important to hold on to the knowledge of craftsmanship. Given that the foundryman makes his living utilizing old technologies, my questions strike a chord, especially when the conversation turns to teaching the next generation.

"If you don't know how to make something, you can't express yourself," Dean says. "When you lay your hands on something, you get personally involved." And in the classes he has taught, instructing middle- and high-schoolers in metalwork, he has seen how kids, especially, respond to this physicality. "Kids just want to touch something. They want reality very badly. They've been sitting in a chair in school. They need to grab something, they need to bend it, they need to cut it. They need to know that they can make an impression on something."

Dean worries that we, as a society, haven't quite grasped all that we are losing to the computer. "Your body is not meant to sit in a damn chair. And these kids are wandering around in a desert—they are parched. What can you do with a computer screen? We're going to have kids with, like, forty-five-pound thumbs and they won't be able to stand up!"

On Dean's first visit to the West Point Foundry, when he was in his twenties, and just learning patternmaking, he found all kinds of wooden patterns among the ruins on the forest floor. It felt magical to connect with the patternmakers from a century ago. "I picked up every one I could find," Dean says, since back then there was no indication that a school like MTU would come in to try to preserve the site's artifacts. Today, what he would really like to see on the foundry property is a trade school for metal and wood, modeled after the North Bennet Street School in Boston.

Founded in 1885, the North Bennet Street School claims to have "pioneered the concept of intensive instruction in a classroom/shop setting for the sole purpose of learning a trade." I'm familiar with the school since Mark Dooley, one of my mother's brothers, recently graduated from its preservation carpentry program. Prior to this recent career shift, Mark had been working in computers for twenty-six years, first as a programmer and later in management at a large, multinational corporation. He still recalls the first mainframe computer he worked on in the 1980s: "It was an IBM 3032, which was not state-of-the-art, but close, with one hundred megabytes, and it took up an entire thirty-by-thirty-foot room." He remembers the rectangular box, painted IBM blue, and the enormous hum in the room, the tapes flying, the lights flickering. This machine had cost several million dollars.

Back then, Mark says, his computer job had elements of craftsmanship that he enjoyed—"the art of programming." He and his colleagues wrote and tested code, and fixed what others had written. When systems he had developed popped up on the old green computer screen, knowing that he wrote it and that it worked gave him immense satisfaction. But with the advent of the microcomputer, the movement away from "home-crafted code" toward "shrink-wrapped software" took some of the fun out of the job. That, combined with outsourcing and consolidations, moved him up into management, which he liked much less.

His position shifted over the years until finally he found himself working primarily with consultants who spent their time "making sure that *their* toast was buttered, that *they* got what they wanted— the raise, the promotion," while he spent most of his energy trying to persuade them to get what his company needed done. He was unhappy working as "a largely faceless staff member for a large company doing work that did no real good for humanity." So when his company reconsolidated, yet again, he decided to take the buyout option and change careers.

Though he had never done more than a little bit of carpentry here and there, including renovations to his own nineteenth-century home in Massachusetts, he decided to switch gears entirely so he could work with his hands. Now, what he enjoys about carpentry is the immediate feedback on the work, which results in a tangible finished product that he can share with "mere mortals"—by which he means that laypeople, rather than just coders of the same ilk, can appreciate what he has produced. What he likes about doing carpentry in the old ways is putting his hands to "something that has longevity and character and a sense of depth and community in it—something that's attached to the quality and integrity of the past."

Dean thinks North Bennet Street's approach is the perfect model for a West Point Foundry metalworking school. "It could be fed by the three community colleges within driving distance of the foundry. We could use the site to teach art and technology, and offer hands-on training. Scenic Hudson could become a leader in teaching environmentally sound manufacturing." Though he has approached Scenic Hudson, the site's current owner, with his idea, not much has happened with it. "If I took six months off work I could probably come up with a business plan," says Dean. But with more work coming in than he can keep up with, that's not likely to happen—at least not anytime soon.

Still, I find it encouraging to hear that Dean's business is doing well, especially in an age when it seems the ethos of craftsmanship is on the outs. As Richard Sennett explains in *The Culture of the New Capitalism*, "Craftsmanship sits uneasily in the institutions of flexible capitalism." The problem, he writes, lies in the investment of time and energy required to "do something well for its own sake." Today's businesses operate at the pace of the consultant who "swoops in and out but never nests," handling "short-term transactions and constantly shifting tasks" that "do not breed that depth." In short, Sennett explains, "the emerging social order militates against the ideal of craftsmanship." In a subsequent book, *Craftsmanship*, Sennett argues that Western civilization has had a "deep-rooted trouble in making connections between head and hand, in recognizing and encouraging the impulse of craftsmanship," despite the benefits that the craftsman's way of working can offer, such as "an anchor in material reality." What happens when "hand and head, technique and science, art and craft are separated," he argues, is that the head suffers, and both "understanding and expression are impaired."

Dean's success runs counter to this trend. As he pages through a photo album of his products, including a variety of traditionally forged ornamental metals, like railings, doors, furniture, grills, lamps, and even brackets for wisteria, he explains the painstaking processes he used to craft these objects. I'm struck not only by their beauty, but by the warmth in his voice when he describes how he made them.

✦ ✦ ✦

The more time I spend on the Hudson, the more I see how the river's history is inextricably linked with the history of craftsmanship in the United States. And one man in particular, I discover, played a pivotal role in its fate: Frederick Winslow Taylor.

Years before he became "Mr. Scientific Management," the "first efficiency expert," at the turn of the twentieth century, Taylor rowed crew on the Squamscott River in Exeter, New Hampshire, the same spot where I savored my first taste of boating. Given the intense pace of my own Exeter existence, it doesn't surprise me to learn that the man who altered the very fabric of Americans' notions about time was a product of Phillips Exeter Academy. The school's infamously grueling workload has taught generations of students to gauge the value of every moment, carefully evaluating how much stealing another few minutes away from that stack of textbooks waiting on your desk will ultimately cost. This notion of time as commodity defined Taylor's work.

Beginning in the 1880s, Taylor inculcated Americans with the notion of efficiency as a core value, thereby helping to transform the United States into the hurried nation it is today. His work, systematizing manufacturing by dividing it up into minute, prescribed movements, threatened the principles of craftsmanship by divorcing workers from the art of their work. As Robert Kanigel explains in *The One Best Way: Frederick Winslow Taylor and the Enigma of Efficiency*, "Traditional craft know-how was being reduced to scientific data and passing from workman to manager, from shop floor to front office."

Taylor lived from 1856 to 1915, precisely when the industrial revolution was at its height. He existed, writes Kanigel in his 1997 biography, in "an age when factories were going up, not coming down; when production, the clamor of things being made, bore the excitement we invest today in Silicon Valley. Hopes for a new era of boundless prosperity surged through American life. . . . Faith in benign science knew no bounds." Taylor felt the intoxication of working in the vanguard of industry. Like the young upstarts in the dot-com era, Taylor envisioned new approaches to common problems, and poured his whole life into creating change.

He systematized machinists' efforts, clocking each precise movement with a stopwatch to determine the most efficient procedures, then used the information to regiment the actions of each worker in the shop. Taylor's system, once adopted, spread to other factories and shops, shifting the very ethos of the nation.

Many workers and labor union bosses were far from enthusiastic about Taylor's new system. As Carroll Pursell explains in *The Machine in America: A Social History of Technology*:

Years of patiently acquired skill could be lost overnight, leaving workers with nothing to sell but their time and muscle. When Taylorism was really successful, the resulting work process was rationalized to the point where skill, initiative, and control were all reduced to their lowest possible level, and workers became changeable parts in the productive machine, contributing time and effort to processes they neither controlled nor understood. For many, the prospect of a small share of the increased productivity in the form of higher piece-rate wages was poor compensation for a work experience drained of initiative, satisfaction, and meaning.

Or, as Dean Anderson puts it, "Once you idiot-proof a job, all you get for workers are idiots."

But managers flocked to Taylorism because his methods offered remedies for real inefficiencies in nineteenth-century factories where work at one end of the shop was often stalled by slowdowns at the other end. In *Clockwork* (1982), Eric Breitbart's documentary about Taylor, early 1900s film footage of a Westinghouse factory reveals a frenzied, chaotic shop space with men climbing in and around equipment piled on the floor. Taylor's goal was to streamline production processes by finding the "one best way" to get each piece of the job done. And instituting these changes helped the United States sustain its position as a global leader in manufacturing.

But some elements of craft don't translate onto the page—they're stored in the muscles and memories of artisans who've performed a task a thousand times before. Taylor's system of having the managers in an office doing all the thinking, while workers were left with only the doing, left an important piece out of the equation: human practice. Taylor didn't set out to destroy craftsmanship, but to create efficiency. He believed knowledge, not muscle power, was the prime productive resource. Today, Kanigel explains, we see the results of his thinking: "The 'knowledge industry' is looked to as the source of most new jobs—while well-paid blue-collar jobs, the kind blending head and hand, disappear."

This split between brain and brawn—which began in the earliest days of industry, at factories like the West Point Foundry—changed the face of production nationwide. Expanding markets and the spread of the wage-labor system were bringing fundamental changes to American society as inventors and engineers worked to devise ways to make products bigger, faster, and cheaper. In the free-market United States, capital reigned supreme, and these national shifts impacted the Hudson River Valley as well. These priorities, along with the increasing value of riverfront land, the widespread movement of manufacturing offshore, and the rise of the global economy set the stage for the next phase of the region's development—as a postindustrial resource for recreation and respite.

Today, advanced manufacturing technologies and materials, overseas shipping efficiencies, and political, economic, and transportation conditions ensure a ready supply of new products. A surfeit of inexpensive goods fosters a consumer culture that pulls us further and further away from engaging with the objects around us in a mechanical way. *If it's broken, chuck it and get a new one. It's too expensive to fix. The parts cost more than a whole new unit.* This disengagement from the objects in our lives deprives us of an opportunity to connect with the physical world.

Back before I wrapped my hands around the fireboat's brass levers, I hadn't given any of this much thought. I didn't realize how much my immersion in virtual work had stripped away my ties with the material world, or grasp how viscerally and spiritually satisfying it would be to make myself useful in a way that produced immediate, tangible results.

Matthew Crawford would understand what I mean. In his essay "Shop Class as Soulcraft," published in *The New Atlantis: A Journal of Technology & Society*, Crawford bemoans the decline of manual competency and craftsmanship in a postindustrial, information age. He cautions that declining tool use seems to "betoken a shift in our way of inhabiting the world: more passive and more dependent."

He shares his frustration over opening the hood on a new car ("especially German ones") only to find "another hood under the hood." I've heard my father voice this very same complaint, grousing about how the computers in today's vehicles thwart a mechanic's ability to make commonsense diagnoses without relying blindly on error codes transmitted over the wires of an On-Board Diagnostic system reader.

These days, there are "fewer occasions for the kind of spiritedness that is called forth when we take things in hand for ourselves, whether to fix them or to make them," Crawford argues. "What ordinary people once made, they buy; and what they once fixed for themselves, they replace entirely or hire an expert to repair, whose expert fix often involves installing a pre-made replacement part."

My dad and my brother often joke about the difference between mechanics and parts swappers. Anyone can keep replacing components until the problem fixes itself, but a true mechanic can think through a hundred cause-and-effect scenarios, identify those most likely, and drill right into the root of the problem—at least on a good day. But nowadays, the impenetrable inner workings of many machines, gadgets, and devices make it harder to deduce anything intelligible from the outside.

What American society is missing, according to John Ratzenberger, is the art of tinkering. Following his days bellying up to the bar as Cliff Clavin, the know-it-all letter carrier on the hit NBC-TV series *Cheers*, John has embarked on a mission to nurture the spirit of tinkering. In conjunction with his Travel Channel show *Made in America*, which features people working in domestic manufacturing, he published a book called *We've Got It Made in America: A Common Man's Salute to an Uncommon Country*, and founded an organization called the Nuts, Bolts & Thingamajigs Foundation. For him, promoting tinkering is a patriotic act.

"By and large, America has been a country of doers, of makers, and of manufacturers who put their hands to something useful every day," he writes. "We had pride in what we did and made, and produced goods that were in demand all over the world." These days, however, all that has changed.

As John sees it, the cultural shift away from making things and working with our hands threatens our national security, weakens our economy, and has the potential to send us down a path toward becoming a third-world nation. I reached out to get John's take on what our country is losing in our shift away from hands-on work.

We met at a restaurant in Providence, Rhode Island, where he had been attending a film festival, and when I witnessed the deference with which the maître d' treated John, I realized the "common man" status he claims in the subtitle of his book regularly meets with challenges. But, celebrity notwithstanding, John treated the staff respectfully, asking our waiter his name, then using it at the end of each "thank you." He seemed secure in the fact that work of all kinds feeds the larger whole—from the busboy to the bus driver to the bus-company executive. What came through loud and clear in our conversation was his sense that negative public perceptions of people who work with their hands have set the country up for a fall.

"It starts with the kids," John began. "Every single industry on the face of the earth started with one person making one thing. And that one person started off as a child who tinkered, whether building a tree house or, like the Wright brothers, messing around with the concept of bicycles and chains and gears. To me, one of the giant dangers is that children don't do that anymore. Soon we won't have any more inventors and innovators—native-born, anyway—who will start new industries." He called this trend an "industrial tsunami." It's heading our way, he said, though few people seem to be anticipating its potentially catastrophic impact.

America's future is in jeopardy, John argues, not just because we aren't raising up the next generation of innovators, but because we don't have young people training for, or even interested in, essential blue-collar work like welding, plumbing, pipe fitting, or bridge building. "A fellow I know in Chicago says he could put a hundred welders to work tomorrow, but he can't find one." And why is that? John blames it on the schools and the media.

"Anytime someone who's skilled manually is depicted on the screen, they're portrayed as either idiots, less than intelligent, or drunken louts. So why would anyone growing up with that image over the last twenty or thirty years want to be that?" This "elitist point of view" has taken hold of the educational system, too, John explained. "Guidance counselors think factory work is for people who are stupid." So when kids do express an interest in hands-on work, they are often discouraged by parents, guidance counselors, and sometimes even their peers.

John recounted a story about a talk he gave at a high school in Erie, Pennsylvania. "I said, 'How many of you are going to college?' Everybody raised their hands except this one kid over in the corner. I said, 'What are you going to do?' He said, a little embarrassed, 'I'm going to go to a tech school.' And everybody started laughing. At first I was pretending to side with the rest of the class. 'What do you want to do at tech school?' He said, 'Auto mechanics,' and everybody went, 'Tee hee hee,' like he was the dope. Then I said, 'Man, that is funny, 'cause in four years you guys will be waiting on tables, paying back your college loans, and he's gonna own his own home. And you're going to be bringing your cars, paying him to fix 'em. So, why is that a bad thing?' But that's the reality these days."

He wishes more kids grew up like he did, "in a family of people who tinkered and puttered, fixed, and mended." That, he said, "is the real genius of America, always has been. People who could just figure something out with seemingly unrelated objects, and make something else." I found myself recalling Robert Fulton and Robert Parrott and John Krevey and other figures along the Hudson River who have marshaled the resources at their disposal to create the next new thing.

"The people in power, especially in the media, I think they think there's a farm out there that's growing people who make things," said John. "They don't realize there are no more shop courses. But even when you tell them that, they don't get it. To them shop courses were where the stupid kids went."

"Shop Class as Soulcraft" essayist Crawford shares John's concern. "Perhaps the time is ripe for reconsideration of an ideal that has fallen out of favor: manual competence, and the stance it entails toward the built, material world," he writes. While the "hard-headed educator will say that it is irresponsible to educate the young for the trades," he or she seems to be missing the important point that not all hands-on work entails getting stuck in a mind-numbing, dead-end job and that some work in the trades cannot be outsourced. Putting it bluntly, Crawford explains, "If you need a deck built, or your car fixed, the Chinese are of no help. Because they are in China."

In the nineteenth century, even the sons of aristocrats took on apprenticeships, although they had no intention of working in the trades. The idea was that manipulating materials exercised important parts of the brain. Some form of hands-on training was considered integral to a well-rounded education. For later generations, this was the idea behind shop classes. But today, as school boards tighten their belts, shop classes (along with art and music classes, which offer other opportunities for hands-on learning) are often the first to get slashed from budgets. Young people today are discouraged from learning manual trades and pushed toward college, supposedly to prepare them for work in the "knowledge economy." I can't help wondering what this remove from material competence is costing our culture.

✦ ✦ ✦

When John Ratzenberger hosts his tinkering camps for kids, or speaks before Congress about the dangers of the debasement of blue-collar work, he says he's operating from a position of patriotism. "My passion is this country. . . . I love this country."

In linking craftsmanship and patriotism, John draws from deep roots. In New York in the 1760s and 1770s, craftsmen were among the first to rally for independence. They organized a Committee of Mechanics that took on some quasi-governmental functions and led the city's revolutionary movement. "These mechanics took Thomas Paine's message to heart and insisted on independence months before more conservative New Yorkers were ready to act," write Paul Gilje and Howard Rock in *Keepers of the Revolution: New Yorkers at Work in the Early Republic*. Many joined militias, the Continental Army, or operated as privateers.

Once the Revolution was over, they demanded that craftsmen occupy a central place in democratic society. They saw the "useful harmony" of the workshop—with its progression from apprentice to journeyman to master—as a model for the entire republic that promised an open, accessible economy that would allow anyone who worked hard to get ahead, explain Gilje and Rock. "Mechanics saw themselves as virtuous manufacturers, and hence the core of the commonwealth. They held politically suspect those who accumulated property without a productive trade, particularly mercantile speculators, bankers, and lawyers." Craftsmanship was seen as the lifeblood of the new nation, the birth of the American dream.

✦ ✦ ✦

During my extend-a-stay college years, I was determined to take full advantage of the semester-abroad program. I studied Italian for a year, then packed my bags for Florence, where I lived for three months, immersing myself in the language and culture—to the extent that one can as an American student, in a single semester. The Stanford program was rigorous, and most of my classes were taught in Italian except for one: art history. The professor, Mr. Verdon, taught us about Italian Renaissance masterpieces through on-site classes all over Florence. A well-connected Roman Catholic priest, Verdon managed to secure us all kinds of behind-the-scenes access.

In the basement of one particular church, he gave us an eye-opening little pop quiz. He pointed out two very different pillars. One was slender, elegant, and covered in magnificent mosaic tile work. The second was sloppy. Fat and lumpy at the base, it looked like a sand castle you'd throw together at the beach. "Which one's older?" he asked us. We all pointed, reasonably, at the lumpy one. No, he corrected. The fine mosaic one was older. So what happened? he asked. No one spoke up. What happened, he explained, was war.

During a period of extended warfare, all attention had strayed away from the building trades, and when the wars ended, there was no one left who knew how to erect a slender column. Wars had devastated the region, interrupting apprenticeships, and the technology had been lost. I had always thought that the progression of time moved society and knowledge forward, but here was proof that human know-how could regress. People had moved back in time, losing skills they once employed to manipulate materials. Of course, I can now grasp that skills do disappear over time. How many of us today could spin wool into thread, or build a wagon wheel, or bake bread from scratch in a wood-fired oven?

When I tell Tim the story about the pillars, he draws a link to ancient pyramids. "Once upon a time, hundreds of thousands of people knew how the pyramids were made," he says. "They all either did it themselves or sat there and watched it happen around them." Today we can only marvel at how some of these engineering masterpieces were produced. "These days," he adds, "we don't know how to fit a rivet." That last example hits close to home.

Nowadays you can buy old textbooks online that offer correspondence-course instruction in all kinds of old ways. But so much of learning to manipulate materials doesn't come through on the page. Mastering manual skills requires learning by doing. And with so many young hands curled around computer-gaming accessories instead of manual tools, I wonder how many versions of that Florentine pillar we, in this country so distracted by computer screens, will forget how to build.

Chapter Fifteen

NAILS IN THE COFFIN
OF INDUSTRY

The Recreational River

AT NINE O'CLOCK on a Monday night in summer 2008, I'm in a wine-colored Subaru, headed with Stephen Fox, a nocturnal landscape painter, to an overlook on Storm King Mountain where we can see the Hudson by the light of the moon.

For the past several years Stephen has been tracking the moon's phases to guide the timing of his wanderings through the Hudson Highlands, where he drives along winding roads, clambers over stone walls, and walks his bike up steep inclines in places where cars aren't allowed, to collect images for what he calls his "nocturnes."

Stephen first discovered the Hudson in 2004 after a wrong turn brought him across the Bear Mountain Bridge. He was struck by the mist coming off the river in the moonlight. I have to explore this, he thought. At first he wondered whether it was "legitimate" to paint land and water so thoroughly explored by other artists, including the Hudson River School's founding father, Thomas Cole. But Stephen found himself drawn to the area, compelled by how "the river changes and doesn't change." A native of Richmond, Virginia, who moved to Brooklyn in 1997, he has since come to see the modern Hudson Valley as "an entirely different world than the one represented so beautifully in those earlier, nineteenth-century paintings."

Stephen didn't realize it at the time, but he was launching into a new period in his work. Three years after his detour, in 2007, he exhibited eleven paintings at the Reynolds Gallery in his hometown, all of which depicted Hudson River scenes at night. He describes them as "investigations of visual silence," explaining that what he seeks to find in the contemporary landscape is "the intersection of nature's grand elements with man's relatively small yet increasingly potent influence upon the land." In this quest he ponders the same questions that Cole and his Hudson River School colleagues contemplated more than a century and a half earlier.

Above the Hudson, 2004. View from an overlook on the east side of the Hudson River, looking south toward Peekskill. *(Oil on canvas by Stephen Fox)*

✦ ✦ ✦

My own appreciation of the Hudson River School artists came through falling for the Hudson itself. When I found myself missing the river on a cold, rainy day in February, I decided to look for it among the paintings at the New-York Historical Society.

Standing in a warm gallery, I caught myself shivering before a painting: *Winter Twilight Near Albany, NY* (1858). "It was the depth of winter and it struck me that I had never seen a winter landscape painted just as I saw it," George Henry Boughton said about his piece. So he gathered his oil paints and crunched over the hard-crusted snow. Then, with cold-cramped hands, he captured the scraggly, leafless branches, the dry grasses and rocks poking through the frozen white, the stillness of the river in its dormancy—its wintertime quiescence. Having worked on the fireboat's machinery in that kind of cold, I could picture him painting until his fingers stopped functioning—until he had to paw his brushes with frozen digits clamped together for warmth.

Boughton had made the riverbank his studio, recording the details that lay before him, pulling the essence of the scene through tiny spaces between the fibers of his canvas. He had captured in paints the ache I so often feel for the icy Hudson, harvesting a truth from his surroundings that carries a lasting message. A critic called it "a perfect piece of winter."

Though painting landscapes from life stemmed from European plein-air roots, a particularly American approach to this type of art took hold in the early 1800s among a loose contingent of painters. Through direct experience of nature, these painters forged a new, self-consciously American vision of the land.

Just as the fledgling nation had recognized the need to establish a domestic manufacturing base as a matter of national security, the country's leading intellectuals clamored for new art that was uniquely American—a matter, in a sense, of national cultural security. New York governor De Witt Clinton was among those calling for active encouragement of the arts. In an 1816 address, he asked, "Can there be a country in the world better calculated than ours to exercise and to exalt the imagination—to call into activity the creative powers of the mind, and to afford just views of the beautiful, the wonderful, and the sublime?"

In 1823, Thomas Cole heeded Clinton's call. He began tramping through the Hudson Valley to make studies from nature, then took his sketchbook back to his tiny Greenwich Street apartment in Manhattan to re-create the most striking scenes from his journeys.

Though it had yet to be named, the Hudson River School movement was born.

"The river focused the sense of divine presence Cole felt in nature," explains Dunwell in *The Hudson: America's River.* "It awoke in him a deeper feeling, a sense of the harmony of creation." Cole considered himself a privileged witness to the divine, equating light, to which he was faithfully attentive, with God's radiance.

In a sense, Cole invented the American landscape. And young painters followed in his footsteps, penciling painstaking sketches from nature. Among this next generation of Hudson River School artists was Frederic Church, who studied under Cole for four years, beginning in 1844, when he was eighteen years old. By age twenty-one Church was an accomplished artist whose outlook was considered quintessentially American.

Sponsorship of the movement came through the patronage of the growing New York City merchant class, many of whom were enjoying newfound prosperity through trade on the newly open Erie Canal. Maintaining extensive collections of American art and funding artists' travels abroad became a status symbol for wealthy businessmen. But the upper classes weren't the Hudson River School painters' only fans. As many as a quarter of a million people visited exhibits at the New York Art Union each year between 1839 and 1851—among them "noisy boys and girls" and "working men by the hundreds," according to an 1848 edition of *Knickerbocker* magazine.

These painters were the rock stars of their day, and their masterpieces galvanized the still-new nation around a common identity: a distinctly American culture captured in the untamed grandeur of the country's vast resources. Europe might have ruins attesting to thousands of years of history, but the newly minted and still-expanding United States boasted acres upon acres of wilderness, revealing the raw work of prehistoric forces and the promise of present-day potential. By offering the country a "recognizable image of itself in art," writes Oswaldo Roque in *American Paradise: The World of the Hudson River School,* Cole, Church, and their compatriots helped inspire national pride and a sense of American uniqueness.

Recording nature directly, Hudson River School painters were able to distinguish themselves from artists who stayed in their studios painting what they imagined nature to be. Yet the school's works were not based solely on fact but also infused with ideology. A century after these artists had captured the valley's color, light, and shadow their paintings were offered as evidence for the need for conservation. Then life began to imitate art.

✦ ✦ ✦

If Storm King had still been named Butter Hill in September 1962, when Consolidated Edison (Con Ed) announced plans to carve out a side of the mountain, the activists fighting to save it might have had a harder time rallying people to their cause. Perhaps we are indebted to Nathaniel Parker Willis, the nineteenth-century writer who went on a naming spree to replace what he considered loathsome or dull designations for Hudson River landmarks (Murderer's Creek became Moodna Creek, Bull Hill became Mount Taurus, and so on) for the fact that Storm King remains intact today.

The controversy began when Con Ed proposed building the world's largest pumped-storage hydroelectric facility by destroying an entire side of the bluff—located in Cornwall, New York, on the west bank of the Hudson about forty-seven miles north of Manhattan. After Con Ed announced its intentions, Chairman Harland Forbes told the *New York Times* that the company anticipated no difficulties. Apparently it had failed to realize that many Americans considered the site to be "sacred ground" writes Dunwell. Con Ed's announcement quickly launched a fight that "assumed the intensity and proportions of a holy crusade." The mythology surrounding this site had existed long before Con Ed dreamed up the Storm King solution to its peak power problem:

> The passage through Breakneck and Storm King had come to symbolize the essence of the Highlands and the Hudson Valley region. . . . The scene of the northern gate, where the river meets the mountains, was painted and sketched more than any other in the Highlands. This was the view that nineteenth-century tourists saw from the plains at West Point; it greeted them from sloops and steamers as they journeyed south across the broad expanse of Newburgh Bay; and it is the image of the river that people today are most likely to remember.

Soon after Con Ed submitted its proposal to the Federal Power Commission (FPC), citizen groups rallied, eventually uniting under a newly formed umbrella organization that came to be known as Scenic Hudson. Originally, the group voiced opposition to the project based on two objections: one, the plant would disfigure the mountain, and two, it would open the door to more big industrial development projects along the river. After the FPC decided in favor of Con Ed in 1964, Scenic Hudson raised funds and hired legal counsel to help it appeal the decision, prompting a series of additional hearings.

As the fight continued, Scenic Hudson "raised every conceivable objection," explains Allan Talbot in his book about the case, *Power Along the Hudson*. "But the central argument was the plant would destroy the scenic beauty of the mountain." Ultimately, the spawning habits of striped bass served as a tipping point against the proposed plant. But such technical and scientific considerations, while relevant, seemed to be raised in service of Scenic Hudson's primary objective, which was to preserve the look of the land.

Scenic Hudson's efforts were successful, not only in thwarting the project, but in pushing the Federal Court of Appeals in New York to make the groundbreaking decision to legitimize aesthetic concerns. The court declared that the FPC must "include as a basic concern the preservation of natural beauty and national historic shrines, keeping in mind that in our affluent society, the cost of a project is only one of several factors to be considered." This call for a review of scenic considerations set an important precedent for environmental cases to come. Another precedent granted environmentalists access to the federal courts by affirming the public's right to participate in decision making about development projects proposed for their communities. The fight to save Storm King has since been lauded as the birth of modern American environmental law.

One of the ways Scenic Hudson had spurred regional, national, and even international opposition to the plant was by employing Hudson River art in its public outreach campaigns. One brochure, reports Raymond O'Brien in *American Sublime: Landscape and Scenery of the Lower Hudson Valley*, used nineteenth-century lithographs to advocate "scenic preservation," the goal of which was "saving landforms that are beautiful today, still beautiful in fact because they were sanctified and mythologized in our romantic past." The key word, I came to learn, was "mythologized."

✦ ✦ ✦

A hundred years earlier, Hudson River School artists also confronted view-scapes altered by the march of technology, including steam trains, lumber mills, tanneries, and other evidence of a country moving away from its agricultural roots toward becoming a world leader in industry. The panoramas many of these artists celebrated—unspoiled landscapes of mountains, water, and trees—depicted the same natural resources upon which the nation's growth depended.

As reflected in his "Essay on American Scenery," Cole understood that development was inevitable. What troubled him, however, was what he saw as careless, unnecessary destruction. When workers laid train tracks on the outskirts of his property in 1835, he dealt with his dismay over the loss of the pristine territory by producing a work that excluded entirely the presence of the railroad. Some of Cole's Hudson River School colleagues, however, seemed to embrace, or at least accept, the changes brought by development with works that expressed "confidence in the harmonious coexistence of progress and nature," and the "ability of the American arcadian ideal to absorb the effects of technology," writes Roque.

In either case, one tenet of the movement, the notion of "composed" landscapes, allowed artists to pick and choose what they included in their renditions from among the rugged cliffs, sloping mountains, and wind-twisted trees. While Hudson River School works are lauded for their naturalistic portrayals of the unbridled wildness of the American landscape, the artists took liberties by blotting out significant industrial features that marred the natural world.

Evidence of their omissions can be found in early photographs. Kevin Avery, associate curator of American paintings and sculpture at the Metropolitan Museum of Art, has compared Sanford Robinson Gifford's 1862 painting, *A Gorge in the Mountains (Kauterskill Clove)*, with an 1860s photograph of the same location that reveals clear-cut land. By the 1860s, many hardwood forests had been destroyed for fuel and the extraction of tannins. Rather than spoil his sylvan vista with evidence of Hudson River industry, Gifford filled in the void with trees. "This place looks better now than it did in the 1860s, when Sanford Gifford painted it," Avery explained.

Likewise, Charles Herbert Moore chose not to include the tunnel that had been blasted through Breakneck Ridge in an 1861 painting, although by that date the Hudson River Railroad had already reached Albany. "What they didn't want to see, they didn't make," explained cultural geographer and Vassar College professor Harvey Keyes Flad.

In a sense, the Storm King battle had been fought and won based on a romanticized vision of the river. The Hudson River School's idealized landscapes had sparked people's passions, prodding them into action. And that's why, when the next big fight between industry and aesthetics came to town, community organizers once again tapped the Hudson River School legacy as a means of rallying action.

✦ ✦ ✦

The city of Hudson is known for its quaint antique stores and the menagerie of different styles of American architecture represented on its main street. But I like it for the remains of industry. Scraggly weeds grow in insistent clumps through the white-tinged limestone ground where the fireboat tied up each summer from 2001 to 2004, in the yard of our waterfront host: St. Lawrence Cement.

Allowing the fireboat to park along the company's bulkhead was likely a gesture intended to improve community relations that had deteriorated drastically since 1999, when the company announced plans to build a mammoth new plant in Greenport, along Hudson's border. The fight had gotten nasty—pitting Stop the Plant neighbor against Support the Plant neighbor. Not since the battle to save Storm King had a conflict this big about Hudson River Valley land use broken out, and many believed the outcome of this struggle would determine the future of industry on the river.

Together with Scenic Hudson, a grassroots advocacy group called Friends of Hudson was spearheading the campaign against the plant, arguing that the negative aesthetic and environmental impacts outweighed any economic benefit the new plant might bring—especially since, by St. Lawrence Cement's own account, the new facility would net just one new job. But plenty of residents supported the plant too, contending that the Friends of Hudson analysis didn't tell the whole story. Construction, for example, *would* bring work to the community, they argued. After all, St. Lawrence Cement had signed a Project Labor Agreement promising the work to local builders. Many who posted "Support the Plant" signs on their lawns hoped to bring back the days when Hudson was a bustling blue-collar town where the stores downtown stayed open late on payday.

This longing was understandable, since today the storefronts along the main drag, Warren Street, proffer art, antiques, and spa treatments, but few products of everyday use to residents. As St. Lawrence spokesperson Dan Odescalchi put it, recalling the now-defunct Universal Atlas Cement Company plant that had once been a source of many local jobs: "Cement put most of the people through college around here, bought most of the homes around here, paid for most of the weddings."

Columbia County, where Hudson is located, had found itself embroiled in an identity crisis that was playing out, to varying degrees, all along the river, as waterfront towns that had been founded by riverfront industries struggled to redefine themselves in a shifting economy. This battle embodied age-old disputes between labor and leisure, using and protecting natural resources, native-born and newcomers, and white- and blue-collar workers.

The cement plant dispute deeply divided the region. Hostilities that "both fostered and were exacerbated by stereotypes decreased the two sides' ability to communicate openly," explains Miriam Silverman in *Stopping the Plant*, published shortly after the New York Department of State handed down its final decision. "Plant supporters were portrayed as being less intelligent, less educated, or having a 'bizarre nostalgia' for the days of industry. Plant opponents were often stereotyped as being rich, gay antiques dealers from New York City." The turf war lasted six years.

For St. Lawrence Cement, a subsidiary of the Swiss and Canadian firm Holcim Ltd., constructing a new, state-of-the-art plant made good business sense. Becraft Mountain, which the company had owned since 1976, offered a plentiful source of limestone—a crucial ingredient of cement manufacture—and its location near the Hudson River offered a ready shipping corridor for moving product to nearby Boston, Albany, and New York City markets.

Over the second half of the twentieth century, cement production in New York State had dropped even as demand increased. More and more cement was imported to the area, which, St. Lawrence advocates argued, denied Hudson River Valley communities the benefits of employment and tax contributions from making it locally. Because of the unnecessary pollution created by the long-distance transportation of imported cement, and the fact that many cement-producing countries, like China and India, didn't hold to the same environmental standards as the United States, company officials contended that overseas production also contributed more pollution globally.

But for Stop the Plant activists, the impact of having a new 1,800-acre industrial city in their backyards outweighed any other consideration. The proposed project, which would occupy an area 20 percent larger than the city of Hudson itself, included a manufacturing plant and limestone mine on Becraft Mountain, and a two-mile tube conveyor system to haul product to a Hudson River dock facility for loading barges. One of the most prominent features of the site would be a forty-story smokestack with a plume that would stretch, according to the cement company's own estimates, more than six miles. The plant would burn 250,000 tons of coal each year, according to the Hudson River environmental group Riverkeeper—the stack emitting twenty million pounds of pollution annually.

In addition to the pollution, antiplant activists worried that the proposed facility would undermine efforts to rebuild the regional economy through tourism. The immense plant might be seen as an eyesore in the area's vistas and therefore detract from the tourist and real estate markets, with serious economic implications. In this, antiplant activists recognized a new model taking shape along the Hudson River. More than a century after manufacturers denuded whole hillsides of hardwoods for tannins and fuel, Hudson riverfront communities claimed heritage tourism and peaceful panoramas as the new lifeblood of local economies.

In their fight against the plant, activists copied the successful Storm King approach, leveraging Hudson River School heritage as a rallying cry for protecting the landscape. As Silverman explains, literature distributed by the Hudson Valley Preservation Coalition entitled "Our Concerns" warned, "This St. Lawrence Cement plant will be a hideous new landmark in a region whose legendary scenery has been immortalized in the paintings of the Hudson River School."

Among the groups active in the Stop the Plant campaign was the Olana Partnership, the nonprofit support arm of the state historic site featuring Frederic Church's former home and studio. Although its proper title is Olana, Church called his Moorish castle "the Center of the World." Built between 1870 and 1891, high upon a hill near the city of Hudson, the site afforded Church sweeping views of the Hudson River and the Catskill Mountains.

Now a National Historic Landmark, Olana is among the most visited tourist sites in the region. Today's visitors can stand in Church's studio and see the vistas that inspired his painting. The Olana Partnership feared the proposed cement plant would dominate its viewshed. It also expressed concern that the six-mile plume might deter tourists, driving away the associated revenues, and could damage the site's buildings, located just three miles away.

Aided by legal precedents set in the Storm King hearings, the New York Department of State ruled against the plant in 2005 on "scenic" grounds. In April, a twenty-page document outlined the reasons why the proposed plant was incompatible with the region, concluding, "It is clear that the SLC proposal . . . would affect historic resources and visual quality of the area." That alone, the report held, was reason enough to reject the proposal.

In the end, the battle over the plant pitted one version of the Hudson Valley's legacy against another. In the fight between scenic beauty and industry, it's perhaps no surprise that the side that is easiest to romanticize won. Stopping the plant was another watershed event in Hudson River history, solidifying the shift away from the river's industrial past and toward a future economy based on landscapes, heritage tourism, and a deep sense of place.

✦ ✦ ✦

The Storm King and St. Lawrence Cement controversies secured citizens' right to have a say in new industrial developments in their backyard, but what would become of the remnants of the Hudson's storied past as a commercial river? If heritage tourism was to become the linchpin of the new river economy, would it include protecting industrial landmarks?

Though Scenic Hudson's funding of the archaeology project on the West Point Foundry site for eight summers exemplified a new model of cooperation between environmental and industrial heritage pursuits, the project came to a close after the students' 2008 dig. Meanwhile other, more intact sites along the river haven't received anywhere near the attention afforded the foundry ruins.

For Rob Yasinsac and Tom Rinaldi, protecting the Hudson River's industrial heritage is an essential part of the valley's future. In April 2008, I met up with Rob and Tom in Yonkers, about fifteen miles north of Times Square in Manhattan, to spend a day with them as they nosed around the city, snapping pictures and checking up on which buildings had vanished since their last visit.

For years, the ruins hunters have been combing the Hudson River Valley collecting images of vanishing industrial landscapes, much in the way Cole and others captured images of disappearing wilderness. Instead of sketchbooks, they carry cameras, usually two apiece, to buildings (and sometimes vessels) that reveal the valley's past. Their collaboration has produced a compendium of endangered "species" along the Hudson, a yearbook of relics, including mills, factories, arsenals, railroad stations, and other crumbling beauties. *Hudson Valley Ruins: Forgotten Landmarks of an American Landscape* reads like a Who's Who of sites they deem worthy of protection.

The highlight of our spring field trip was a stop at the Yonkers Power Station, one of the most significant turn-of-the-century industrial structures still remaining on the Hudson. I had seen this building many times through the fireboat portholes. Later, from the wheelhouse of the tug, I finally took in the commanding brick structure all at once, admiring its rows of arched windows, the red terracotta trim, and the two round stacks that convey the very essence of the building's function: power.

Turns out, the river offers the best view of the building, which is

Yonkers Power Station, as viewed from the river in July 2002. *(Photo by Rob Yasinsac, www.hudsonvalleyruins.org. From Rinaldi and Yasinsac, Hudson Valley Ruins)*

simply too massive to take in from the waterfront park beside it. But I was grateful for the stillness of examining the structure from the land, since I could take my time looking, without worrying about the wheel or the levers at the control stand.

"This is one of the most distinct and important landmarks on the

Hudson River between New York and Albany," said Tom, and Rob agreed. In fact, Rob and two other Yonkers preservationists had filed a landmark application with the city in hopes of protecting it from demolition. The city's Landmarks Preservation Board had recommended the designation, but the planning board rejected it, and the application has since stalled in the city council.

"I don't understand how a planning board could look at this and say it is not a landmark," Tom grumbled. "It's got an architectural pedigree, and it holds an important place in the cultural history of the region."

The problem, replied Rob, was that the city planners didn't seem to be able to envision more than two options: ongoing abandonment or demolition. Unless someone tears down the building, they think it will sit here empty for another four decades, he explained. "They're not considering the fact that maybe there is someone out there who will refurbish it."

Models of successful reuse of decommissioned power plants and factories abound. One of the most striking domestic examples stands in Baltimore's Inner Harbor, where another early-twentieth-century power station was converted into the centerpiece of a shopping district. In London, the Tate Modern art museum occupies a former plant on the south bank of the river Thames. And along the Hudson, another art museum, Dia:Beacon, occupies a nearly 300,000-square-foot former box-printing factory in Beacon, New York.

Though Rob and Tom are young, thirty-one and twenty-nine respectively, they've witnessed profound changes along the Hudson. "Even in the seventies and eighties, when it was still pretty dirty, people wanted a view of the river," said Tom. "The river went from a transportation artery of commerce to a dumping ground. And today, now that the river's cleaner, it's still the economic stimulus threading through all the towns on both sides." The river, mostly used now for recreation, he explained, ties all these communities together.

Rapid population growth and efforts to clean up pollution mean riverfront property is in ever-greater demand, which has brought new attention to long-abandoned structures. These buildings could be redeveloped, put to new use, or preserved, but instead are often viewed as "eyesores"—symbols of stagnation—and destroyed. Up and down the river, as the ruins hunters explain in their book, "the region pens brochures promoting its rich history with one hand yet dashes that history away with the other."

Rob and Tom discovered their mutual interest while they were both still in college, each maintaining his own separate ruins Web site. After meeting over spring break in 1999, they decided to team up. These days Tom attends Columbia University's Graduate School of Architecture, Planning and Historic Preservation, and Rob works as a museum associate and interpreter at Philipsburg Manor in Sleepy Hollow, sometimes donning period garb—a frock coat or a milling apron. One of the Hudson River's earliest milling, farming, and trading complexes, Philipsburg Manor dates from the seventeenth century and is now a museum.

Together, Rob and Tom hope that sharing their documentation of structures in jeopardy will raise public awareness of industrial landmarks, and encourage them to be saved. When the sites don't survive, though, they take comfort in the fact that at least their images offer a lasting record of ruins destined to disappear. In their shared passion, Rob and Tom join the ranks of photographers like Berenice Abbott and Peter Moore (whose wife and editor Barbara Moore runs the fireboat's gift shop, selling souvenirs that help fund boat restoration), who each captured the haunting beauty of New York's Pennsylvania Station before its 1966 demise, which sparked the modern historic preservation movement.

The final chapter of *Hudson Valley Ruins* features the Yonkers Power Station. It makes a fitting endnote to their book, given the building's striking presence and architectural and industrial significance, which marks a crucial transition in turn-of-the-century railroad technology. Built in 1906 for the New York Central and Hudson River Railroad, the plant helped facilitate the transition from steam locomotives to electric trains in New York City. At the time, electricity remained a limited commodity. Thomas Edison had built his first Manhattan power station in 1882, but the output it provided was nowhere near enough to supply New York Central. So the railroad company decided to supply its own power. The Yonkers plant was an integral component of a three-part upgrade to the metropolitan rail system—a huge capital-improvements project that also included another power station in the Bronx and a newly constructed Grand Central Terminal.

Designed by the Minnesota-based architectural firm Reed and Stem, the Yonkers station housed twenty-four boilers powered with coal fed from two overhead bunkers, each with 3,500-ton capacity. On the northern side of the building stood four 5,000-kilowatt, thirty-five-foot-tall Curtis turbogenerators—units that supplied alternating current to a series of substations where it was converted to direct current and fed to trains via a new device known as the third rail.

"See the wharf down there?" asked Tom, pointing toward the river. "That's where the coal barges came in. The boilers were in the south side. The coal got burned in the boilers, the smoke went up the stack, and the steam got piped into the room under the north gable where it was forced through the turbines, generating the power that wound up in the third rail to run the trains."

When it was completed, the Yonkers Power Station stood as a triumphant expression of the architecture and engineering of its day. In their book, Rob and Tom call it "the prototype for the last traditional industry to establish a presence in the valley: electric power generation." As other industries declined, power plants mushroomed up along the waterfront, eventually "growing so intrusive that they became a menace to the quality of life on the river." Examples included Central Hudson Gas and Electric's Danskammer plant, which opened in 1952; the Con Ed nuclear power plant at Indian Point, just south of Peekskill, which opened in 1963; and subsequent plants in Tomkins Cove (since demolished), Bowline Point, and Roseton, north of Newburgh. Power plant construction along the Hudson continues into the twenty-first century, with the opening of the Athens Generating Plant, which went into service in 2004.

The Yonkers station finally closed in 1963, after new technologies enabling modern plants to operate more efficiently had rendered it obsolete. Unlike some later plants, however, the Yonkers Power Station had been carefully designed, architecturally, to complement its surroundings. Rob and Tom hope this fact will increase the likelihood that at least parts of the plant will remain intact in some new incarnation.

For now, the power plant's cathedral-like rooms have been emptied of machinery. All the turbines have been removed, and rainwater pools in the spaces left behind. Green mosses grow over their empty mounting beds, and rust spreads over orphaned gears in the floor. Daylight spills through the many-paned, arched windows, revealing the brush and vines overtaking the brick facade. One power plant visitor who posted photographs online commented:

> Just navigating the space was a challenge, but much of the work was done ahead of time. Missing sections of stairways covered with metal grates, makeshift ladders and ramps all over the place. With all the catwalks and stairways and ladders, I felt as if I was transported into a video game.

So far, the future of the Yonkers Power Station looks promising. Mark Peckham tells me that the New York State Historic Preservation Office has deemed it eligible for National Register listing. This determination does not guarantee protection—it just means that any state or federal agency involved in an undertaking at this property (including funding, licensing, permitting) will now be required to contact the preservation office, which will consult on how to "avoid, minimize, or mitigate adverse effects to the plant," Mark explains. "We would hope that it would also set the stage for an adaptive reuse, which is the only way we are really going to be able to provide for long-range preservation.... Whether you find beauty in this behemoth or not," he adds, "its history is compelling and its loss would be a huge waste of well-built steel and masonry in a prime waterfront location. As preservationists say, 'The greenest building is the one that is already built.'"

Since the beginning of the industrial age, the people of the Hudson River Valley have struggled to strike a balance between natural vistas and the visible presence of industry. Drawn to river landscapes by their complexity, both artists and documentarians have captured glimpses that show the choices society makes over time. Their depictions reveal the eternal tensions between nature and humankind, past and future, industry and recreation.

✦ ✦ ✦

Nocturnal landscape artist Stephen Fox knows exactly where he wants to stop. He has driven around these same twists and turns up Storm King Mountain on many a moonlit night. When the winding two-lane leads us to a particular high point in the road, Stephen pulls off onto a wide shoulder and parks the car.

We step out of the Subaru onto the mighty Storm King, and across the river I can see Breakneck Ridge. As Stephen sets up his camera on a tripod, he tells me that reaching the top of the ridge requires scrambling over the rocks on all fours. One night when he was out shooting pictures, he climbed up at dusk, then realized there was no way he could make it down in the dark, even with his flashlight and headlamp. So he watched for the moon to rise, shot his pictures, then lay down on the rocks, his daypack under his head, to wait for morning light. "I got more bug bites than I've ever gotten in my life," he says, adding, "Who knows what the Hudson River School painters had to do, what insects they had to contend with, to get their landscapes."

I nestle myself into a rounded depression in one of the pieces of cut stone assembled here, keeping quiet so that Stephen can concentrate on his gear. Like Rob and Tom, Stephen's sketchbook is his camera. He snaps dozens of digital photos, sometimes hundreds in a single night. At home, on the computer screen, he pieces together sections of the landscape into a choppy, makeshift panorama, hunting for the shapes and qualities of light that seem right. Then, after constructing a single image from the many, he tacks the photo to the wall in his studio and prepares to paint.

While I wait in the moonlight, my eyes adjusting to the dark, a convergence of Hudson River activity unfurls before me. I can make out the shape of a tugboat pushing a loaded barge north, the boat's deckhouse outlined in blue lights. Then the headlights of a passenger train appear, the engine speeding up the Hudson's eastern shore, pulling its cars full of people. A second tug materializes, heading south, its yellow deck lights lined up in a row. This second tug is towing an empty barge, and it passes the other tug port to port, on the one-whistle side. At that moment, a clatter signals the approach of another train, this one on our side of the river, at the base of this mountain. A string of freight cars, the multiple colors of their shipping containers barely discernible in this light, shoots south down the Hudson's western shore. The scene before me embodies the mixed-use river of today—the tugs and barges, the trains hauling freight and people, the village of Cold Spring twinkling across the river, with its pleasure boats bobbing on moorings, and artists and spectators like us, who have come to watch the ever-busy river by the light of the moon.

Chapter Sixteen

Full Speed Ahead

⤳

DURING OUR YEAR in the shipyard in Bridgeport, the *John J. Harvey* crew learned a lot about independence. But what ended up saving the boat, allowing her to run for another season, was community.

I had no business being on deck when we pulled into New York harbor under tow. I should have been down in the engine room, answering bells. But having all hands available proved to be important as we arrived alongside Krevey's barge in his new spot, Pier 66. Negotiations with the Hudson River Park Trust had secured him a place in the park, so he had towed his car float barge a few blocks north, to the foot of a restored float bridge—the type that would have been used to offload a barge like his in decades past. The slip was silted in with mud, so after an hour of maneuvering, we finally had to tie up the boat cockeyed, the stern jutting out at a weird angle. Though this was her new home, the fireboat was so far from shore that Matt, captain of the *Cornell*, the tug that had towed us back to New York, had to drop us off a few piers away. We gathered our things and each wandered off on our own ways, consumed by the city that I wasn't sure had missed us while we were gone. My limbs felt heavy, my stomach sick. I had no idea what was going to happen next. The boat was still not able to move under her own power.

Months went by and I didn't set foot on the fireboat, which had become like the sick relative you don't want to visit in the hospital. Everything we had given hadn't been enough. What I didn't realize, though, was that fireboat *John J. Harvey* was bigger than all of us, and that someone in New York harbor had been watching, knew the boat's predicament, and was in a position to help.

Caddell Dry Dock and Repair Co. has been fixing commercial, military, recreational, and historic vessels in New York harbor for more than a century. Since its founding in 1903, the company has seen wood boats replaced by steel, rivets by welding, and steam engines by diesel. One of the few remaining full-service shipyards in the New York region, Caddell's operation boasts six dry docks, and the staff of 200 workers service more than three hundred vessels annually.

At the helm is president Steven Kalil, who began working for the company in 1975, when he was hired as a carpenter's helper. One cold winter morning he tried to quit, but John Bartlett Caddell II, grandson of the founder, invited him to work in the office instead. He learned the ropes of managing the yard, and gradually took over the day-to-day operations.

When all hope for the fireboat seemed lost, Kalil stepped in, offering to remove the shafts and replace the cutless bearings under a special payment arrangement. This wasn't the first time Caddell had supported historic vessels under Kalil's leadership, but this generous deed saved the *John J. Harvey*.

Just as America's earliest settlers embraced a system of bartering and shared labor that was crucial to their survival, the maritime community, too, depends on cooperative effort to withstand the rigors of change along the waterfront. In other ways, too, there are signs of old traditions being put to work in new ways up and down the Hudson.

✦ ✦ ✦

John Ratzenberger's tinkering message has already reached the Hudson River Valley, and his cosponsorship of a hands-on camp for teenage girls points to a possible next wave of industry springing up in the valley. Since 2007, his Nuts, Bolts & Thingamajigs foundation has helped fund a free weeklong camp, hosted by an Ulster County career and technical center, called Girls Get S.M.A.R.T. (Summer Manufacturing and Robotics Training) for young women in grades seven through ten. Located in Port Ewen (home of the tugboat-cradling

Madonna), just a couple of miles downriver from Kingston, the camp brought together twenty-three young women in August 2008 to learn about alternative energy. By the end of their week they had programmed a robotic solar car, built model houses, and studied wind, solar, and hydroelectric power.

This brief camp was just a small taste of the alternative-energy training that will soon be coming to the region's high schools and community colleges. In January 2009, New York State governor David Paterson announced a $5 million initiative, the Clean Energy Training Consortium, for green-energy job training and research to help reach the goal of converting 45 percent of the state's energy use to alternative sources by 2015—creating 50,000 green-sector jobs in the process. The initiative will fund training, particularly in Dutchess and Ulster counties, both along the Hudson, and with this investment, the governor hopes to make New York State a leader in green energy generation.

As part of the plan, the New York State Energy Research and Development Authority will build a Center for Efficient Building Science and invest $1 million in a training program for solar-panel installation at several career centers and community colleges, including Ulster County's. Perhaps one of the young women from the Get S.M.A.R.T. program, inspired to learn even more about solar power, will complete the training and land herself a "green-collar" job.

✦ ✦ ✦

As Consolidated Edison learned with Storm King Mountain and St. Lawrence Cement discovered in Hudson, launching industrial projects along the Hudson River comes with complications. One man who has managed to surmount these challenges is Carver Laraway, who recently established a new enterprise called P&M Brick–Port of Coeymans Marine Terminal, fifteen miles south of Albany.

Every September when we head to Waterford for the Tugboat Roundup, I slow the *Gowanus Bay*'s engines as we pass by Coeymans to catch a glimpse of all that has changed over the past year. Fascinated by this new industry springing up along the riverbanks, Bob, Karl, Tim, and I follow the site's progress, tallying new inlets and bulkheads constructed, scoping out buildings renovated or replaced, and tracking the paths of earthmovers in seemingly perpetual motion as they mold and reshape the land.

"Here's what it looked like," says Laraway, during my visit to his operation in January 2009, as he flips through an album of photographs that document the changes over the past seven years. "Hiroshima." The property that Laraway and his business partner, Eli Weis, had purchased had been home to the last remaining brickmaking operation on the Hudson River.

The complex of buildings they inherited from Powell and Minnock Brick Company, which closed down in November 2001, included a number of large kiln sheds, some with rusted steel siding and others with crumbling or missing wood planks. Laraway didn't have a specific plan in mind when he bought the site, but early on looked into retrofitting the kiln equipment and reopening the brick business. When he found it would be cost prohibitive, he considered putting up 1,800 condominium units, but then decided against it. "We thought, No way, it just doesn't fit. You can put houses anywhere, but this place was just sitting here screaming for industrial use. Our vision is to put three hundred to four hundred people to work, and we have fifty to sixty people here so far."

After spending three years securing permits from the Department of Environmental Conservation, Laraway's team began shoreline remediation in July 2007, and finished the following summer. Today the operation has grown to include a warehousing and delivery service for bulk minerals, space and services for small manufacturing businesses, and a division that reclaims old building materials for reuse.

Workers have renovated the old, tumbledown kiln sheds, resheathing them with new steel painted a pale yellow, topped with green roofs. Today these vast buildings provide 160,000 square feet of warehouse space to hold salt, bauxite, gypsum, and other minerals that benefit from dry storage. Cement companies and municipalities contract to have ships drop off their products for storage here, then the port facility delivers them as needed.

Laraway's expansion plans include providing facilities and equipment to about twenty different small manufacturing enterprises, each with thirty to forty employees. "We have to encourage industry in this country or there will be no place for people to work," he says. Ideally he wants to find more tenants like the Fort Miller Company, a small manufacturer that exemplifies the type of business that can benefit most from the port's unique facilities.

Fort Miller leases a 15,000-square-foot building for making precast concrete products. Because of the on-site access to the Hudson, the company can ship its finished paving slabs by barge to avoid having to truck oversized, overweight loads by road. Instead of nine hundred trucks making the 150-mile trip to New York City, says Laraway, the company can load up nine barges that can be towed by the engine of one tugboat.

Reducing fuel use and emissions by shipping via water instead of over roads is a trend that Laraway wants to encourage with the port, citing the long legacy of waterways bearing the heaviest loads. "The river has always been the gateway to the Northeast," he says, adding that he hopes more businesses will use the transport capabilities the river has always historically provided.

When Laraway and Weis first purchased the former brickyard, some local community members worried he would create a landfill on the site. "I made a commitment," he says. "I won't take garbage here. But do I believe in recycling? Absolutely. We all have to do our part." Today he uses the facility to reclaim building materials from demolition sites for reuse in new construction and other products. "Just think about all the minerals that are extracted from the earth, and what do we do? We landfill them. How stupid. I can take a house and give you back ninety percent of it. You can take every bit and make a product out of it. In today's economy, this is where we have to look."

While some have called the new Port of Coeymans a downriver Port of Albany, Laraway says the two are not competitors. "We'll find our own niche," which he envisions will include precast cement and concrete manufacture, bridge and other steel construction (following the success of Manhattan's 145th Street Bridge, built here in 2005), and clean-energy technologies. "I would love to be the service center for all the windmills," Laraway says. "If these windmills are being imported, they need a place to come. We could house them here, along with the parts, and could service them, say, if a bearing went, or if a blade failed."

Laraway has lots of ideas, but no matter which of them ultimately come to fruition, he recognizes that the core value of his port property is the Hudson itself. "The river," he says, "is the hub of it all."

✦ ✦ ✦

To honor the 400th anniversary of Henry Hudson's historic voyage in fall 2009, the historic-vessel community has been dreaming up ways to bring people out onto the river to show them how and why the Hudson is still "the hub of it all." Plans include a "Working on Water" tour featuring more than a dozen historic boats and barges— the descendants of Hudson's *Halve Maen* and Fulton's *North River Steamboat*—to commemorate the Hudson's history as America's first river of commerce, and to celebrate its present-day role as a mixed-use waterway, valued as a resource for both work and play.

The boats will make whistle-stops in riverfront towns, inviting the public to watch performances, view exhibits, participate in hands-on maritime educational programs, tour (and sometimes ride) the vessels, and otherwise reconnect with the river. Working on Water is, in essence, an expanded version of the fireboat's annual Hudson River trips, accompanied by a whole fleet of old-boat friends. As details get hashed out on conference calls and in e-mail debates, I remember why we do this. One important reason is community.

✦ ✦ ✦

Another reason is to share with others some of the joy we get from running boats. One of my happiest days at the helm of the *Gowanus Bay* was a rainy Thursday in late May 2008, cruising through the mouth of Rondout Creek into the Hudson River with a dozen first-graders aboard. The children were students from the Woodcrest School—members of an international community rooted in early Christian values called Bruderhof, located in Rifton, about four miles south of Kingston. The kids had arrived wearing yellow slickers, excited about the boat ride that was the culmination of their unit of study on maritime themes.

At the mouth of the Rondout, I headed south, thinking that the Esopus Lighthouse, just a few miles away, would prove to be a helpful landmark for their learning. On the way there, the children filed through the wheelhouse in twos and threes, each taking a turn at the helm. Since they were too short to see out, I set up a stool, then hoisted them up one by one for a turn to play captain—the girls in kerchiefs with long dresses under their raincoats, the boys in plaid shirts and plain pants. I instructed them how to spin the wheel slowly, one click at a time, then wait for the boat to respond, explaining that it takes some time for the boat to listen to the rudder.

When we reached the lighthouse, I rounded up, pointing the boat back north, and cut the engine. The children gathered on the stern, preparing to release the little wooden boats they had each made by hand. Finely shaped, sanded smooth, and painted bright primary colors, each one had a small cylindrical figure to represent a paddler. An engraved metal tag at the bottom listed the name of the child artisan and a message for whomever might intercept the little boat on its way to the sea: "Please put me back in the water."

After scanning the river up ahead, I turned around to watch the children throw the boats overboard. I worried for a moment that if they landed wrong, the tiny rowers might make their voyage upside down. But these little vessels had been carefully designed—weighted at the bottom so they would right themselves.

Back at the dock, the teachers presented the crew with five plates full of homemade cookies, and a stack of handmade cards from the children, each inscribed with careful cursive messages of thanks. Then they gathered their students into a semicircle for the recitation from memory of mariner-themed poetry. Each child, depending on his or her personality, belted out or whispered a part at the appropriate time. Then they sang several sea chanteys filled with gloriously arcane language, echoing another place in time.

✦ ✦ ✦

Less than a week later, I was back in Manhattan, firing up engines on the fireboat, which was running once again. She had come out of Caddell with repaired shafts and new bearings, ready to take on the season.

It was Memorial Day 2008. And since we had spent last Memorial Day in the shipyard, missing the chance to leave flowers at what remains of Pier 42, this year's ceremony felt even more important.

Tim had begun the tradition. His days with the Glen Rock Fire Department had driven home the importance of remembering the fallen. Each year, a committee was charged with flag detail—putting flags on the gravesites of all who had once served the department. It was a matter of duty. Placing the flowers on the pilings "is the opportunity for us, as the veteran, historic vessel, to honor our own," explains Tim. "And by honoring one, we honor them all."

✦ ✦ ✦

Each year we come to remember pilot John Harvey, whose fate on February 11, 1930, continues to haunt me, even as I learn the details of his death.

When fireboat *Thomas Willett* steamed around the corner of Pier 42, the rising column of smoke pouring from the stern of the steamship *Muenchen* drew the pilot's attention, but not entirely. Standing at the helm of a 132-foot vessel, he still had to maintain control.

"No notice was given," noted officials attending the fire, "that there were contained in said hold number six any cargo or cargoes of an explosive nature or character. . . . No permit to carry explosive material had been obtained from the fire commissioner of the City of New York by the owners or agents of the said steamship."

But the smoldering cargo exploded. The blast that tore apart sections of the *Muenchen*'s hull and superstructure also tore off the *Willett*'s pilothouse, blowing it seventy feet in the air before it plunged into the water, with pilot John Harvey still inside.

At least four other firefighters also hit the frozen water, amid cakes of floating ice. "Debris shot fifty feet in the air when the explosion came," recounted Lieutenant Harold Duryea, who was among several firefighters who had been preparing the deck guns to douse the flames. "I was picked up like a feather and knocked overboard. It was plenty cold in the water." He and the other firefighters were quickly recovered. But two hours after the explosion, police with grappling hooks were still hunting for the pilot's body.

Though John Harvey's brother, Lieutenant James Harvey of the Detective Bureau, was on the pier working among the two hundred police officers charged with restraining the crowd of ten thousand onlookers, he was kept unaware that his brother had gone missing. Finally, four hours after the blast, pilot Harvey's body was recovered off Pier 41, one city block away, and carried to his home at 82 Jane Street.

The *Muenchen* burned for nearly twenty-four hours before an army of firefighters and a fleet of fireboats managed to extinguish the blazes. At four o'clock the following day, firefighters boarded the half-sunk liner to search out traces of smoke or flames. Later, the chief fire marshal pronounced the cause of the fire to be "spontaneous ignition." After the firefighters left, *Muenchen* crew members boarded the vessel and made a surprising discovery in Hold Four: seven thousand canaries, given up for dead, all alive and chirping.

On February 14, 1930, the Fire Department of New York Drum Corps and Color Guard, along with a detail of fifty firefighters in full uniform, including six pallbearers from among the *Willett's* crew, marched behind the hearse carrying Harvey's body from his home to the church for his funeral.

The following year, on March 10, 1931, when construction began on a new fireboat—the largest and most powerful in the world—high up in the fire department, a decision was made. For the first time a fireboat would be named for a man from the ranks: John J. Harvey.

✦ ✦ ✦

One disadvantage of experiencing the Hudson by workboat is how quickly everything passes by. A speed boater would laugh at the notion of a ten-knot boat feeling fast, but the growing ranks of river kayakers would understand what I mean. After all, they paddle along at whatever pace feels right for the moment, their legs actually under the waterline in the boat, the river just an arm's reach away.

There's a park I like to visit to sit and watch the river go by slowly. It overlooks the Esopus Lighthouse, and in late August the shallows get consumed with vegetation that sprawls out over the surface. At dead-low tide, the slimy rocks at the water's edge dry out in the sun. Later, when the tide changes, they are swallowed up again as the advancing sea pushes north. I watch this happen as the river fills in. I can't see the moon but I know it's the force pulling the water back upriver like a blanket over bare shoulders.

To my right a jet-black cormorant hunts for fishy creatures, picking through a brownish patch in the plants. In the sky, a huge bird with a broad wingspan and a white head—an eagle—soars out over the river. It crosses the path of a sailboat riding the northerly wind, the bird's size discernible by the distance and perspective granted by the lighthouse sitting stolid in the middle of the river.

This trick of scale reminds me of the view from an airplane when you're low enough to make out houses, but high enough that you can't see people. It offers a sense of self as speck in the grand unfurling of time.

A newcomer stands on the deck of the *Muenchen*, watching the approach of the awesome metropolis, preparing to take her first steps, like millions before her, onto American soil. Black powder traces on the stone that lines a Delaware and Hudson Canal Lock remind us of the blaster whose job was to explode rock safely. Between the saplings at the West Point Foundry site, a student unearths a "Home Rule" pipe, left untouched for more than a century. A moonlit overlook reveals to generations of artists, like Stephen Fox, the confluence of divergent Hudson River uses. Aboard the *K. Whittelsey*, Steve Trueman shakes hands in the dark with the ghost of the man who built his engine. And in the engine room of fireboat *John J. Harvey*, I trace the footpaths worn, over seventy-eight years, into the pattern on the diamond-plate floor.

NOTES

In chronicling my personal history and that of the Hudson River and fireboat *John J. Harvey*, I have relied on primary and secondary sources—including books, newspapers, court records, interviews, e-mails, Web sites, transcripts, audio recordings, charts, logbooks, notes, and journals—and have cross-referenced multiple sources to confirm my own and others' recollections of days past. I have shifted the timing—though not the content—of a couple of conversations, and have changed some names. Though many people helped me to piece together the details, these stories are, in the end, told from my perspective.

PROLOGUE

1 Information about the SS *Muenchen* fire comes from documents I found at the National Archives and Records Administration's New York regional office, including the *Muenchen* passenger manifest and claims records from the United States District Court, Southern District of New York, as well as various newspaper sources: "17 Liners Laden with Passengers Will Dock Today," *New York Herald Tribune*, February 11, 1930; "Muenchen Burns, Sinks at Her Pier; 2 Dead, 8 Injured," "North German Loss Heavy in Series of Fires," "Visiting Chiefs Watch Fire from Hotel Roof," "German Sailor and His Schnapps Parted by Blast," *New York Herald Tribune*, February 12, 1930; "Blasts and Fire Wreck Liner Muenchen; Ship Sinks at Pier, Imperils Hudson Tube," "Eyewitness Tells of Blasts," "Ship Fire Clogs the Hudson Tubes," "Jersey Crowds View Fire," *New York Times*, February 12, 1930; Byron Darnton, "German Ship Burns, Sinks at Dock After Blasts; 7 Hurt; N.J. Tube Closed," *New-York Evening Post*, February 11, 1930; "Begin Today to Raise Shell of Muenchen," *New York Times*, February 13, 1930; "Find No Arson Clue in Burning of Ship," *New York Times*, February 14, 1930; "Body Found in Muenchen," *New York Times*, April 5, 1930; *Report of the Fire Department of the City of New York* (New York: Lecouver Press Co., 1911), 105.

1 *tiny wooden cage:* Information about how the canaries were captured and transported overseas came from author's e-mail correspondence with bird dealer Max Geisler's grandson, Fred Geisler, November–December 2006.

CHAPTER ONE: NAMESAKE

8 *raw footage: Classic Fireboats in Action: Harbor Fires—New York & New Jersey 1900–1950*, videocassette (Webster Groves, MO: The Ahrens-Fox Video Library, 1996).

12 *half a million commuters:* Neal Bascomb, *Higher: A Historic Race to the Sky and the Making of a City* (New York: Doubleday, 2003), 117.

13 *seventeen liners:* "17 Liners Laden with Passengers Will Dock Today," *New York Herald Tribune*, Feb. 11, 1930.

13 *a "horizontal city":* Kevin Bone, "Horizontal City," in Kevin Bone, ed., *The New York Waterfront: Evolution and Building Culture of the Port and Harbor* (New York: The Monacelli Press, 2004), 87.

15 *at the foot of Twenty-third Street:* Information about fireboat *John J. Harvey*'s construction came from, among other sources, various *New York Times* articles: "Plant Starts Work on City's Fireboat," March 10, 1931; "Rivets Fireboat Today," June 23, 1931; "Fireboat Named for Hero," August 19, 1931; "New Fireboat to Be Launched Oct. 6," September 21, 1931; "To Launch New Fireboat," October 5, 1931; "Launch Fireboat Today," October 6, 1931; "New Fireboat Powerful," December 18, 1931. Also, *Classic Fireboats in Action: Harbor Fires–New York & New Jersey 1900–1950*, videocassette (Webster Groves, MO: The Ahrens-Fox Video Library, 1996).

16 Information about the construction of the Empire State Building came from: Geraldine B. Wagner, *Thirteen Months to Go: The Creation of the Empire State Building* (San Diego, CA: Thunder Bay Press, 2003); Neal Bascomb, *Higher: A Historic Race to the Sky and the Making of a City* (New York: Doubleday, 2003); Kenneth T. Jackson and David S. Dunbar, eds., *Empire City: New York Through the Centuries* (New York: Columbia University Press, 2002); John Tauranac, *The Empire State Building: The Making of a Landmark* (New York: Macmillan, 1997); Thomas Kelly, "75 Years: Performing Miracles with Wrench and Rivet," *New York Times*, April 23, 2006.

CHAPTER THREE: A TALE OF TWO VOYAGES

36 *body in a physical way:* Janet Zandy, *Hands: Physical Labor, Class, and Cultural Work* (New Brunswick, NJ: Rutgers University Press, 2004), 3–4.

39 *naming it River Mauritius:* Russell Shorto, *The Island at the Center of the World: The Epic Story of Dutch Manhattan, the Forgotten Colony That Shaped America* (New York: Doubleday, 2003), 38.

39 *"Great River of the Mountaynes":* Hudson quoted by deLaet, "New World," in Franklin Jamison, ed., *Narratives of New Netherland, 1609–1644* (New York: Charles Scribner's Sons, 1909), 49. As quoted in Frances F. Dunwell, *The Hudson: America's River* (New York: Columbia University Press, 2008), 3.

40 *southernmost portion:* Shorto, *The Island at the Center of the World*, 43.

44 *longest in the world:* Edward Flaxman, *Great Feats of Modern Engineering* (1938, reprint: Manchester, NH: Ayer Publishing, 1967), 47.

44 *granite-clad, Gothic-style towers:* Sharon Reier, *The Bridges of New York* (Mineola, NY: Dover Publications, 2000), 100.

45 *an average of 4.6 feet:* Jeffrey Levinton, "The Hudson River Estuary—The Basics," BIO/GEO 353—Marine Ecology—2008, State University of New York at Stony

Brook, http://life.bio.sunysb.edu/marinebio/fc.1.estuaries.html (accessed April 13, 2009).

45 *a hundred million years ago:* Tom Lewis, *The Hudson: A History* (New Haven, CT: Yale University Press, 2005), 16.

46 *fjord, or "drowned river":* Arthur G. Adams, *The Hudson River Guidebook* (New York: Fordham University Press, 1996), 5.

47 *September 11, 1609:* Russell Shorto, "The Streets Where History Lives," *New York Times,* February 9, 2004; Robert Juet, *Journal of Hudson's 1609 Voyage,* 1625 Edition of *Purchas His Pilgrimes* (modified version), transcribed by Brea Barthel for the New Netherland Museum (PDF), 24 http://www.halfmoon .mus.ny.us (accessed April 2, 2009).

47 *"a very good Harbour":* Juet, *Journal of Hudson's 1609 Voyage,* 24.

47 *led a mutiny:* Lewis, *The Hudson,* 49.

47 *Verenigde Oostindische Compagnie:* Shorto, *The Island at the Center of the World,* 30.

48 *"soft Ozie ground":* Juet, *Journal of Hudson's 1609 Voyage,* 24.

49 *"Snipe" is a navy term:* Tom Thomas, "The Navy Snipe," http://oldsnipe.com/ SnipeBegin.html (accessed April 2, 2009).

50 *"Historic Fireboat Visits City":* Beatriz Rivera-Barnes, "Historic Fireboat Visits City," *Poughkeepsie Journal,* August 18, 2001.

55 *"end for shipping to goe in":* Juet, *Journal of Hudson's 1609 Voyage,* 27.

56 *raise awareness of historic boats:* Jeff Buell, "Old Ship Visits Capital District," *Troy Record,* August 20, 2001.

CHAPTER FOUR: FIREBOAT *JOHN J. HARVEY* SERVES AGAIN

57 *"We looked to our right":* Tom Sullivan, interview by David Tarnow, "All Available Boats: Harbor Voices from 9/11," http://transom.org/shows/2002/200209 .boats.html.

58 *300,000 people:* Norman Brouwer, "All Available Boats," *Seaport: New York's History Magazine,* Spring/Summer 2002, 10.

66 *"covered in and breathing in":* Kate Fenner, songwriter and performer, "Twin Griefs" from the CD *Horses & Burning Cars,* B.Music CR8955, © 2003.

CHAPTER FIVE: APPRENTICESHIP:
"MAKE YOURSELF USEFUL"

73 *"exceeding valor in aiding":* Representative Carolyn B. Maloney of New York, Extensions of Remarks, 107th Cong., 1st Sess., *Congressional Record* 148, No. 8 (February 6, 2002), E99–E100.

76 *625 volts:* New York City Transit, "Subways," http://www.mta.info/nyct/facts/ ffsubway.htm (accessed April 2, 2009).

77 *formalized craft apprenticeships:* W. J. Rorabaugh, *The Craft Apprentice: From Franklin to the Machine Age in America* (New York: Oxford University Press, 1986), viii.

78 *Conditions in colonial America:* Rorabaugh, *The Craft Apprentice,* 4–15.

CHAPTER SIX: RED SKIES IN MORNING

96 *"Dedicated to the history"*: Tugboat Enthusiasts Society, "Welcome to the T.E.S. Website," http://www.tugboatenthusiastsociety.org (accessed April 2, 2009).

106 *"Old Barney"*: Longbeachisland.com, "A History of the Barnegat Lighthouse," http://www.longbeachisland.com/history.html (accessed April 2, 2009).

CHAPTER SEVEN: ON THE HARD:
THE INEVITABLE DECLINE OF OLD THINGS

110 *term "planned obsolescence"*: Giles Slade, *Made to Break: Technology and Obsolescence in America* (Cambridge, MA: Harvard University Press, 2006), 72.

110 *published a pamphlet*: Bernard London, *Ending the Depression Through Planned Obsolescence* (New York: self-published, 1932), 6–7. As quoted in Slade, *Made to Break*, 73–74.

111 *Technological one-upmanship*: Slade, *Made to Break*, 261.

111 *five to seven million tons*: Silicon Valley Toxics Coalition, *Poison PCs and Toxic TVs: California's Biggest Environmental Crisis That You've Never Heard Of* (SVTC: San Jose, 2001), 8. As cited in Slade, *Made to Break*, 262.

111 *more than 130 million*: Slade, *Made to Break*, 263.

111 *"a veneration of newness"*: Susan Strasser, *Waste and Want: A Social History of Trash* (New York: Henry Holt, 1999), 5.

111 *"suffering from overproduction"*: "Production and Consumption," *U.S. Economist and Dry Goods Reporter*, May 6, 1876. As quoted in William Leach, *Land of Desire: Merchants, Power and the Rise of a New American Culture* (New York: Pantheon, 1993), 36. As quoted in Slade, *Made to Break*, 9.

111 *"a uniquely American invention"*: Slade, *Made to Break*, 3–4.

112 *household laundering*: Slade, *Made to Break*, 13.

112 *white-collar jobs*: C. Wright Mills, *White Collar: The American Middle Class* (New York: Oxford University Press, 1956). As cited in Carole Turbin, *Working Women of Collar City: Gender, Class, and Community in Troy, New York, 1864–86* (Chicago: University of Illinois Press, 1992), 28.

112 *Hannah Montague of Troy*: Don Rittner, *Troy: A Collar City History* (Charleston, SC: Arcadia Publishing, 2002), 96.

112 *thirty-three shirt, collar, and cuff factories*: Turbin, *Working Women of Collar City*, 46.

112 *produced 150 million*: Slade, *Made to Break*, 13.

113 *Ford "stood steadfast"*: Slade, *Made to Break*, 33.

113 *practice of "repackaging"*: Slade, *Made to Break*, 36.

114 *Home to Remington rifles*: Citytowninfo.com, "Bridgeport, CT, Facts," http://www.citytowninfo.com/places/connecticut/bridgeport (accessed April 2, 2009).

114 *Phineas Taylor*: Kathleen Maher, "P. T. Barnum (1810–1891): The Man, the Myth, the Legend," The Barnum Museum, http://www.barnum-museum.org/manmythlegend.htm (accessed April 2, 2009).

119 *The formation of rust is gradual*: A. Campbell Holms, *Practical Shipbuilding: A Treatise on the Structural Design and Building of Modern Steel Vessels* (New York: Longmans, Green and Co., 1918), 439.

Chapter Eight: A View from the Factory Floor

124 *11,000 American soldiers:* "Scenes of Wretchedness, Disease, and Woe": *Aboard the Prison Ship* Jersey, in Paul A. Gilje and Howard B. Rock, eds., *Keepers of the Revolution: New Yorkers at Work in the Early Republic* (Ithaca, NY: Cornell University Press, 1992), 172.

128 *Manhattan Island to the Piermont Marshes:* Donald Squires and Kevin Bone, "The Beautiful Lake: The Promise of the Natural Systems," in Kevin Bone, ed., *The New York Waterfront: Evolution and Building Culture of the Port and Harbor* (New York: The Monacelli Press, 2004), 21.

129 *cliff face of thick diabase:* United States Geological Survey, "NYC Regional Geology, 39. The Palisades," http://3dparks.wr.usgs.gov/nyc/parks/loc39.htm (accessed April 2, 2009).

129 *quarrymen blasted out:* Frances F. Dunwell, *The Hudson: America's River* (New York: Columbia University Press, 2008), 217.

129 *"morning, noon and night":* Palisades Interstate Park Commission (PIPC), *Sixty Years of Park Cooperation*, 17. As quoted in Dunwell, *The Hudson: America's River*, 217.

129 *progressive New Jersey women's:* Barbara H. Gottlock and Wesley Gottlock, *New York's Palisades Interstate Park* (Portsmouth, NH: Arcadia Publishing, 2007), 8–9.

130 *Hudson's "working character":* Lawrence Downes, "The Rural Life; One Hudson Morning," *New York Times,* May 27, 2007.

130 *largest brickmaking center:* George V. Hutton, *The Great Hudson River Brick Industry: Commemorating Three and a Half Centuries of Brickmaking* (Fleischmanns, NY: Purple Mountain Press, 2003), 7.

130 *any brick you see in Manhattan:* Hutton, *The Great Hudson River Brick Industry*, 12.

131 *archipelago of small islands:* The Center for Land Use Interpretation, *Up River: Man-Made Sites of Interest on the Hudson from the Battery to Troy* (New York: Blast Books, 2008), 82–83.

131 *Raw materials were mixed by foot:* Daniel DeNoyelles, *Within These Gates* (Thiells, NY: D. DeNoyelles, 1982), 3.

131 *James Wood, an Englishman:* DeNoyelles, *Within These Gates*, 7, 17; Hutton, *The Great Hudson River Brick Industry*, 24–25.

132 *cut down an acre of trees:* Maury Klein, *The Power Makers: Steam, Electricity, and the Men Who Invented Modern America* (New York: Bloomsbury Press, 2008), 18.

132 *363-mile-long Erie:* New York State Canal System, "The Erie Canal: A Brief History," http://www.nyscanals.gov/cculture/history (accessed April 2, 2009).

132 *Excavation of the D&H:* Larry Lowenthal, *From the Coalfields to the Hudson: A History of the Delaware & Hudson Canal* (Fleischmanns, NY: Purple Mountain Press, 1997), 47–52.

132 *remembrances of a man:* Lowenthal, *From the Coalfields to the Hudson*, 266.

133 *The canal was built:* Lowenthal, *From the Coalfields to the Hudson*, 71.

133 *one photograph of the men:* Lowenthal, *From the Coalfields to the Hudson*, 63.

134 *first eleven boats:* Manville B. Wakefield, *Coal Boats to Tidewater* (South Fallsburg, NY: Steingart Associates, 1965), 7–8.

135 *Dutch word* haverstroo: Arthur G. Adams, *The Hudson River Guidebook* (New York: Fordham University Press, 1996), 150.

135 *New Netherland Museum:* "The New Netherland Museum," The New Netherland Museum, http://blacktulipwebdesign.com/halfmoon/index.htm (accessed April 2, 2009).

135 *Irving said it was named:* Washington Irving, *A History of New York—from the Beginning of the World to the End of the Dutch Dynasty, by Diedrich Knickerbocker* in the Kinderhook edition of *The Works of Washington Irving* (New York: G. P. Putnam's Sons, 1880). As quoted in Adams, *The Hudson River Guidebook,* 167.

135 *nasal promontory:* Adams, *The Hudson River Guidebook,* 188; Dunwell, *The Hudson: America's River,* 256.

136 *more than 177 feet deep:* Dunwell, *The Hudson: America's River,* 21.

136 *Martelaer's Rock:* Lincoln Diamant, *Chaining the Hudson: The Fight for the River in the American Revolution* (New York: A Lyle Stuart Book Published by Carol Publishing Group, 1989), 7.

137 *America was born on the Hudson:* Russell Shorto, *The Island at the Center of the World: The Epic Story of Dutch Manhattan, the Forgotten Colony That Shaped America* (New York: Doubleday, 2003), 3.

137 *resolved to send "experienced":* 2nd Continental Congress resolution as quoted in Diamant, *Chaining the Hudson,* 85.

137 *By fortifying the highlands:* Diamant, *Chaining the Hudson,* 7.

137 *"the continent's chief ":* Richard M. Ketchum, *Saratoga: Turning Point of America's Revolutionary War* (New York: Henry Holt and Company, 1997), 19.

138 *"command the Hudson":* Dunwell, *The Hudson: America's River,* 26.

138 *Patriots first fortified:* Diamant, *Chaining the Hudson,* 14.

138 *a chain on wooden rafts:* Diamant, *Chaining the Hudson,* 85–122.

138 *Engineer Tadeusz Kosciuszko:* Tom Lewis, *The Hudson: A History* (New Haven, CT: Yale University Press, 2005), 139.

138 *The links were made:* Diamant, *Chaining the Hudson,* 157.

138 *willingness to switch sides:* Lewis, *The Hudson,* 141–142; Dunwell, *The Hudson: America's River,* 43.

139 *urban renewal:* Tim Logan and John Doherty, "The Promised Land, Chapter One: Promised Land," *Times Herald-Record* (Middletown, NY), January 29, 2006, http://archive.recordonline.com/news/special_reports/newburgh (accessed April 10, 2009).

CHAPTER NINE: TOWING WITH TOM

147 *first commercially viable steamboat:* Alice Crary Sutcliffe, *Robert Fulton and The Clermont* (New York: The Century Co., 1909), http://www.hrmm.org/diglib/sutcliffe/chapter4-1.html (accessed April 2, 2009).

147 *crowd had gathered:* Information about Robert Fulton and his steamboat comes largely from Kirkpatrick Sale, *The Fire of His Genius: Robert Fulton and the American Dream* (New York: Simon & Schuster, 2002).

147 *great shipping port:* Sale, *The Fire of His Genius,* 8.

147 *first attempts, on the Seine:* Sutcliffe, *Robert Fulton and The Clermont.*

148 *a methodical, scientific approach:* Brooke Hindle and Steven Lubar, *Engines of Change: The American Industrial Revolution 1790–1860* (Washington, DC: Smithsonian Institution Press, 1986), 75.

148 *exclusive right:* Hindle and Lubar, *Engines of Change,* 84.

148 *transforming even people's concept of time:* Tom Lewis, *The Hudson: A History* (New Haven, CT: Yale University Press, 2005), 161.

149 *"All were still incredulous":* Sutcliffe, *Robert Fulton and The Clermont.*

149 *a little past two:* Sale, *The Fire of His Genius,* 21.

149 *eight hours later:* Robert Fulton, Letter to the Editor, *The American Citizen* (New York, NY), August 20, 1807. As quoted in Sutcliffe, *Robert Fulton and The Clermont.*

149 *thirty-six hours:* George Matteson, *Tugboats of New York: An Illustrated History* (New York: New York University Press, 2005), 19.

149 *"single most important instrument":* Sale, *The Fire of His Genius,* 14.

149 *more than 150 vessels:* Sale, *The Fire of His Genius,* 182.

150 *schooners carried cargoes of grain:* Lewis, *The Hudson,* 160.

151 *986-foot freighter:* Exxon Valdez Spill Trustee Council, "Oil Spill Facts: Questions and Answers," http://www.evostc.state.ak.us/facts/qanda.cfm (accessed April 2, 2009).

153 *overturned their hold:* Sale, *The Fire of His Genius,* 181.

153 *ticket prices plummeting:* Matteson, *Tugboats of New York,* 29.

153 *steam ferries doubled as towboats:* Matteson, *Tugboats of New York,* 24–25.

154 *turn a profit solely by towing:* Matteson, *Tugboats of New York,* 24–25.

154 *towing "on the hawser":* Paul E. Fontenoy, *The Sloops of New York: A Historical and Design Survey* (Mystic, CT: Mystic Seaport Museum, 1994), 64. As cited in Matteson, *Tugboats of New York,* 32.

154 *the side-wheel towboat* General McDonald: Matteson, *Tugboats of New York,* 33.

155 *larger companies with the capital and flexibility:* Matteson, *Tugboats of New York,* 214.

158 *specially built icebreaker:* Stuart Murray, *Thomas Cornell and the Cornell Steamboat Company* (Fleischmanns, NY: Purple Mountain Press, 2001), 24–25.

158 *135 icehouses:* U.S. Bureau of the Census, Tenth Census, 1880, v. 22 (Washington, DC: Government Printing Office, 1888); reprinted as: Henry Hall, *The Ice Industry of the United States: With a Brief Sketch of Its History* (South Dartmouth, MA: Early American Industries Association, 1974), 24–26; Lewis, *The Hudson,* 244–247.

159 *wooden structures:* Hall, *The Ice Industry of the United States,* 27.

CHAPTER TEN: "ARE YOU LICENSED?"

171 *stereotype vulnerability:* For more on "stereotype vulnerability," see research conducted by Stanford University Lucy Stern Professor of Psychology Claude Steele and NYU associate professor of applied psychology Joshua Aronson, *Journal of Personality and Social Psychology* (in press).

CHAPTER ELEVEN: LOVE OF LABOR

182 *shallow tidal embayments:* Donald Squires and Kevin Bone, "The Beautiful Lake: The Promise of the Natural Systems," in Kevin Bone, ed., *The New York Waterfront: Evolution and Building Culture of the Port and Harbor* (New York: The Monacelli Press, 2004), 26–27.

182 *These same high tides:* Squires and Bone, "The Beautiful Lake," 27.

183 *New York City first established clear policies:* Michael Z. Wise, Wilbur Woods, and Eugenia Bone, "Evolving Purposes: The Case of the Hudson River Waterfront," in Kevin Bone, ed., *The New York Waterfront*, 196.

183 *Slaughterhouses and leather tanneries:* Wise, Woods, and Bone, "Evolving Purposes: The Case of the Hudson River Waterfront," 198.

183 *slashed in half:* George Matteson, *Tugboats of New York: An Illustrated History* (New York: New York University Press, 2005), 209.

183 *reduce ferry traffic:* Wise, Woods, and Bone, "Evolving Purposes: The Case of the Hudson River Waterfront," 199.

183 *"a fragmented terrain":* Mary Beth Betts, "Masterplanning: Municipal Support of Maritime Transport and Commerce 1870–1930s," in Kevin Bone, ed., *The New York Waterfront*, 39.

183 *Manhattan Waterfront:* Narration, Harold McCracken, narration writer, *Manhattan Waterfront*, Van Bueren Corp., released by RKO Radio Pictures, 1937, http://www.archiveorg/details/ManhattanWat (accessed April 11, 2009).

184 *blinded by their own profit seeking:* Keith D. Revell, *Building Gotham: Civic Culture and Public Policy in New York City, 1898–1938* (Baltimore: JHU Press, 2005), 59.

184 *"outlaw frontier":* Malcolm Johnson, "Mobsters, Linked to Vast International Crime Syndicate, Rule New York by Terror," *New York Sun*, November 8, 1948. Republished in Malcolm Johnson, *On the Waterfront* (New York: Chamberlain Brothers, 2005), 3.

184 *tacked hundreds of millions:* Haynes Johnson, foreword to Johnson, *On the Waterfront*, viii.

185 *containerization was cemented:* Marc Levinson, *The Box: How the Shipping Container Made the World Smaller and the World Economy Bigger* (Princeton, NJ: Princeton University Press, 2006), 1.

185 *Westway:* Wise, Woods, and Bone, "Evolving Purposes: The Case of the Hudson River Waterfront," 217.

189 *at least 75 percent:* Walter Licht, *Industrializing America: The Nineteenth Century* (Baltimore: JHU Press, 1995), 3.

190 *once-famous Chelsea Piers:* Wise, Woods, and Bone, "Evolving Purposes: The Case of the Hudson River Waterfront," 198.

190 *authority over the waterfront:* Betts, "Masterplanning," 42.

190 *a row of magnificent buildings:* Wise, Woods, and Bone, "Evolving Purposes: The Case of the Hudson River Waterfront," 198; "Public Relations at Chelsea Piers: History," Chelsea Piers, http://www.chelseapiers.com/prhistory.htm (accessed April 14, 2009).

191 *arrival at Pier 54:* "Public Relations at Chelsea Piers: History," Chelsea Piers, http://www.chelseapiers.com/prhistory.htm (accessed April 14, 2009).

192 *tug nestled between two car floats:* Thomas R. Flagg, *New York Harbor Railroads in Color*, vol. 1 (Kutztown, PA: Morning Sun Books, 2000), 5.

192 *5,300 cars per day:* Flagg, *New York Harbor Railroads in Color*, 5.

194 *A Thousand Days:* Reid departed New York harbor on April 21, 2007. For more information about his voyage see http://www.1000days.net.

CHAPTER TWELVE: SINKING: REPAIRS AND REPARATIONS

200 *Nine of Her Crew Killed:* "Nine of Her Crew Killed," *New York Times*, December 19, 1895.

200 *Wrecks of Great Fire-Scathed Ships:* "Wrecks of Great Fire-Scathed Ships," *New York Times*, July 2, 1900.

200 *Old Ferryboat Sunk:* "Old Ferryboat Sunk by a Sea-going Barge," *New York Times*, December 30, 1906.

201 *a top-secret basement: Cities of the Underworld: New York*, History Channel, May 28, 2007; Susan Orlean, "Grand Central Passion," *National Geographic*, December 2005.

205 *John Jervis:* Frances F. Dunwell, *The Hudson: America's River* (New York: Columbia University Press, 2008), 168.

205 *"wild, visionary, and unpromising":* John B. Jervis, "The Hudson River Railroad: A Sketch of Its History, and Prospective Influence on the Railway Movement," *Hunt's Merchant Magazine*, March 1850. As quoted in Dunwell, *The Hudson: America's River*, 169.

205 *raised $3 million: The Hudson River and the Hudson River Railroad* (Bradbury and Guild, 1851), Catskill Archive, http://www.catskillarchive.com/rrextra/abnyh.html (accessed April 2, 2009).

206 *track bed to hug the riverbank: The Hudson River and the Hudson River Railroad* (Bradbury and Guild, 1851).

206 *fifteen-mile stretch:* Frances F. Dunwell, *The Hudson River Highlands* (New York: Columbia University Press, 1991), xiv.

206 *"the first known public outcry":* Dunwell, *The Hudson: America's River*, 171.

Chapter Thirteen: Shaking Hands with Dead Guys: Preservation and the Long Good-bye

213 *John Ratey:* John J. Ratey, *A User's Guide to the Brain: Perception, Attention, and the Four Theaters of the Brain* (New York: Vintage, 2002). As cited in *Evocative Objects: Things We Think With*, ed. Sherry Turkle (Cambridge, MA: The MIT Press, 2007), 90.

219 *"Does history matter?":* The National Trust (UK), "Why History Matters," History Matters report, http://www.nationaltrust.org.uk/main/w-history-matters .pdf (accessed April 14, 2009).

219 *"unending dialogue":* Edward Hallet Carr, *What Is History?* (New York: Viking, 1967), 35.

223 *Verrazzano:* The Italian Historical Society, "Giovanni da Verrazzano," http://www.italianhistorical.org/verrazzano.htm (accessed April 2, 2009).

227 *"honorable discharge":* David Lear Buckman, *Old Steamboat Days on the son River: Tales and Reminiscences of the Stirring Times That Followed the Introduction of Steam Navigation* (1907, reprinted: Astoria, NY: JC & AL Fawcett, 1989), 76.

Chapter Fourteen: Citizen Craftsmen: The Art in Craft

230 *establishment of a military school:* Benson J. Lossing, *The Hudson* (1866; reprint: Hensonville, NY: Black Dome Press, 2000), 235.

230 *foundry's initial proprietors:* Elizabeth Norris, "An Historical and Industrial

Archaeology Strategy for the West Point Foundry Site, Cold Spring, New York" (master's thesis, Michigan Technological University, 2002), 61.

231 *created the Mechanics Institute*: "Mechanics—Apprentices," in Paul A. Gilje and Howard B. Rock, eds., *Keepers of the Revolution: New Yorkers at Work in the Early Republic* (Ithaca, NY: Cornell University Press, 1992), 50–51.

231 *General Swift had returned*: Charles R. Isleib and Jack Chard, *The West Point Foundry and the Parrott Gun: A Short History* (Fleischmanns, New York: Purple Mountain Press, 2000), 10.

231 *Gouverneur Kemble*: J. N. Paulding as cited in William S. Pelletreau, *History of Putnam County, New York: With Biographical Sketches of Its Prominent Men* (Philadelphia: W. W. Preston, 1886), 615.

231 *James K. Paulding*: Isleib and Chard, *The West Point Foundry and the Parrott Gun*, 12.

232 *secured two hundred acres*: Proceedings of the New York State Historical Association, The Seventeenth Annual Meeting, vol. XV (New York: New York State Historical Association, 1916), 196.

232 *thirty-six-foot waterwheel*: Marvin Wilson, *Thirty Years of Early History of Cold Spring and Vicinity, with Incidents. By One Who Has Been a Resident Since 1819* (Newburgh, NY: Schram Printing House, 1886), 27.

232 *made a corporate body*: Pelletreau, *History of Putnam County*, 559.

232 *government provided an advance*: Margaret L. Raoul, "Gouverneur Kemble and the West Point Foundry," in *Americana, American Historical Magazine*, vol. 30, no. 3 (New York: American Historical Society, 1936), 464, as cited in Edward Rutsch, Brian H. Morrell, Herbert J. Githens, and Leonard A. Eisenber, "The West Point Foundry Site, Cold Spring, Putnam County, New York, November 1979," unpublished manuscript (Newton, NJ: Cultural Resource Management Services, 1979).

232 *designing the company's structure*: Gouverneur Kemble's diary, June 6–July 1, 1817, as cited in Michael Deegan, "Living on the East Bank of the West Point Foundry: An Archaeological Investigation of the East Bank House Ruin, West Point Foundry Site, Cold Spring, New York" (master's thesis, Michigan Technological University, 2006), 24.

232 *total of skilled mechanics*: Anthony Wallace, *Rockdale: The Growth of an American Village in the Early Industrial Revolution* (New York: Alfred A. Knopf, 1980), 219.

232 *protect its monopoly*: Deegan, "Living on the East Bank of the West Point Foundry," 24.

232 *lengths to which foundry recruiters went*: Cold Spring (NY) *Recorder*, February 4, 1937, as quoted in Deegan, "Living on the East Bank of the West Point Foundry," 25.

233 *"There wasn't a manual"*: Patrick E. Martin, professor of social sciences, Michigan Technological University. Interview by telephone with author, May 15, 2008.

233 *first products were ordnance*: Isleib and Chard, *The West Point Foundry and the Parrott Gun*, 15.

234 *first American locomotives*: Emory Edwards, *Modern American Locomotive Engines: Their Design, Construction and Management, a Practical Work for Practical Men* (New York: S. Low, Marston, Searle & Rivington, 1883), 95.

234 *the foundry had expanded*: Norris, "An Historical and Industrial Archaeology Strategy," 65; Kathy Daley, "Cold Spring: The Birth of a Village," *The Sunday Star* (Peekskill, NY), August 7, 1983.

234 *soup-to-nuts approach:* Norris, "An Historical and Industrial Archaeology Strategy," 49, 59–61.

234 *company reached its peak:* Pelletreau, *History of Putnam County, New York,* 561.

235 *foundry produced twenty-five guns:* Harper's Weekly, "West Point Foundry," vol. 5, no. 246, September 14, 1861, 580. As quoted in Norris, "An Historical and Industrial Archaeology Strategy," 53.

235 *the Parrott gun:* Isleib and Chard, *The West Point Foundry and the Parrott Gun,* 16, 19, 27.

235 *reduced government contracts:* Deegan, "Living on the East Bank of the West Point Foundry," 31.

235 *receivership:* Isleib and Chard, *The West Point Foundry and the Parrott Gun,* 32.

236 *"deep breathing of furnaces":* Lossing, *The Hudson,* 246.

240 *"Craftsmanship sits uneasily":* Richard Sennett, *The Culture of the New Capitalism* (New Haven, CT: Yale University Press, 2006), 105.

240 *"deep-rooted trouble":* Sennett, *The Craftsman* (New Haven, CT: Yale University Press, 2008), 9.

240 *"anchor in material reality":* Sennett, *The Craftsman,* 11.

240 *"hand and head":* Sennett, *The Craftsman,* 20.

240 *"Mr. Scientific Management":* Robert Kanigel, *The One Best Way: Frederick Winslow Taylor and the Enigma of Efficiency* (New York: Penguin Books, 1997), 2.

240 *"first efficiency expert":* Kanigel, *The One Best Way,* 1.

241 *Americans' notions about time:* Information on Frederick Winslow Taylor's influence on American culture comes from Kanigel, *The One Best Way.*

241 *"Traditional craft know-how":* Kanigel, *The One Best Way,* 179.

241 *"an age when factories":* Kanigel, *The One Best Way,* 12.

242 *"patiently acquired skill":* Carroll W. Pursell, *The Machine in America: A Social History of Technology* (Baltimore: JHU Press, 1995), 211–212.

242 *"The 'knowledge industry' ":* Kanigel, *The One Best Way,* 9.

243 *"betoken a shift":* Matthew B. Crawford, "Shop Class as Soulcraft," *The New Atlantis: A Journal of Technology & Society,* No. 13, Summer 2006, 7.

243 *"another hood under the hood":* Crawford, "Shop Class as Soulcraft," 7.

244 *"fewer occasions":* Crawford, "Shop Class as Soulcraft," 7.

244 *"a country of doers":* John Ratzenberger and Joel Engel, *We've Got It Made in America: A Common Man's Salute to an Uncommon Country* (New York: Center Street, 2006), 1–2.

247 *"Thomas Paine's message":* Paul A. Gilje and Howard B. Rock, eds., *Keepers of the Revolution: New Yorkers at Work in the Early Republic,* 2.

247 *"useful harmony":* Gilje and Rock, *Keepers of the Revolution,* 3.

Chapter Fifteen: Nails in the Coffin of Industry: The Recreational River

252 *leading intellectuals:* Oswaldo Rodriguez Roque, "The Exaltation of American Landscape Painting," in Metropolitan Museum of Art, *American Paradise: The World of the Hudson River School,* (New York: The Metropolitan Museum of Art, 1987), 21.

252 *"Can there be a country"*: Roque, "The Exaltation of American Landscape Painting," 22.
252 *Cole heeded Clinton's call:* William Dunlap, *A History of the Rise and Progress of the Arts of Design in the United States* (1834, reprint: New York: Dover Publications, 1969), vol. 2, 357. As cited in Roque, "The Exaltation of American Landscape Painting," 22.
253 *"river focused the sense"*: Dunwell, *The Hudson: America's River* (New York: Columbia University Press, 2008), 86.
253 *a privileged witness:* Lewis, *The Hudson*, 197.
253 *"noisy boys and girls"*: Dunwell, *The Hudson: America's River*, 93.
253 *recognizable image:* Roque, "The Exaltation of American Landscape Painting," 24.
254 *Nathaniel Parker Willis:* Dunwell, *The Hudson: America's River*, 141.
254 *anticipated no difficulties:* "Huge Power Plant Planned on Hudson," *New York Times*, September 27, 1962. As quoted in Dunwell, *The Hudson: America's River*, 279.
254 *"sacred ground"*: Dunwell, *The Hudson: America's River*, 281.
254 *"passage through Breakneck"*: Dunwell, *The Hudson: America's River*, 281.
255 *"destroy the scenic beauty"*: Allan R. Talbot, *Power Along the Hudson: The Storm King Case and the Birth of Environmentalism* (New York: Dutton, 1972), 3.
255 *the FPC must "include"*: Scenic Hudson Preservation Conference v. FPC, 354 F.2d 608, 624 (2nd Cir. 1965). As quoted in Miriam D. Silverman, *Stopping the Plant: The St. Lawrence Cement Controversy and the Battle for Quality of Life in the Hudson Valley* (Albany, NY: State University of New York Press, 2006), 29.
255 *"saving landforms"*: Raymond O'Brien, *American Sublime: Landscape and Scenery of the Lower Hudson* (New York: Columbia University Press, 1981). As qouted in Silverman, *Stopping the Plant*, 37.
256 *"Essay on American Scenery"*: Thomas Cole "Essay on American Scenery," 1835, reprinted in John W. McCoubrey, *American Art, 1700–1960: Sources and Documents* (Englewood Cliffs, NJ: Prentice-Hall Publications, 1965). As quoted in Roque, "The Exaltation of American Landscape Painting," in *American Paradise*, 39.
256 *workers laid train tracks:* Roque, "The Exaltation of American Landscape Painting," 40.
256 *"harmonious coexistence"*: Roque, "The Exaltation of American Landscape Painting," 40.
257 *"place looks better now"*: Kevin J. Avery, "The Hudson River School: The Influence of the Environment, Then and Now" (lecture, Henry Tepper, moderator, New-York Historical Society, February 1, 2007).
257 *"What they didn't want to see"*: Harvey Keyes Flad, "The Hudson River School: The Influence of the Environment, Then and Now" (lecture, Henry Tepper, moderator, New-York Historical Society, February 1, 2007).
258 *"Cement put most of the people"*: Silverman, *Stopping the Plant*, 47.
258 *Hostilities that "both fostered"*: Silverman, *Stopping the Plant*, 21.
259 *cement production in New York:* Silverman, *Stopping the Plant*, 4–5.
259 *area 20 percent larger:* Silverman, *Stopping the Plant*, 3–4, 6; Lisa W. Foderaro, "Taking Sides in the Hudson Valley; Plant Raises Issues of Pollution and Economic Change," *New York Times*, June 27, 2003.
259 *250,000 tons of coal:* Riverkeeper, "Development, What We're Doing: St. Lawrence Cement," http://www.riverkeeper.org/campaign.php/development/we_are_doing/770-st-lawrence-cement (accessed April 19, 2009).

259 *twenty million pounds of pollution:* Silverman, *Stopping the Plant*, 78.
260 *"hideous new landmark":* Silverman, *Stopping the Plant*, 37.
260 *the Olana Partnership:* Silverman, *Stopping the Plant*, 37, 150.
260 *on "scenic" grounds:* Silverman, *Stopping the Plant*, 105–106.
263 *long-abandoned structures:* Thomas E. Rinaldi and Robert J. Yasinsac, *Hudson Valley Ruins: Forgotten Landmarks of an American Landscape* (Lebanon, NH: University Press of New England, 2006), 1–2.
264 *Built in 1906:* Rinaldi and Yasinsac, *Hudson Valley Ruins*, 286–288.
265 *"last traditional industry":* Rinaldi and Yasinsac, *Hudson Valley Ruins*, 286, 292.
266 *"navigating the space":* Paul Berge, "Yonkers Power Station," PBergephotography .com, September 3, 2007, http://pbergephotography.com/2007/09 (accessed April 13, 2009).

Chapter Sixteen: Full Speed Ahead

270 *weeklong camp:* Anne Pynburn, "Girls get S.M.A.R.T. at Ulster BOCES," *Ulster County Press* (Stone Ridge, NY), August 11, 2008. As posted on nutsandbolts foundation.org, Nuts, Bolts & Thingamajigs Foundation, http://www.nutsand boltsfoundation.org/Girls-get-SMART.cfm (accessed April 13, 2009).

BIBLIOGRAPHY

Adams, Arthur G. *The Hudson River Guidebook* (New York: Fordham University Press, 1996).

Bascomb, Neal. *Higher: A Historic Race to the Sky and the Making of a City* (New York: Doubleday, 2003).

Bone, Kevin, ed. *The New York Waterfront: Evolution and Building Culture of the Port and Harbor* (New York: The Monacelli Press, 2004).

Bruegel, Martin. *Farm, Shop, Landing: The Rise of a Market Society in the Hudson Valley, 1780–1860* (Durham, NC: Duke University Press, 2002).

Buckman, David Lear. *Old Steamboat Days on the Hudson River: Tales and Reminiscences of the Stirring Times That Followed the Introduction of Steam Navigation* (1907, reprinted: Astoria, NY: JC & AL Fawcett, 1989).

Carr, Edward Hallet. *What Is History?* (New York: Viking, 1967).

Center for Land Use Interpretation. *Up River: Man-Made Sites of Interest on the Hudson from the Battery to Troy* (New York: Blast Books, 2008).

Crawford, Matthew B. "Shop Class as Soulcraft," *The New Atlantis: A Journal of Technology & Society*, No. 13, Summer 2006.

Deegan, Michael. "Living on the East Bank of the West Point Foundry: An Archaeological Investigation of the East Bank House Ruin, West Point Foundry Site, Cold Spring, New York" (master's thesis, Michigan Technological University, 2006).

DeNoyelles, Daniel. *Within These Gates* (Thiells, NY: D. DeNoyelles, 1982).

Diamant, Lincoln. *Chaining the Hudson: The Fight for the River in the American Revolution* (New York: A Lyle Stuart Book Published by Carol Publishing Group, 1989).

Dunwell, Frances F. *The Hudson: America's River* (New York: Columbia University Press, 2008).

———. *The Hudson River Highlands* (New York: Columbia University Press, 1991).

Edwards, Emory. *Modern American Locomotive Engines: Their Design, Construction and Management, a Practical Work for Practical Men* (New York: S. Low, Marston, Searle & Rivington, 1883).

Flagg, Thomas R. *New York Harbor Railroads in Color*, vol. 1 (Kutztown, PA: Morning Sun Books, 2000).

Flaxman, Edward. *Great Feats of Modern Engineering* (1938, reprint: Manchester, NH: Ayer Publishing, 1967).

Ford, Edwin Millard with Friends of Historic Kingston. *Images of America: Kingston* (Portsmouth, NH: Arcadia Publishing, 2004).

Fried, Marc B. *The Early History of Kingston and Ulster County, N.Y.* (Kingston, NY: Ulster County Historical Society, 1975).

Gilje, Paul A., and Howard B. Rock, eds. *Keepers of the Revolution: New Yorkers at Work in the Early Republic* (Ithaca, NY: Cornell University Press, 1992).

Gottlock, Barbara H., and Wesley Gottlock, *New York's Palisades Interstate Park* (Portsmouth, NH: Arcadia Publishing, 2007), 8–9.

Hindle, Brooke, and Steven Lubar. *Engines of Change: The American Industrial Revolution 1790–1860* (Washington, DC: Smithsonian Institution Press, 1986).

Holms, A. Campbell. *Practical Shipbuilding: A Treatise on the Structural Design and Building of Modern Steel Vessels* (New York: Longmans, Green and Co., 1918).

Hutton, George V. *The Great Hudson River Brick Industry: Commemorating Three and a Half Centuries of Brickmaking* (Fleischmanns, NY: Purple Mountain Press, 2003).

Ingersoll, Ernest. *Illustrated Guide to the Hudson River and Catskill Mountains* (1910, reprinted as *Handy Guide to the Hudson River and Catskill Mountains 1910* (Astoria, NY: JC & AL Fawcett, 1989).

Isleib, Charles R., and Jack Chard. *The West Point Foundry and the Parrott Gun: A Short History* (Fleischmanns, New York: Purple Mountain Press, 2000).

Jackson, Kenneth T., and David S. Dunbar, eds. *Empire City: New York Through the Centuries* (New York: Columbia University Press, 2002).

Johnson, Malcolm. *On the Waterfront* (New York: Chamberlain Brothers, 2005).

Kanigel, Robert. *The One Best Way: Frederick Winslow Taylor and the Enigma of Efficiency* (New York: Penguin Books, 1997).

Ketchum, Richard M. *Saratoga: Turning Point of America's Revolutionary War* (New York: Henry Holt, 1997).

Klein, Maury. *The Power Makers: Steam, Electricity, and the Men Who Invented Modern America* (New York: Bloomsbury Press, 2008).

Levinson, Marc. *The Box: How the Shipping Container Made the World Smaller and the World Economy Bigger* (Princeton, NJ: Princeton University Press, 2006).

Lewis, Tom. *The Hudson: A History* (New Haven, CT: Yale University Press, 2005).

Licht, Walter. *Industrializing America: The Nineteenth Century* (Baltimore: JHU Press, 1995).

Lossing, Benson J. *The Hudson* (1866; reprint: Hensonville, NY: Black Dome Press, 2000).

Lowenthal, Larry. *From the Coalfields to the Hudson: A History of the Delaware & Hudson Canal* (Fleischmanns, NY: Purple Mountain Press, 1997).

Magee, Mike, MD, ed. *All Available Boats: The Evacuation of Manhattan Island on September 11, 2001* (New York: Spencer Books, 2002).

Matteson, George. *Tugboats of New York: An Illustrated History* (New York: New York University Press, 2005).

Metropolitan Museum of Art. *American Paradise: The World of the Hudson River School* (New York: The Metropolitan Museum of Art, 1987).

Murray, Stuart. *Thomas Cornell and the Cornell Steamboat Company* (Fleischmanns, NY: Purple Mountain Press, 2001).

O'Brien, Raymond J. *American Sublime: Landscape and Scenery of the Lower Hudson Valley* (New York: Columbia University Press, 1981).

Pelletreau, William S. *History of Putnam County, New York: With Biographical Sketches of Its Prominent Men* (Philadelphia: W.W. Preston, 1886).

Proceedings of the New York State Historical Association, The Seventeenth Annual Meeting, vol. XV (New York: New York State Historical Association, 1916).

Pursell, Carroll W. *The Machine in America: A Social History of Technology* (Baltimore: JHU Press, 1995).

Ratzenberger, John, and Joel Engel. *We've Got It Made in America: A Common Man's Salute to an Uncommon Country* (New York: Center Street, 2006).

Reier, Sharon. *The Bridges of New York* (Mineola, NY: Dover Publications, 2000).

Revell, Keith D. *Building Gotham: Civic Culture and Public Policy in New York City, 1898–1938* (Baltimore: JHU Press, 2005).

Rinaldi, Thomas E., and Robert J. Yasinsac. *Hudson Valley Ruins: Forgotten Landmarks of an American Landscape* (Lebanon, NH: University Press of New England, 2006).

Rittner, Don. *Troy: A Collar City History* (Charleston, SC: Arcadia Publishing, 2002).

Rorabaugh, W. J. *The Craft Apprentice: From Franklin to the Machine Age in America* (New York: Oxford University Press, 1986).

Rutsch, Edward, Brian H. Morrell, Herbert J. Githens, and Leonard A. Eisenber. "The West Point Foundry Site, Cold Spring, Putnam County, New York, November 1979," unpublished manuscript (Newton, NJ: Cultural Resource Management Services, 1979).

Sale, Kirkpatrick. *The Fire of His Genius: Robert Fulton and the American Dream* (New York: Simon & Schuster, 2002).

Sanderson, Dorothy Hurlbut. *The Delaware & Hudson Canalway: Carrying Coals to Rondout* (Ellenville, NY: The Rondout Valley Publishing Co., 1965).

Sennett, Richard. *The Craftsman* (New Haven: Yale University Press, 2008).

———. *The Culture of the New Capitalism* (New Haven, CT: Yale University Press, 2006).

Shorto, Russell. *The Island at the Center of the World: The Epic Story of Dutch Manhattan, the Forgotten Colony That Shaped America* (New York: Doubleday, 2003).

Silverman, Miriam D. *Stopping the Plant: The St. Lawrence Cement Controversy and the Battle for Quality of Life in the Hudson Valley* (Albany, NY: State University of New York Press, 2006).

Slade, Giles. *Made to Break: Technology and Obsolescence in America* (Cambridge, MA: Harvard University Press, 2006).

Steuding, Bob. *Rondout: A Hudson River Port* (Fleischmanns, NY: Purple Mountain Press, 1995).

Strasser, Susan. *Waste and Want: A Social History of Trash* (New York: Henry Holt, 1999).

Talbot, Allan R. *Power Along the Hudson: The Storm King Case and the Birth of Environmentalism* (New York: Dutton, 1972).

Tauranac, John. *The Empire State Building: The Making of a Landmark* (New York: Macmillan, 1997).

Turbin, Carole. *Working Women of Collar City: Gender, Class, and Community in Troy, New York, 1864–86* (Chicago: University of Illinois Press, 1992).

Turkle, Sherry, ed. *Evocative Objects: Things We Think With* (Cambridge, MA: The MIT Press, 2007).

U.S. Bureau of the Census, Tenth Census, 1880, v. 22 (Washington, DC: Government Printing Office, 1888, reprinted as Henry Hall, *The Ice Industry of the United States: With a Brief Sketch of Its History* (South Dartmouth, MA: Early American Industries Association, 1974).

Wagner, Geraldine B. *Thirteen Months to Go: The Creation of the Empire State Building* (San Diego, CA: Thunder Bay Press, 2003).

Wakefield, Manville B. *Coal Boats to Tidewater* (South Fallsburg, NY: Steingart Associates, 1965).

Wallace, Anthony. *Rockdale: The Growth of an American Village in the Early Industrial Revolution* (New York: Alfred A. Knopf, 1980).

Wilson, Marvin. *Thirty Years of Early History of Cold Spring and Vicinity, with Incidents. By One Who Has Been a Resident Since 1819* (Newburgh, NY: Schram Printing House, 1886).

Zandy, Janet. *Hands: Physical Labor, Class, and Cultural Work* (New Brunswick, NJ: Rutgers University Press, 2004).

ACKNOWLEDGMENTS

WRITING MAY BE a solitary pursuit, but making a book is definitely a group sport. I am overwhelmed with gratitude for all who have provided support along the way.

First and foremost, I owe an enormous debt to the people who have helped keep fireboat *John J. Harvey* afloat through the ten years since she was auctioned off by New York City. Many more people have contributed their sweat, time, and resources to the boat's upkeep than are reflected in the preceding pages. I especially want to thank my crewmates, particularly those whom I have not yet mentioned: John Browne, John Doswell, Thorner Harris, Peter Hobbs, Barbara Moore, Jean Preece, Bruce Rosenkrantz, and Karl Schuman. It is an honor to work with you. Other *Harvey* supporters whose contributions have been significant to me personally include, but are by no means limited to, Karl (Corky) Anderson, Rick and Renee Batchelder, Liz Bergin, Scotty Conder, Rose Craig, Bob Cunningham, Joe Dempster, Craig Denecke, Andrew Furber, the Ivory family, Jean Kondek, Angela Krevey, the Lenney family, Florent Morellet, Sue Mortgu, Julie Nadel, Maggie Bergin O'Connor, Garry Pace, Carl Selvaggi, Richard Siller, Randy Simon, Dick and Denise Solay, Eric and Evelyn Stallings, Mort Starobin, John Treatout, the Weisler family, and Dawn Wray, as well as the Kennedy Engine Company and the FDNY Marine Division. For more information on fireboat *Harvey* or to make a donation, please visit www.fireboat.org.

For lending support in countless ways, including help with Marine Division and fireboat history, I want to extend a special thank-you to Bob Lenney, Huntley Gill, Al Trojanowicz, and Chase Wells.

I am profoundly grateful to Tim Ivory—a brilliant mechanical mind and a gifted teacher—for his infinite patience with my endless questions and for his consistent faith in me. His willingness to share this adventure has opened up whole new worlds.

In addition to those mentioned in the text who so generously shared their stories, a number of others offered their time, insights, and expertise, including James Ring Adams, Sandy Balick, Gwen Billig, Debbie and Michael Biltonen, Lucey Bowen, Norman Brouwer, Fabio Chizzola, Joseph Curto, Ralph Erenzo, Jennifer Grossman, Mary Habstritt, Bryce Kirk, Venetia Lannon, Tom Lewis, Brian Maher, Julie Nadel, and Gerry Weinstein. People who provided research assistance include Chris at the National Archives; Tammis Groft at the Albany Institute of History & Art; Sarah Judd at the New York City Fire Museum; Danny May and Ed Fahey at the Mann Library; the Putnam County Historical Society & Foundry School Museum; Craig Williams, John Scherer, and Geoffrey Stein at the New York State Museum; as well as Eric Breitbart, Carter Craft, Shirley Dunn, Fred Geisler, Field Horne, Diane McNamara, Pat Murphy, Stephen Osborn, Robert Pfeil, and Elizabeth Wales. Thank you also to Richard and Cathy Andrian, Jonathan Atkin, Bernie Ente, and Sarah Lyon for photography assistance, to Mark Peckham for so graciously sharing his illustrations, and to Christine Rigden, Kathy Murray, Carolyn Tice, Lilly Bommarito, Barry Eager, Elin Schroeder-Goering, and Matt, Mark, Sharon, and Sue Dooley for genealogical assistance.

I also want to thank the Mid-Hudson Library System, and David Smith, librarian to the stars, who opened doors to the wonders of the New York Public Library, including the Wertheim Study. A special shout-out to Jodi Jaecks, who valiantly jumped in with all manner of research and transcription assistance. And I can't forget Keith Blount, developer of Scrivener (www.literatureandlatte.com/scrivener.html), the powerful software that helped me manage mountains of information.

I'm grateful to John and Alice Carlson for the use of their beautiful farmhouse in Ontario, to Carlo Adinolfi for the Hudson hideaway, to John Voelcker and Dave Provost for sharing their mountain home, and to Tania Amrod for the Hudson River view.

And for corporeal and spiritual maintenance, I offer heartfelt thanks to David Harnick, M.D., Dale Kimberlin, Maria Elena Maurin, Asa Coddington, Jeff Rossman, Inez Anders, and Stephen Cope, as well as to Scenic Hudson for establishing Esopus Meadows Preserve and Lighthouse Park, the riverfront respite that sustained me throughout the writing of this book.

I must also extend my appreciation for the musicians who accompanied me through long, lonely writing hours, including Hossein Alizadeh and Djivan Gasparyan, Hasna el Becharia, Jim Campilongo, Duke Ellington, Hassan Hakmoun, Baaba Maal, Youssou N'Dour, Ajda Pekkan, Suba, Ali Farka Touré, and Luther Wright.

Numerous friends and colleagues have generously lent their support, including Amy Laura Cahn, Beth Connelly, Trevor Corson, Hilary Davidson, Joel Derfner, Jay Dixit, Leslie Elman, Liz and Ryan Enschede, Ben Fine, Lori Heddinger, Katia Hetter, Erin Keating, Nelson Kim, Sharon Lintz, Amanda McBaine, Ellen Neuborne, Kim Severson, Jenna Schnuer, Dred Scott, Myrna Shinbaum, Jenny Strasburg, Rob Sudduth, and Ted Weinstein. I am indebted to the many generous teachers I've had over the years, including Elizabeth Merrick, Donna Minkowitz, Chris Robinson, and Karen Rowe, and to authors Julia Cameron, Natalie Goldberg, and Anne Lamott for their books' dependable guidance, available at all hours, day or night.

I am grateful to Barbara Sjoholm and Seal Press for publishing my essay "Below Decks" in *Steady As She Goes: Women's Adventures at Sea*, which informed my understanding of my marine engineering journey, and to Lloyd Graff for allowing me to explore topics in *Today's Machining World* that helped fuel my thinking about manufacturing and hands-on work.

Thanks to James Gregorio for his wise counsel, Joel and Heidi Roberts for their high-energy strategizing, Stuart Krichevsky for his early encouragement, Christa Bourg and Bridget DuLong for wise proposal advice, Deb Robson for editing early versions of this material, and Kate Dowling and Erika Casriel for thoughtful feedback. Mountains of gratitude to John Voelcker for lending sharp insights and a keen editorial eye to hundreds of manuscript pages on painfully tight deadlines, and Nancy Rawlinson (www.nancyrawlinson.com) for invaluable editing and structural guidance.

This book could not have found a better home than at Free Press, and I couldn't have asked for a more diligent, dedicated, hard-working publishing crew, including Andy Dodds, Eric Fuentecilla, Caitlin Hayes, Carisa Hays, Edith Lewis, Donna Loffredo, and Jennifer Weidman. I am tremendously grateful to Martha Levin for her faith in this project and to Leslie Meredith for her deep, thoughtful, and wise edits and her invaluable ability to view the material from thirty thousand feet at moments when I found myself blindly scrabbling through the details.

David Black runs a top-notch agency, and I cannot thank Joy Tutela enough for being such a vehement advocate, sage adviser, faithful shoulder, and steadfast champion.

There are no words sufficient to express my gratitude to my family. Thank you, Mom and Dad, for grounding me in what matters, and teaching me how to pave my own road. Thank you, Ellen and Harold, for your patience, generosity, and support. Thank you, Bridget, Jim, Josh, Molly, Zach, Andrew, Shannah, Grace, and Ryan for sharing all the complicated joys of family.

Thank you, Ben, for walking with me through the many years when b**k was still a four-letter word, and for standing by me as I discovered exactly why it merits that designation—selflessly giving more help and support than I ever could have imagined. Without you this book would not be.

INDEX

❧

Page numbers in *italics* refer to illustrations.

ABOUT THE AUTHOR

Jessica DuLong, a U.S. Coast Guard–licensed merchant marine officer, is one of the world's only female fireboat engineers. She's also a journalist whose work has appeared in *Newsweek International, Rolling Stone, Psychology Today, CosmoGIRL!, Parenting, Today's Machining World, Maritime Reporter & Engineering News,* and other publications. Her passion for the Hudson River took shape at her post in the diesel exhaust–filled engine room of retired New York City fireboat *John J. Harvey,* where temperatures climb to 130 degrees. The 1931 vessel, dubbed "Ambassador of the Hudson," now operates as a living museum, offering free public trips around New York harbor and an annual whistle-stop tour up the Hudson River, with DuLong at the engine-room controls.

Learn more about fireboat *John J. Harvey* at www.fireboat.org.

For more information about the author, visit www.jessicadulong.com.